ROBERT KIRKMAN

Conversations with Comic Artists
M. Thomas Inge, General Editor

Robert Kirkman: Conversations

Edited by Terrence R. Wandtke

University Press of Mississippi / Jackson

The University Press of Mississippi is the scholarly publishing agency of the Mississippi Institutions of Higher Learning: Alcorn State University, Delta State University, Jackson State University, Mississippi State University, Mississippi University for Women, Mississippi Valley State University, University of Mississippi, and University of Southern Mississippi.

www.upress.state.ms.us

The University Press of Mississippi is a member of the Association of University Presses.
Copyright © 2021 by University Press of Mississippi

First printing 2021
∞
Library of Congress Cataloging-in-Publication Data

Names: Kirkman, Robert, interviewee. | Wandtke, Terrence R., editor.
Title: Robert Kirkman: conversations / edited by Terrence Wandtke.
Other titles: Conversations with comic artists.
Description: Jackson: University Press of Mississippi, 2021. | Series: Conversations with comic artists series | Includes bibliographical references and index.
Identifiers: LCCN 2021008824 (print) | LCCN 2021008825 (ebook) | ISBN 978-1-4968-3481-2 (hardback) | ISBN 978-1-4968-3482-9 (trade paperback) | ISBN 978-1-4968-3483-6 (epub) | ISBN 978-1-4968-3484-3 (epub) | ISBN 978-1-4968-3485-0 (pdf) | ISBN 978-1-4968-3486-7 (pdf)
Subjects: LCSH: Kirkman, Robert—Interviews. | Cartoonists—United States—Interviews. | LCGFT: Interviews.
Classification: LCC PN6727.K586 Z46 2021 (print) | LCC PN6727.K586 (ebook) | DDC 741.5/973 [B]—dc23
LC record available at https://lccn.loc.gov/2021008824
LC ebook record available at https://lccn.loc.gov/2021008825

British Library Cataloging-in-Publication Data available

Works by Robert Kirkman

FUNK-O-TRON
Battle Pope

IMAGE
The Astounding Wolf-Man
Capes
Guardians of the Globe
Haunt (cowritten with Todd McFarlane)
The Infinite
Invincible
Oblivion Song
Outcast
Savage Dragon: God of War
Super Dinosaur
SuperPatriot
Tech Jacket
Thief of Thieves (cowritten with Nick Spenser and others)
The Walking Dead

MARVEL
Captain America: Avengers Disassembled
Fantastic Four: Foes
Destroyer
The Irredeemable Ant-Man
Jubilee
Marvel Team-Up, vol. 3
Marvel Zombies, Marvel Zombies: Dead Day, Marvel Zombies 2
Ultimate X-Men: Phoenix?, Magical, Cable, Sentinels, Apocalypse

CONTENTS

INTRODUCTION

ANOTHER EXTRAORDINARY COMIC BOOK EVERYMAN

In the beginning (of the American comic book industry), people were largely unaware of the creator(s) that shaped that world. Because they were uncredited nonowners of their creative work, it would be years before EC and Marvel would begin to sell comics by showcasing the personalities of their big talents. Even then, the superhero became dominant, and company-owned characters were more important to the average reader than the minds and hands behind the scenes. Last but not least, if any type of creator garnered fan followings in the early days of the comic convention and the direct-market comic shop, it would be the artist rather than the writer. With all this stated, the comic book writer slowly but surely came to the forefront with writers like Alan Moore, capable not only of creating a fan following but also of reshaping the industry through the power of near-celebrity status. Beyond the historical development that led to this point in the twenty-first century, Robert Kirkman now represents this situation at its most pronounced as a writer of titles like *Invincible* and *The Walking Dead*, a partner of the creator-rights company Image Comics, and a founder of the multimedia production house Skybound Entertainment.

Before proceeding further, it should be acknowledged that few comic book writers are as well known to the American public as Stan Lee: the Marvel writer, producer, and icon who, in part, initiated this kind of celebrity status for comic book creators. And yet even without Hitchcock-style cameos in superhero movies, Robert Kirkman is the one comic book writer who rivals Lee in terms of recognition and influence. Like Lee, he is recognizable beyond the comic con circuit thanks to the transmedia success of properties like *The Walking Dead* and his savvy, self-effacing presence on high-profile late-night talk shows as well as on AMC's *The Talking Dead*. And like Lee, he has crafted fictive worlds that inspire fan devotion and make more money than practically any other independently owned properties in the history of American comics. While this near-equal prominence might be an argument in itself for serious attention to Kirkman, it is important to also note the significant ways that he differs; within these differences reside an even more significant rationale for showcasing Kirkman through his interviews in this volume of the "Conversations with Comic Artists" series.

Lee is a self-consciously fashioned company man associated with the 1960s rebirth of superhero comics; but more famously, he represents the Marvel superhero industry that has become more oriented to producing summer blockbusters than comic books while continuing to treat their creators as factory workers and mascots. Kirkman is a fanboy consumer-turned-creator associated with the 2000s flourishing of comic book creators' rights; but more particularly, he represents Image Comics, a company like Dark Horse that has expanded genre offerings and increased the audience diversity for comic books while treating their creators as artists and rights-holders. A standard-bearer for the new comic book mainstream where superhero comics no longer dominate, Kirkman owns his properties as well as his multiplatform entertainment company, Skybound. And while that company also produces film, television, and video-game entertainment, Kirkman continues to write prolifically with an intense, clearly espoused devotion to the comic book. Kirkman's journey has become the new ideal for contemporary comic book creators: from an obscure, in-debt, self-publishing comic book creator to a new type of company man who is an independent, respected, and affluent writer and producer of horror, crime, science fiction, and superhero stories.

THE FAN AND THE CREATOR: FOREVER UP AND COMING

While Stan Lee was quite an extraordinary comic book creator and businessman, he continued to regard and promote himself as an everyman—and Robert Kirkman also continues in that tradition. Raised in Cynthiana, Kentucky, Kirkman uses his small-town upbringing as a consistent reference point: from his discovery of DC and Marvel comic books at Walmart to his first visit to a comic shop in Lexington to his job working as a clerk in a comic book, game, and collectible shop.[1] Moving straight from high school to the work force, he was well acquainted with the material necessities of life when he considered producing an independent comic (inspired by Eric Larsen's *The Savage Dragon* and the Image "revolution"). With Todd McFarlane's departure from Marvel and the establishment of Image as a creator-owned comics company, Kirkman disregarded the rocky state of the direct market and showcased his abilities as a writer by financing his own title: an irreverent parody of action comics called *Battle Pope*. Maxing out his credit cards, Kirkman and childhood friend and artist Tony Moore crafted stories of a hard-drinking, sex-addicted Pope living in the aftermath of God's judgement and the release of demons from hell. Chosen by God to assist Michael in the defense of the good people on earth, Pope Oswald is endowed with a '90s-era superhero physique, many overlarge weapons, and a partner in the form of God's nose-picking, nerdy son Jesus.

Battle Pope reveals Kirkman as a keen developer of character within the context of a parody that comfortably moved from broad, low humor to incisive, self-referential commentary. While a bit sloppy in its execution and working with sexist teen comedy tropes in a way not quite satiric, it effectively pokes fun at superhero and horror comic tropes and even mounts effective criticisms of organized religion (even though that may not have been Kirkman's intention): "I never wanted to do any biblical stuff in the book just because to me it was a superhero book that happened to be about Jesus and Battle Pope fighting demons and Lucifer" (Abrams 55). *Battle Pope* was Kirkman's earliest attempt to play to the market by developing something both absurd and controversial so that it would be picked up by Diamond Distribution (who at the time had a stranglehold on the direct market): "I had my pie-in-the-sky dreams of the Catholic League hunting me down and getting me on CNN and people going into comic stores in droves to see what this thing was about. That was the purpose of the thing being what it was" (Abrams 53).

Although a synthesis of many genres, *Battle Pope* relied heavily on a buddy-movie formula to make the tough guy Pope Oswald and the oversensitive oaf Jesus into unlikely friends; moreover, the generic plot conventions became a means to the end of exploring characters and their relationships: particularly that of unexpected and extended families. For instance, in addition to Pope Oswald and Jesus, the group eventually includes Michael, a demon, an elderly landlord, and others who work to collectively overcome obstacles (like the rift between Pope Oswald and God after he sleeps with the big-busted "virgin" Mary). In one of his earliest interviews, Kirkman would display his everyman honesty alongside his tendencies as a consummate salesman: "It only seemed logical to publish it ourselves. Not that I didn't send out submissions to other publishers—I did. Image, Dark Horse, and Oni didn't seem interested, but it was always the plan to do it ourselves. So far it's worked out pretty well—I can't seem to keep Diamond in stock!" (Connor).[2] In fact, the comic book didn't sell well enough to pay his bills, but his "Funk-O-Tron" title did attract a cult following and make others think of him as a viable player in the comic book industry.

EVERYTHING CHANGES WHILE EVERYTHING STAYS THE SAME (WITH SUPERHEROES)

In many ways, Kirkman's continued life as a fanboy caused him to make connections to comic book creators that he loved like Eric Larsen (enabled in part by the robust convention and internet culture of 1990s); these connections eventually helped him write his way out of debt through work with Image: the publisher that had fundamentally shaped his aesthetics and whose culture he would enthusiastically join. Kirkman's earliest work with Image included several derivative superhero series that fit comfortably into the Image superhero universe, but they would not be the basis for Image's long-term foothold in comics. In fact, Kirkman himself would identify his work with Eric Larsen's character in the *SuperPatriot* series as one of the means by which he and artist Corey Walker became acclimated to the rudiments of comic book narrative as well as working within an industry's narrative universe. However, in short order, Kirkman would be part of a change at the young company in two important ways. With *Invincible*, he crafted a superhero story that self-consciously deployed DC and Marvel prototypes (as well as the Image's grim and gritty take on them) and yet questioned the superhero tropes in play. And with *The Walking Dead*, he crafted a horror story that harkened to the controversial past of comics (as well as George Romero's take on zombies) and yet paved a way to a new mainstream audience for comic books as comic books and as transmedia entertainment.

With Image's attempt to promote a superhero universe with clearly interlocking superhero titles, the proposal for *Invincible* was the easier proposal to sell. As mentioned earlier, Kirkman developed a keen sense of how to negotiate between his own storytelling sensibilities and the market: appealing to publishers and readers. Abandoning his passion project "Science Dog" (about a superintelligent talking dog), he pitched a coming-of-age superhero story that utilized his strengths: character development and humor. Mark Grayson, a teenager and the only child of the superhero Omni-Man, manifests superpowers similar to his father and finds himself in need of his father's unique guidance. Catapulted into a world of superheroes where secret identities are maintained and absurd threats are fought, he relies on his iconic father (a clear stand-in for Superman in the Image universe). However, this Golden Age superhero setup is thrown into complete turmoil when he discovers his father has brutally murdered the Guardians of the Globe (a clear stand-in for the Justice League).

Rather than an extraterrestrial with benevolent intentions, Omni-Man has been sent to Earth to prepare the planet for colonization. This early twist in the series brought up a question of audience for the series that had been characterized as an all-ages alternative to the grim and gritty content represented by Image's early output (with titles like Todd McFarlane's *Spawn*). Kirkman states, "Jimmy Olsen could get his head blown off tomorrow. I'm not going to show it on panel, and it's not going to be gratuitous, and I'm not trying to do a gritty and depressing superhero comic, but that guy could go tomorrow" (Fahey). While depicting graphic violence, the series continued to work as a redress of the grim and gritty revenge plot with a continued focus on family drama and an often-humorous tone in line with the nostalgic era of the 2000s (with titles like Mark Waid's *Astro City*). *Invincible* negotiates an interesting space between the concerns related to growing up in a broken family and the consequences of living in a world where conventional law cannot prevent the brutal oppressions of people with superpowers. In particular, the series examines changes to Mark's values as he becomes a father and leader of a family and as he become a superhero and a leader of a nation.

With a realistic passage of time and aging of characters, the series moves beyond the repetitive, constantly reset myth of superheroes (described as the "oneiric climate" by Umberto Eco). And with domestic concerns, the series moves beyond the Western loner hero who works only through redemptive violence (described as the superhero's American monomyth by Robert Jewett and John Shelton Lawrence). Although devoted to superhero stories in general, Kirkman states that superhero "comics are based on male power fantasies" (Abrams 79). While the series satisfies in conventional terms, having interstellar battles with would-be colonizers of earth, *Invincible* also deals with the problematic morality of stories typically solved with one big punch. In addition to partnering with the former supervillain and eco-terrorist Dinosaurus and prioritizing Dinosaurus's environmental goals, Mark leaves earth in the hands of the former superhero and authoritarian ruler Robot; after Robot's violent takeover of the superhero community, Robot keeps himself from public view and provides the world with everything superheroes were supposed to provide: universal peace, prosperity, education, and more.

By making "Science Dog" Mark's favorite comic early in the series, Kirkman would take jabs at the mainstream comics industry, but his most potent criticisms were built into the story itself: questioning superhero stories that never end or examine their moral implications. In regard to radical changes undone by the perennial superhero reboot, Kirkman states, "I know that *Civil*

War being what it is, Captain America will be alive again soon and Iron Man and he will be best friends, . . . and all the consequences of *Civil War* will be undone . . . That's how it works" (Abrams 76). In *Invincible*'s "Reboot?" arc, Kirkman not only reveals that the return to Mark's origin is a fantasy induced by aliens but also that the fantasy has cost him five years of time and caused *irreversible* loss.

A GOOD HORROR COMIC NEVER DIES: HOW SURVIVAL IS MORE HORRIBLE THAN ZOMBIES

Arguably much more significant to Kirkman's early career would be *The Walking Dead*, a series proposal nearly rejected because zombies were then considered a monster of little interest in the twenty-first century. Although that near-rejection now seems ridiculous, Kirkman worked around the problem by pitching a zombie outbreak that results from an alien invasion. As the series gained a loyal following, he never had to put into place the "alien invasion" explanation that he considered a ruse from the start. The success of this graphically violent horror comic demonstrated fundamental change in a time beyond the Comics Code that had prohibited content associated with crime but more specifically with horror. Moreover, *The Walking Dead* demonstrated a shift in the interests of the comic book reading public away from superhero stories that continued to make much more money in other media incarnations. This title comfortably sat alongside other successful genre titles that also distanced themselves from the American comic book history of the superhero like *The Sandman*, *Sin City*, *Fables*, and *Y: The Last Man* from publishers like Vertigo, Dark Horse, and Image. Through *The Walking Dead* and a few other works like the film *28 Days Later* and the novel *World War Z*, zombies and their apocalyptic world again made their way to the forefront of popular culture: flexible metaphors to represent many cultural anxieties.

With Rick Grimes wakening to a world overrun by flesh-eating zombies, Kirkman again sets up a heroic figure whose stereotypical arc will be frustrated by circumstance. As a small-town sheriff wounded in action, Rick possessed many qualities of the reluctant cowboy walking the line between civilization and the wilderness. Kirkman's great contribution to the idea behind zombie stories (which would pave the way for the television adaptation of the series) was to recognize that this end-of-times disaster story was better as a story that never ended. Billed as "a continuing story of survival horror," the fan engagement came less from a desire to see zombie attacks and more from a desire to see the long developmental arcs of characters like Rick living through the zombie apocalypse. The real horror then resulted from the "heroes" who became monstrous in the name of survival: a change made completely believable in narrative terms. Kirkman states, "I think the main theme about *The Walking Dead* is that deep down we really are all rotten people . . . The whole book really is just based on me thinking 'Wow, this would be really screwed up if it happened to me'" (Fahey).

One of the often-cited highlights from the first years of the series was a speech in which Rick refers to his fellow survivors, not the zombies, as the walking dead. Clearly unafraid to kill his darlings, the series made everyone including Rick seem expendable and by extension forced the reader to understand the uncivilized depths to which sympathetic characters sink. In regard to Rick, Kirkman states, "To a certain extent, he's a vicious killer, but he's still fairly likable and he has a reason for everything he does. If this was the kind of book where he could be rescued and taken to some kind of utopia, I seriously doubt he'd be able to adjust to that kind of society after everything he's been through" (Abrams 83). Again dealing with family issues, Rick often prioritizes the needs of his wife, son, and makeshift survivor group over those of other survivors and the idea of civilization. While the zombies provide a constant threat, the figures often identified as villains (or the true monsters in the series) are the authoritarian leaders who rise during this apocalypse like the Governor, Neegan, and Alpha. And yet, they are not so much villains as antagonists to Rick's group and often can be better understood as foils or doubles for Rick.[3]

When the hostilities of a climactic battle with another survivor group are suspended, Rick softens and nearly convinces the power-mad Neegan with his advocacy of the peace-and-cooperation characteristic of civilization—and then slits Neegan's throat. For Kirkman, the idea of the monstrous in all people makes the zombie a potent metaphor[4] for systematic failures and cultural anxieties: "I think zombies were popular during the Cold War and zombies are popular again because of the threat of terrorism and how we all live in fear right now. I think when we're living in an environment where we're told to go out and buy plastic sheets and duct tape like we're building nuclear bunkers in our backyard, we start to think about the end of the world, and that's become popular in fiction" (Abrams 87).

While obviously working against the old Comics Code standards and harkening back to EC horror, Kirkman also operates at a level described by H. P. Lovecraft: evoking a dread of the horror already with and within us. Kirkman demonstrated many talents within this series, particularly with an attention to dialogue most would associate more with playwrights than comic book writers. Though not short on action or graphic violence, the series was just as likely to employ words to describe graphic violence as to employ visuals. Rarely using flashbacks or dream sequences, Kirkman relied on the horror of the immediate experience conveyed in words and thereby in the imagination of the readers. Consequently, Kirkman made the series less about frightening monsters and more about horrifying ideas like the coherent ways in which we define ourselves (revealing that Kristeva's horror concept, the abject, exists not so much in the bodies of rotting corpses as in the minds of human beings).

Through *Invincible* and *The Walking Dead*, Kirkman would establish important patterns for himself as a storyteller including a focus on interpersonal dynamics, an understanding of compositional theory, and a sense of comics as pronounced collaboration. In terms of interpersonal dynamics, Kirkman states, "I think that plot is terrible and boring. Plot is really just so that it's not people talking in rooms the whole time. But the character stuff, that's the part that interests me. I think if you really pay attention I think that most of my plots are really half-assed. Well, you've gotta go over here and you've gotta do a thing. Great. And now we can just sit around and talk about our feelings" (Harper). While many Kirkman fans would take issue with his assessment of his plots, this statement suggests that his genre-based starting points are just a means to an end (and the complexity he loves in characters have the power to undermine the conventional gratuities of genre).

In terms of compositional theory, Kirkman states, "I try to organize my thoughts into a rough outline. . . . [but] I'm not bound to that plot outline, I veer from it quite a bit—I've even completely changed the last half of a couple issues at the last minute because I've changed my mind. . . . It's all up in the air until it's typed up" (Frisch, "Interview") and "I have a rule on killing characters. . . . If I ever kept a character around because I thought it would be good for the story, I'd feel like I was cheating. That's not how death works. It's supposed to be quick and sudden and disruptive" (Frisch, "Nine Questions"). In opposition to the careful planning associated with high literature, Kirkman adopts and defends a practice much more in line with the scatological practices of pulp writers driven by a deadline, shaped by the thrill of plot twists, and derided by defenders of traditional art culture.

Further along those lines, Kirkman refuses the godlike control of the author and elevates the importance of contributions of artists with whom he works: a collaboration essential to the medium's visual narrative. In reference to that collaboration, Kirkman reveals his artists joke with one another about

This exchange between Rick and Abraham represents the text-heavy drama characteristic of Kirkman's style. From *The Walking Dead*, Book 5, by Robert Kirkman and Charlie Adlard; Image Comics, 2010.

his scripts: "It'll be because I say things like, 'This guy's got a brick and he's getting ready to throw it through a window. I don't know, maybe he should have a crowbar to throw through the window because that might look cooler. Really, it's up to you.' . . . I like the free-flowing, I'm-having-a-discussion-with-the-artist style" (Abrams 72). Ultimately, Kirkman always gives credit to his artists with an almost accidental humility that clearly undermines a traditional, preindustrial, literary notion of the writer as a singular genius. However, while he loves this dynamic working relationship and the medium itself, his love of comic books does not uniformly lead to a love of the comic book industry.

THE SICKNESS UNTO DEATH: THE INDUSTRY'S "CONTINUING STORY OF SURVIVAL HORROR"

With these successes to his name, Kirkman would work for a short time with Marvel on some of the company's most notable characters: the X-Men, Avengers, Captain America, and Spider-Man. Providing often quirky and critical takes on superheroism with *The Irredeemable Ant-Man* and the "League of Losers" arc in *Marvel Team-Up*, Kirkman's most popular story for Marvel would also feature zombies (furthering a storyline suggested by Mark Millar in *Ultimate Fantastic Four*). With a title referring to the label given to Marvel fans, *Marvel Zombies* presented the Marvel superhero universe overrun by a zombie virus. Told from the perspective of the zombie superheroes (almost all Marvel superheroes had succumbed to the virus), the series examined the all-consuming Marvel universe and the mindlessness of beings driven to consume; the series subtly and humorously commented on Marvel's superhero industry (somewhat like George Romero's critique of consumer culture through the mall setting of *Dawn of the Dead*). Although this meaning may have been subliminal for Kirkman, it would serve as a precursor for Kirkman's definitive break from the company-owned properties of superhero companies DC and Marvel.[5] In love with superheroes in general (and some in particular), Kirkman would be frustrated by the editorial and contractual limitations placed on him in narrative, creative, and vocational terms.

Subsequently, Kirkman joined past advocates for creators' rights like Dave Sim, Scott McCloud, and (in a literal way) Todd McFarlane at Image. Through a video manifesto posted online, Kirkman began his life as a partner at Image Comics by making a definitive statement against the corporate practices of DC and Marvel; he identified their model as a threat that undermined the long-term success of comics publishing. He effectively described the situation seen a decade later when DC and especially Marvel would treat comic books only as research and development for other more profitable superhero ventures.[6] This would become an enduring motivation for his expanding life as a creator, corporate leader, and independent businessman. For Kirkman, the essential argument against storytelling within the context of an international corporation is that product management prohibits individual ownership and innovative storytelling. In regard to independent-creator ownership, Kirkman states, "I'm not answering to stockholders, and I am not perpetuating a property. I am not obligated to keep someone in the same costume because there's a lunchbox on the shelf, or keep him with his girlfriend because there's a movie coming out where they're together" (Fahey).

Kirkman would continue to love comic books as comic books and not see them as research and development for a more profitable media venture. This would not prevent him from eventually expanding his creative work (like *The Walking Dead*) as a transmedia phenomenon, but he would negotiate between his own control and the freedom of his collaborators (much as he had done with comic book artists). Moreover, Kirkman would see the potential in transmedia adaptation and technological innovation as a business means to reach the goals of personal ownership and artistic integrity. Kirkman states, "As we move into the digital era I think that the problems that we've had with distribution, getting books out to a larger audience, are going to go away . . . we're not going to try to sell original material to an audience that's predisposed to keeping their runs of Daredevil intact . . . that'll make for a better comic book industry because people will be doing more original stuff" (Adams).

THE ZOMBIE APOCALYPSE WILL BE TELEVISED, NOVELIZED, AND VIDEO GAME-IZED

While Kirkman would remain passionately devoted to comics and continue working actively as a comics writer, he also developed *The Walking Dead* as a television series with Hollywood producer Frank Darabont (famous for his film adaptations of works by Stephen King). Eventually landing on the cable network AMC, the success of the series would be multifaceted, certainly increasing Kirkman's net worth and taking his creator-owned properties to new heights of desirability for adaptation. However, his approach to the properties would be fundamentally different than that of larger conglomerates, refusing to force his works into other media forms simply because the market indicated they could earn big money in the short run. To more effectively manage adaptations of his work and to also develop original projects in comic books and other media forms, Kirkman founded Skybound Entertainment with film and television producer David Alpert in 2010. Within the context of Skybound, creator's rights became more than a legal right and guided the company's ethos.

Moving away from the authoritarian control associated with a conglomerate like Disney (which purchased Marvel in 2009), Kirkman encouraged something like the open-ended writer/artist partnerships in his comic books (with products as a creative negotiation between owners and adapters). In particular reference to *The Walking Dead*, he maintained some level of creative control over the television series but practiced the art of adaptation in an interesting way. As the series brought the comic book's new zombie craze, graphically violent horror, and dystopic antiheroism to the mainstream, Kirkman didn't treat his comic book as an authoritative text. Unlike other creator-controlled projects like J. K. Rowling's *Harry Potter* series, he allowed experimentation with the narrative; the comic book served as a basic roadmap, but new characters were introduced, new subplots altered major events, and central characters died years before their comic book demise. Clearly stating that the original version was not authoritative and the most recent version was not his "director's cut," Kirkman worked with a love of variants characteristic of both folklore and the postliterate digital narratives.

In general reference to Skybound, Kirkman further developed business skills that first manifested themselves in rudimentary ways in his life as a self-publisher; he recognized the potential of his own material and that of others created under the Skybound umbrella as brands. At the same time, he didn't fall into the bottomless pit of product development that led to merchandising in the form of socks and Happy Meals featuring his characters. Similar to Pixar, a collective of creatives, the company fostered innovation in new comic book work as well as work in film, television, animation, and video games. Central to the company's approach was to develop work in one area that might be extended (and not just adapted) in another media form, but the multimedia presence of every property was not an essential end goal. Kirkman states, "There's this soulless corporate idea of transmedia, but there's also an organic, almost accidental transmedia, which I think is a bit truer. . . . While we are working in video games and TV and movies and comics, not everything we do has to plug into every one of those sections of the entertainment world. We're just trying to make the best stuff possible" (Crescente). Each media form was understood as having its own characteristics, with each suited (or not suited) to represent the specifics of individual projects.

In addition, in his life as a fan and a young writer, he had participated in and benefitted from the comic book–convention fan culture that encouraged the breakdown of the producer/consumer dichotomy. Consequently, the Skybound business model would be based on a consistent outreach to fans as much more than mindless buyers: understanding their interests and opinions as a viable influence on (and not a violation of) Skybound's products.

WITH THE SKY AS THE LIMIT, FEET ARE ON THE GROUND AND HANDS IN THE WRITING

In addition to superhero company giants like DC and Marvel and unexpected independent successes like Eastman and Laird's *Teenage Mutant Ninja Turtles* in the twentieth century, Kirkman would move to the forefront as a comic book creator with properties that successfully moved into the mainstream. Disapproving voices would claim that he stumbled upon the new monster of choice with *The Walking Dead*, but approving voices would claim that he succeeded by instituting creator-centered practices with Skybound: practices like those of EC Comics (nearly erased from existence by the Comics Code) that encouraged satisfaction, creativity, and innovation. Whether or not the latter is the reason for the success of TellTale's *The Walking Dead* video game (both popular and critically acclaimed), it could be argued that Kirkman's enduring position as a company man who advocates for creator's rights is probably due to still being in the creative mix of things as a very active comic book writer.

Unlike other comic book creators who transitioned entirely to multimedia production, Kirkman continued to write critically acclaimed comics work. Kirkman states, "I get this a lot with the whole 'You're in television now. Why would you slum it in comic books?' It's one of the most offensive things that happens to me in interviews. . . . It's a medium that's driving all of entertainment now. We should have a little more respect for it. I feel honored to be able to continue to do comics" (Harper). Continuing the long arcs of comic book series of *Invincible* and *The Walking Dead*, Kirkman would add to his excessive workload with other genre work such as *Super Dinosaur* (adolescent science adventure, 2011), *Thief of Thieves* (crime drama, 2012), *Outcast* (horror/thriller, 2014), and *Oblivion Song* (science fiction with fantasy elements, 2018). Often resistant to the high-culture argument for comics as art and an object of academic study, Kirkman would more often articulate his understanding of comic books as a unique medium (in ways not dissimilar from comics luminary Will Eisner). Kirkman states, "Comics are a medium that is dependent on an individual; ten people can read the same comic and all get a different experience out of it . . . the pacing and so many other things, the inflection on dialogue and all this other stuff, is based on you. That freedom for an audience member to kind of control their experience is really awesome and unique" (Crescente). And as time passes, Kirkman becomes more willing to explore the deeper themes of his works and moves beyond his earlier claims that he simply subverted expectations for the sake of entertainment value.

Both *Outcast* and *Oblivion Song* continue to explore issues characteristic of his earlier works, including the relationships in extended families, the aberrant in normal psychology, and the monstrous in everyday life. But in each case, Kirkman, who had largely avoided religion and politics, now identified these ideas as giving rise to the specific narrative contours of these titles. In *Outcast*, Kyle Barnes fights the demon possession in those around him with the help of true believer Reverend Anderson, but they both discover that demon possession is not what they expected. In addition to tackling religion and belief in general in a serious way avoided by *Battle Pope*, Kirkman creates a sympathetic bias for the conclave that forms around Kyle. From the outside viewed as a cult, the group becomes a vehicle to examine the power of belief and the question of truth in a post-Christian world obsessed with the mechanics of power.

In *Oblivion Song*, scientist Nathan Cole uses technology to travel to another world called Oblivion to rescue people from a part of Philadelphia replaced by a part of Oblivion and its monsters years earlier. As the series unfolds, Nathan's fixation grows not only from his brother being one of the missing but also from his experiments being the likely reason for the disaster. With the tragedy being localized and the protagonist being burdened with survivor's guilt, *Oblivion Song* becomes a more definite exploration of the post-9/11 concerns of American culture. Kirkman states, "You kind of think about things like 9/11 or income inequality or global terrorism; people just get used to things in a really odd way. It's the greatest strength and the greatest weakness of us as a civilization. We are very adept at normalizing things and going, 'Okay, this is the foundation of our lives now and let's forget about that other stuff and move on.' And it's sometimes not the best thing to do" (Harper). Kirkman had joked about fans' preference for living in the "simpler times" of the world of *The Walking Dead* but literally explores this possibility when some people caught in the "transference" of Philadelphia choose to stay in the monster-filled world of Oblivion. With these works, Kirkman cements himself as one of the foremost comic book writers using genre conventions as a means to understand trauma in the postindustrial world.

ENDINGS AND NEW BEGINNINGS: BEING OUT-OF-TOUCH IN THE BEST WAYS

After bringing *Invincible* to a close in 2017, the series has received critical attention as one of the great superhero epics of all time (while being developed as film and animation projects). And after bringing *The Walking Dead* (the "zombie movie that *never ends*") to a close in 2019, the series has become a new standard for long-form comics narrative, revisionist horror drama, and multiplatform company success; of course, *The Walking Dead* story would continue to unfold in multiple television series and video games. While the number of viewers has dropped for the shows, that is likely due to a migration from scheduled cable station content to online streaming service content; *The Walking Dead* is still one of the highest rated cable dramas. With the conclusion of these long-running comics series, critics and scholars began putting together retrospective pieces on them and on Kirkman. To some, this seemed like an important moment to find answers to questions raised about Kirkman's worldview as a traditional white male or an unconventional proponent for diversity, as a small-town gun advocate or a progressive reformer revealing the consequences of violence, etc.—especially because neither of the series ends with the bloody death of civilization and existential bleakness that many had predicted.

In fact, many characterized the ending of *Invincible* as harkening back to a Golden or Silver Age optimism evinced at the beginning of the series, something that Kirkman identified as of interest long before. Kirkman states, "If you look at what kids had growing up in the '60s and '70s and at the excitement in the world at the time . . . I mean, we don't have . . . an excitement in being an American that we had back then, so yeah, there are all kinds of things that are not making the imagination as it was back then. Now we live in a bitter society that's not very optimistic" (Abrams 76). Likewise, while Rick is ignobly killed in a minor conflict shortly before the end of *The Walking Dead*, many suggested the flash-forward demonstrated the more important (triumphant and not tragic) survival of Rick's often-challenged dream of human civilization through the containment of the zombie threat and the reestablishment of a functioning right-minded government.

However, these characterizations are too simplistic. Kirkman himself provided an afterward to the last issue of *The Walking Dead* that reminded readers of his compositional process by suggesting the ending would have been much bleaker had he ended at another point.[7] With a long-form narrative developed less due to a long story-arc plan and more due to rereading his past work and riffing on it,[8] Kirkman's work can be justifiably understood differently at different points in his various series; and Kirkman's endings can be justifiably understood differently with different emphases from a variety of readers at the end.[9] Moreover, these endings are only brighter by relative degrees, with *The Walking Dead* flash forward in particular. Focusing on a much older Carl (Rick's son), the final issue offers a picture of a future where the zombie threat is now quite easily contained; however, it still offers several points at which a rebuilt society, increasing in size and complexity, may still fall apart due to problems within the individual and collective (one of Kirkman's points of focus within the series).

While some may find this all to add up to thematic inconsistency (especially if judged by classical compositional standards), others may identify it as complexity. And it certainly works to encourage the fan culture that debates the relative merits of various arcs of Kirkman's series and even explores alternate routes that could have been taken by the comic book, television shows, or video game. Along those lines, the literal, commercial details of the ending of *The Walking Dead* created a stir among fans buying individual issues of the series, as the final issue wasn't promoted as the final issue (and solicitations to stores were created for following issues that would never be produced). This works in several interesting ways to 1) intentionally continue to subvert the narrative and provide unexpected twists to the horror narrative; and 2) artificially create a collector's item–buying frenzy characteristic of comic-store phenomena of Kirkman's youth.

But perhaps most importantly, it also asserts Kirkman's control over a creation that has become increasingly influenced by other creators and fans focused on other manifestations of *The Walking Dead*. Kirkman states, "But the 'I own this' stuff is interesting, where somebody could be in a comic shop and be like, 'Well, that's not right. That's not Carl.' Whatever. I fucking made Carl; I can do whatever I want with him. . . . If I want the story to be something that you don't like, that's my right. It's a fascinating journey to be on with *The Walking Dead* 'cause there are so many people that have their opinions, watching it, and there are so many people behind the scenes that are working on it. It's a very, very weird experience" (Harper). Interestingly, this statement comes from an interview in which Kirkman also celebrates a cantankerous fan-letter writer as an integral part of his creative life. Clearly, the negotiation of creator's rights and fan "ownership" is an evolving issue in the understanding of the contemporary comics world and, interestingly, is an evolving issue in Kirkman's understanding of his own work.[10] Despite his sense of his own position as no longer "up and coming," Kirkman in many ways is still at the contentious center of ideas in popular culture.

The conflict between Carl and the Hershel, the zombie-showman, shows how hard-won lessons have already been lost. From *The Walking Dead*, Book 16, by Robert Kirkman and Charlie Adlard; Image Comics, 2019.

A FEW NOTES BEFORE WALKING AWAY: THE UNLIKELY TRIUMPH OF ROBERT KIRKMAN

The end of *The Walking Dead* represents a conundrum at the center of Kirkman's identity as a creator: he's an optimist who in narrative terms can't quite believe in his optimism. This applies to his own success and in interviews, Kirkman recognizes his accomplishment, influence, and net worth and yet still demonstrates some level of surprise. With *Outcast* concluding its final arc in 2020, Kirkman continues his success as a writer with the popular *Oblivion Song* and maintains his busyness by adding the young series *Die! Die! Die!* and *Fire Power* to his schedule. Skybound expands its various media offerings through collaborations with Jon Goldman (film), David Alpert (television), and Catherine Winder (animation)—among other notable creators working those and other media areas—and Skybound expanded its offices beyond Beverly Hills to Vancouver in 2016. And the overarching doubt of blind optimism even more noticeably drives his creative work, which questions narrative tropes undergirding society's unexamined life. Understanding himself as a blue-collar joe who inexplicably made it big, his work explores the territory between the ideas of Romanticism and postmodernism—although he never uses these terms himself. However, the idea of subversion is one to which Kirkman often returns, and it applies to both his business practice and his compositional strategy.

In the following interviews, which span his career, the evolution of Kirkman as an important comic book creator and media producer can be seen. Always willing to share his thoughts in plain and unpretentious terms, he speaks as a writer, collaborator, genre expert, industry insider, creator rights advocate, multimedia adapter, and producer. Last but not least, Kirkman speaks as a humorist, an aspect that might seem less significant but does much more than make his interviews readable; while his wit demonstrates he clearly has fun, he also uses it as a vehicle to self-consciously spoof his own work and more importantly, to incisively critique the comic book world and related media industries. Like Stan Lee in importance, Robert Kirkman is even more a brand in himself, representative of a different time period in comics history; hopefully, this volume will serve as a worthwhile and important point of departure into a study of his work.

In regard to the interview selection, it should be mentioned that a variation on one question connects many of the interviews: how would you survive a zombie apocalypse? Otherwise, each interview has distinctions that merit its inclusion. Leighton Conner's interview is an early conversation that showcases a young Kirkman and his enthusiastic advocacy of *Battle Pope*; as a bonus, it also features Tony Moore, Kirkman's earliest artistic collaborator. Sean Fahey's interview covers the early success of *The Walking Dead*, an interesting discussion of horror, and Kirkman's initial optimism about his working relationship with Marvel. Marc-Oliver Frisch's first of two interviews deals with Kirkman's creative process and some early ruminations on the economics of comics sales; and the second interview offers follow-up to the first and asks questions that further reveal *The Walking Dead* as an international phenomenon. D. J. Kirkbride's interview is a free-wheeling conversation that encourages Kirkman to be funny (and invent a fictitious past with Brian Michael Bendis). The Simon Abrams interview is an incredibly extensive retrospective that develops deep context illuminating Kirkman's work and career. John Joseph Adams and David Barr Kirtley's podcast interview focuses on Kirkman's world as it expands to include Skybound Entertainment, *The Walking Dead* television show, and his growing dissatisfaction with Marvel and DC.

Aaron Sagers' interview sets Kirkman alongside Max Brooks, author of *World War Z*, arguably the other most significant figure in the twenty-first century revival of the zombie (no pun intended). Evan O. Albert's interview comes from a Lexington publication and provides some local perspective on the Kentucky boy who made it big. Brian Crecente's interview connects Kirkman's work as a writer to his work as the founder of Skybound and focuses on creative work in other media forms like video games. Jesse Schendeen's interview is specifically focused on *The Walking Dead* #150 and provides a window into the way traditional comic book collectors interface with Kirkman. Abraham Riesman's interview looks at Skybound's documentary on the comics industry and elicits Kirkman's opinions as a creator activist. David Harper's podcast interview places Kirkman's continued devotion as a comic writer within the context of his multiplatform work and his relationship to his ever-expanding constellation of fans. And Milton Griepp's interview poses questions about marketing decisions that seem to work against the short-term money-making potential of comic books still published on a monthly basis. To honor a part of Kirkman's creative life that he identifies as crucially important, an appendix also features short interviews with several of Kirkman's most significant collaborators: Ryan Ottley (*Invincible*), Paul Azaceta (*Outcast*), and England's former comic laureate, Charlie Adlard (*The Walking Dead*).

Ultimately, this introduction represents a few of my own ideas on the interviews gathered in this collection, and while I hold those ideas dear, the main point of this collection is to encounter his words firsthand in order to develop your own ideas from and about Kirkman. The selection of interviews represents the chronological spread of his career and focuses on different aspects of his career: not only covering conversations on most of the series that he has written but also covering conversations on many of his ideas as a businessman. In addition, the selection is drawn from a variety of publications and podcasts led by interviewers who complicate a simplistically drawn continuum that places scholars on one end and fans on the other. And in the end and perhaps more importantly, I believe the volume works well as a whole not only because of Kirkman's important place in comic book history but also because of the way the selection represents his fun, engaging, and insightful personality.

Notes

1. Although the differences that preceded are more significant, it should be noted that Kirkman regularly identifies himself as small-town guy; this is a way that his everyman status differs from that of Stan Lee (almost always associated with New York): "[Cynthiana] was a small town, and I was aware of maybe six kids in the whole middle school that read comics. I could talk to them, but as far as neighborhood kids—I lived out in the country, so I maybe had two neighborhood friends who were within bike-riding distance" (Abrams 46).

2. These concerns would continue throughout his career: "I wouldn't say I was a sell-out, but I did try to think of commercial ways to make my books appeal to a broader audience at the creation stage" (Abrams 66) and "Anything that I can do to help the retailer to help sell my product, it all just comes back to me in the end. So I'm helping them and I'm helping me by helping them. Anything I can do to get a project on a solid footing as early as possible is to me a worthwhile endeavor" (Harper).

3. Heroism is hard for these characters to maintain in the absence of a meaning for living beyond survival (or even an explanation for the zombie outbreak): "The thing about *The Walking Dead*, though, is that it is about normal people in Atlanta, and they're in the woods—in a camp—and they're stealing canned goods from grocery stores, and hanging out in the woods fighting zombies every now and then. Those people would never find out what happened" (Fahey).

4. "I think zombies are the closest reflection to what we are" (Fahey).

5. Kirkman did resist Marvel imperatives in other ways, such as not participating in universe-wide crossovers in *Marvel Team-Up*: "As a writer, I try to avoid it, which is usually pretty foolish [in terms of immediate sales]. When I was writing *Marvel Team-Up*, *House of M* was going on. I could have done a *House of M* issue; I could have done three *House of M* issues. I just kept thinking, 'I'm going to have a long run on this book

and when I look back on my run, I don't want to have to look back on my run and think, 'Well, issues #18–20 are *House of M*, so in order to understand those issues in my run, you have to go back and find those *House of M* trades and figure out what that stuff is about.' I just wanted the reader to be able to sit down with #1–25 and think, 'I picked up issues #1–25 and it all makes sense.' . . . For me, as a reader, the veil has been lifted." (Abrams 76)

6. Years later, Kirkman would continue to articulate his love of comics and thereby fight against the idea of using comics primarily as a means to an end. "I have to make it strictly a comic. It would be very easy for me, because I am well-versed in how productions go at this point, to go, 'Oh, well, I'll make this monster smaller, so it can be a guy in a suit, instead of a CG thing.' Or, 'Let's change the world this way, so that it'll work better on a set.' There's different things that I could do to make a production easier, but that would be limiting to the comic space. The beauty of doing a comic is that you don't have those limitations. I'm always very mindful of anytime anything like that creeps into my head of, 'It would be better if you did this.' I end up pushing myself in the opposite direction because I want to stay, quote, true to the streets, unquote, if that makes any sense. I don't want to feel like I'm a Hollywood sellout by structuring my comics for other mediums" (Griepp).

7. An earlier interview seems to indicate something similar. "I'm indifferent [to Rick]; I don't like or dislike him. One of the things I wanted to show with Rick is how far people can go and what limits they can be pushed to and how much they can change over time. Over the course of *The Walking Dead*, Rick has gone from being an optimistic small-town cop to beating people to death with his bare hands when he feels his family is threatened." (Abrams 83). However, plot mechanics mean Rick doesn't live to be part of the full return of civilization.

8. "I know the first issue better than I know the twelfth issue because I'm constantly looking back and paying attention to what's going on and monitoring things. And I do that on all my books" (Harper).

9. With an honesty not characteristic of many well-established writers in their interviews, Kirkman has expressed regrets (making the Marvel's gay character Freedom Ring into an incompetent superhero) and acknowledged course corrections (making *The Walking Dead*'s katana-wielding Michonne as a contrast to the series more passive female characters).

10. Kirkman on short arcs versus long arcs and pleasing the fans versus pleasing himself: "I don't like it when an entire story is self-contained in six issues, followed by another completely self-contained arc. I want things to build in my stories . . . and build up to payoff, so that people feel rewarded by reading long runs of the books. . . . I think dropping things in a story that reflect to old stories makes a new reader want to hunt down back issues. So that's how I do things, the way I prefer. That's really all I can do.

I'm writing this stuff all day, every day. I'm the one that has to be kept happy" (Frisch, Interview).

Works Cited

Abrams, Simon. "The Robert Kirkman Interview." *Comics Journal*, no. 289, April 2008, 41–96.

Adams, John Joseph, and David Barr Kirtley. "The Geek's Guide to the Galaxy Podcast, Episode 25: Interview with Robert Kirkman." *Io9*, 11 November 2010. https://geeks guideshow.com/geeks-guide-to-the-galaxy-podcast-episode-25-interview-with-robert -kirkman-transcript/.

Connor, Leighton. "Robert Kirkman and Tony Moore: *The Death Cookie* Interview." *The Death Cookie*. July ,2000. http://www.deathcookie.com/index.php/features/ interviewslist/99-dc-interview-vault-robert-kirkman-a-tony-moore.

Crescente, Brian. "The Kirkman Effect: How an Undead Army May Recreate Entertainment." *Polygon*, 30 March 2015. https://www.polygon.com/features/2015/3/30/8311735/the -walking-dead-invincible-outcast-fear-the-walking-dead-interview-robert-kirkman.

Fahey, Sean. "Interview: Robert Kirkman." *Thor's Comic Column* hosted by *CHUD.com*. 22 March 2004.

Frisch, Oliver. "Interview with Robert Kirkman." *Comicgate*, November 2005. http://archiv .comicgate.de/interviews-in-english/interview-with-robert-kirkman.html.

Frisch, Oliver. "Nine Questions with Robert Kirkman." *Der Tagesspigel*. March 2010. https://www.tagesspiegel.de/kultur/comics/interview-der-tod-kommt-schnell-und-ploet
zlich/1764602.html.

Griepp, Milton. "ICv2 Interview: Robert Kirkman, Parts 1 & 2." *ICv2*, 28 January 2019. https://icv2.com/articles/news/view/42363/icv2-interview-robert-kirkman-part-1.

Harper, David. "Off Panel 47: The Comic Life with Robert Kirkman." *SKTCHD*, 19 March 2018. https://sktchd.com/podcast/off-panel-147-the-comic-life-with-robert-kirkman/.

Kirkbride, D. J. "Science Dog and Zombies: An Interview with Robert Kirkman." *Silver Bullet Comics*. 23 January, 2006.

CHRONOLOGY

1978   Born November 30 in Lexington, Kentucky; his immediate family eventually includes a younger brother (five years junior) and a younger sister (thirteen years junior).

1988   Moves to Cynthiana, Kentucky.

1991   Meets Tony Moore and future wife Sonia in seventh grade. DC's "Death of Superman" story runs through 1993, indicating a change in the marketplace for collector comics and content for mainstream superhero stories. Image Comics is founded with six associated studios (comics initially published through Malibu Comics). Erik Larsen's *Savage Dragon* published by Image.

1997   Graduates high school, moves to Lexington, Kentucky. Father moves to Florida with Kirkman's brother and sister. Works at Red Rock Collectibles and Kentucky Lighting and Supply company. Provides illustrations for Hex Games' QAGS (the Quick Ass Game System).

1999   Creates first comic *Between the Ropes* (cowritten with Robert Sutton) on wrestling; rejected by Diamond.

2000   *Battle Pope* with Tony Moore self-published under Funk-O-Tron (ran through 2002 as a series of limited series).

2001   Interviews Erik Larsen for *PencilJack.com*.

2002   Marries Sonia. *SuperPatriot* (created by Erik Larsen) miniseries (#1–4) with Cory Walker published by Image. *Tech Jacket* miniseries (#1–6) with E. J. Su published by Image.

2003   *Masters of the Universe: Icons of Evil* (eight one-shots) with various artists published by CrossGen. *Invincible* with Cory Walker published by Image (Ryan Ottley would become the ongoing artist) (runs through 2018, issue #144). *Walking Dead* with Tony Moore published by Image (Charlie Adlard would become the ongoing artist) (runs through 2019, issue #193). *Capes* miniseries (#1–3) with Mark Englert published by Image.

2004   Receives his first Eisner Award nomination for *Invincible*. Hired by Marvel to write *Sleepwalker* series but canceled before debut; completed material appeared in *Epic Anthology*. *Savage Dragon: God of War* miniseries (#1–4) with Mark Englert published by Image. *Captain America* (#29–32) with Scot Eaton published by Marvel. *Jubilee* miniseries (#1–6) with Derec Donovan published by Marvel.

2005   *Marvel Zombies* (an *Ultimate Fantastic Four* spin-off) with Sean Phillips published by Marvel (followed by the prequel *Marvel Zombies: Dead Days* and the sequel *Marvel Zombies 2* in 2007). *Marvel Team-Up, Vol. 3* (runs through 2006, issue #25) with various artists published by Marvel. *Fantastic Four: Foes* miniseries (#1–6) with Cliff Rathburn published by Marvel.

2006   Peter Parker Kirkman is born April 25 to Kirkman and his wife, Sonia. *Ultimate X-Men* (begins with #66 and runs through 2008, issue #93) with various artists. *The Irredeemable Ant-Man* (runs through 2007, issue #12) with Phil Hester and Cory Walker published by Marvel. "Weekend Off," *Tales of Army of Darkness* (one-shot) with Ryan Ottley published by Dynamite. Kirkman's San Diego Comic-Con disagreement with Todd McFarlane leads to *Haunt* (2009).

2007   Receives another Eisner Award nomination, the first for *The Walking Dead*. *The Astounding Wolf-Man* with Jason Howard published by Image (runs through 2010, issue #25).

2008   Becomes partner at Image Comics. Posts his "comic book manifesto" video. *Battle Pope* adapted into eight animated webisodes for Spike TV.

2009   *Haunt* (runs through 2011, #18) with Todd MacFarlane, Greg Capulo, and Ryan Ottley published by Image. *Destroyer* miniseries (#1–5) with Cory Walker published by Marvel (MAX line).

2010   Wins the Eisner Award and Harvey Award for *The Walking Dead*. *The Walking Dead* television series developed with Frank Darabont for AMC (Kirkman writes first season episode "Vatos" and writes one or two episodes every season through season five). Creation of the Beverly Hills-based Skybound with David Alpert (multimedia studio associated with Image that brings together Kirkman's previous and subsequent creator-owned work). *Guardians of the Globe* (an *Invincible* spin-off) with Benito J. Cereno III published by Image (runs through 2011, issue #6).

2011   Moves to Los Angeles, California. Daughter is born to Kirkman and his wife, Sonia. Named the comics-industry Person of the Year by *The Beat*. *Super Dinosaur* (ongoing) with Jason Howard published by Image. *The Infinite* miniseries (#1–4) with Rob Liefeld, published by Image. *The*

Walking Dead: Rise of the Governor (first in a series of text-only novels) cowritten with Jay Bonansinga, published by Thomas Dunne Books.

2012   Sued by Tony Moore for greater compensation for his role in the creation of *The Walking Dead*. *Thief of Thieves* cowritten with Nick-Spenser (and others), with Shaun Martinborough, published by Image (Andy Diggle takes over as writer with #20). Skybound produces *Clone* comic book by David Schuler and Juan Jose Ryp (other comic books titles to follow from Skybound would include *Birthright* and *Witch Doctor*). Telltale produces single-player video game *The Walking Dead: The Game* for various platforms.

2013   Skybound partners with Darin Ross to produce the Kickstarted video game *Superfight,*

2014   *Outcast* with Paul Azaceta published by Image Comics. *The Walking Dead* television series reaches all-time ratings high with an average of 14 million viewers.

2015   Receives his first Bram Stoker Award nomination for *Outcast*. *Fear the Walking Dead* television series (a spin-off of *The Walking Dead*) developed with Dave Erikson for AMC. Skybound produces the interactive VR series *Gone* for Samsung Milk.

2016   Highway signs dedicated to Kirkman in hometown of Cynthiana, Kentucky. Skybound produces the television show *Outcast* for Cinemax (runs for two seasons through 2018). Skybound produces the feature film *Air*. Skybound expands with the Vancouver-based Skybound North.

2017   Wife, Sonia, opens Ashford Acres, a bed and breakfast in Cynthiana, Kentucky. Skybound produces the television documentary *Robert Kirkman's Secret History of Comics* for AMC. Skybound develops exclusive content deal with Amazon to include an adaptation of *Invincible*.

2018   *Oblivion Song* with Lorenzo de Felici published by Image. *Die!Die!Die!* with Scott M. Gimple and Chris Burnham published by Image. Skybound expands with Skybound Games and continues *The Walking Dead* game series after the collapse of Telltale Games.

2019   *The Walking Dead* comic series ends surprisingly with #193 (comic stores have solicitations for #194 and #195).

2020   *Fire Power* with Chris Samnee published by Image.

NOTE: Most years are indisputably correct but Robert Kirkman keeps most things about his private life very private (such as his daughter's name). I have done my best to respect this choice and only included personal details discussed in interviews. In terms of early dates, some years are extrapolated from said interviews (e.g., meeting Tony Moore in seventh grade). Whenever possible, those years have been corroborated by Kirkman's friends and associates.

ROBERT KIRKMAN

Robert Kirkman and Tony Moore:
The Death Cookie Interview

LEIGHTON CONNER / 2000

From *The Death Cookie*, July 2000. Reprinted by permission of Leighton Connor

PART ONE: KIRKMAN

Death Cookie: Give me the lowdown on *Battle Pope*.

Robert Kirkman: The *Battle Pope* miniseries is about the not-so-holy Pope of the not-so-distant future and his quest to rescue Saint Michael with the help of Jesus. It's got lots of action and lots of jokes, so it should be pretty entertaining. I think I might have thrown a couple of chicks in there for eye candy, too. Buy lots!

DC: How did the series come to be?

RK: Tony and I met in middle school, and have been friends ever since. We always liked comics and wanted to someday work on them. Last summer I was digging through some old papers of mine (I keep EVERYTHING) and I found a picture of a "para-military" type Pope I drew my senior year in high school. I looked at it and thought "BATTLE POPE," and then it hit me. I plotted the first issue based on that old sketch, laid out all the pages and mentioned the idea to Tony. He dug it pretty well, and we started on the book less than a month later. It only seemed logical to publish it ourselves. Not that I didn't send out submissions to other publishers—I did. Image, Dark Horse, and Oni didn't seem interested, but it was always the plan to do it ourselves. So far it's worked out pretty well—I can't seem to keep Diamond in stock!

DC: We'll get back to *Battle Pope* in a minute, but I want to get your thoughts on another matter. It's well-documented that you're a big fan of the comic book *Savage Dragon*. What did you think of the big turning point issue #75 that came out a few months back?

RK: I'm not ashamed to admit that I was a little disappointed. There wasn't much resolved, and it was too much of a BIG FLASHY ACTION sequence to feel like the last Dragon issue in this continuity. I've since gotten 76, and I must say that I missed the supporting cast immensely. This new stuff is going to take a little getting used to. I still LIKE it, mind you; it's just not the same. The ART was GREAT though.

DC: Speaking of Erik Larsen's art, have you seen his recent work at Marvel?

RK: I've LOVED it! I enjoyed the *Spider-Man* art a little more than the *Thor* stuff—John Beatty is a GOD! As far as the entire package, *Thor* was a better book, although art-wise there were a few proportion problems. Of course you must realize that Erik HAD to draw BOTH books in two weeks! So the art is bound to suffer a little.

DC: So you liked that pseudo-Kirby style he adopted for *Thor*?

RK: Erik's "Kirby style" isn't much of a stretch from his normal stuff. So I like it; I can't wait for his Fantastic Four project.

DC: How do you feel about Jack Kirby?

RK: I'm a little young, so I find that while I like Kirby's stuff quite a bit, I like the people who try to "ape" him better. Ladronn, Timm, etc.

DC: What other comics creators do you like?

RK: Bob Fingerman, Walt Simonson, Frank Miller, Alan Moore, Warren Ellis, Garth . . . SHIT, doesn't EVERYONE put the SAME names as their answer to these questions! I also like Eli Stone's stuff, Larry Young's work on *Astronauts in Trouble*, and I've been known to enjoy a Rob Liefeld book from time to time.

DC: Are there any creators who have influenced you in the creation of *Battle Pope*?

RK: Other than the obvious Erik Larsen-ness seen in my layouts, none really. I prefer to swipe from television and movies—it's harder to notice that way.

DC: I'm not complaining, but based on the first few pages of *Battle Pope* #1, particularly the line "I christen thee—Pope!" I'm guessing that neither of you is Catholic and that you didn't do a whole lot of research on Pope-related stuff. Is that the case?

RK: Well I'll admit that neither of us is Catholic, BUT . . . I studied the Catholic religion for almost three years before starting the script for BP. I know it inside and out, but you must realize I only had one page for that scene and I couldn't squeeze in the talent or the bikini competition. So I cut straight to the raffle. And STILL only had room to show the end of it. (Tony likes big panels.)

DC: Around page five or so of issue 1, where God judges and condemns everyone, *Battle Pope* reads a bit like a Jack Chick tract. Are you familiar with Mr. Chick's work?

RK: I have seen Jack Chick tracts but most of my knowledge of them is second hand. Any similarities are purely coincidental.

DC: How have sales been so far? In how many countries is the comic available?

RK: Sales have been very good for a small press book, and VERY VERY good for two unknown guys working out of a bedroom in my house with NO money. Seriously, folks, all you need to make a comic is a good idea and Tony Moore.

We are available in all English-speaking countries that Diamond distributes to. We were working out a deal with an Italian company that was going to publish the book in Italian AND French, but I have had no contact with him in a week or two, so I'm assuming the deal fell through.

DC: One of the best parts about *Battle Pope* is the snappy dialogue (like the classic "You been swimmin?") How long does it take you to come up with good dialogue? And do you write the dialogue before or after Tony has drawn the pictures?

RK: The good dialogue like "you been swimming" is often written before we even start an issue. I'll think of something funny and create a scene around it. Most of the dialogue, though, is written after Tony finishes penciling a page. There is a nice descriptive step by step of how we make this comic in issue 2.

DC: If you're going to make a habit out of getting interviewed, you need to get prepared for the really tough questions people are going to ask. So I'm going to help you out by asking a tough question. The age-old question of evil is, if God is all-powerful and all-good, why is there evil in the world? As it relates to *Battle Pope*, I think a more appropriate question is why does God sent agents to help out on Earth? Couldn't he take care of these things himself?

RK: My thought on that is that God doesn't exist, at least how we perceive him he doesn't. I don't really believe in all this hocus pocus. Evil exists because God doesn't. Of course I could be wrong, but so could EVERYONE else.

In *Battle Pope*, God has turned his back on the world. He is no longer involved in it, but he still LOVES the people inhabiting it. So he sends Saint Michael to protect the people on it. He could do it himself, but he condemned them—God can't go back on his word. No one would take him seriously then. Besides we all know God works in mysterious ways.

DC: That's a pretty good answer. Here's an easier question: Is *Battle Pope* basically a single story that will be finished at the end of the miniseries, or do you have further plans for the character?

RK: We have LOTS of future plans for the character! I'd like to get to a point where we do two miniseries a year at some point. But I realize the "gag" part of *Battle Pope* will eventually wear off and the character will have to be put to sleep. I can see about five *Battle Pope* miniseries existing, the last one being "the death of" because that would be cool and fun to do. This ain't *Cerebus*.

DC: You and your cocreator really gush about each other in the letters page to issue 1. Come on, let's be honest here. What's one thing about Tony Moore that really annoys you?

RK: Tony wastes SOOOOO much time in between pages that this miniseries could have come out in winter. He has tons of other stuff to do, mind you, but the boy sleeps at least sixteen hours a day, no shit. Tony can do twelve pages in one week and then two the next, and then wonder why I'm saying, "Why aren't there more pages here?" If he wasn't THE MOST TALENTED PERSON I'VE EVER MET, I might not put up with his irresponsibility. But in Tony's defense, NO ONE in the industry, and I mean NO ONE, could have brought more to this project than Tony. Not Frank Miller; not Erik Larsen; NO ONE. I can't imagine this book without him.

PART TWO: MOORE

DC: Give me the lowdown on Funk-O-Tron. How did the company come to be?

Tony Moore: Well, it was really kinda simple. Kirkman and another buddy of ours, Robert Sutton, had an idea for a somewhat satirical book that they had wanted to cultivate as an idea to market towards all the freaks that bought into the whole wrestling resurgence (which sadly I think they were part of). Anyway, they wanted to self-publish it, and wanted to know if I wanted in on the action. Of course I was so ecstatic I almost peed, and within a few days we all drove over to the state capitol and bought our LLC license, and so Funk-O-Tron was officially born.

DC: The artwork in *Battle Pope* #1 is very good, especially considering that this is the first comic from a brand-new company. What kind of art training do you have?

TM: Thanks! I'm glad you enjoyed it! Well, I've been drawing since I was old enough to shit, but as far as formal education goes, I attended the Art Academy of Cincinnati for a year before transferring to the University of Louisville, where I am currently very, very close to getting my BFA in fine art.

DC: What experience do you have in the comics field? The letters page mentions that you were working on a comic called *Talon* for Nifty Comics. Can you tell us a little about that?

TM: Mmmmm . . . well, outside of that whole Talon thing, I've done a few pinups and a ten-page short story for Beta 3 Comics' "Sniper and Rook." So I'm still relatively green. Anyway, a few years ago, I was approached by the head of Nifty about doing the art for a series he wanted to launch. He had seen my work on Wizard's Cafe DNA website and thought I'd be a good match. I looked over some scripts and stuff and said sure. So, I finished two issues and then didn't hear from him for a very long time, so I dropped it and focused my energies on BP. I don't regret it, though; it was great practice to kinda nail down my storytelling before getting into anything serious. I highly suggest it for any serious budding comic artists with the time to commit. It's great practice with a remote possibility of actually becoming something. Not a bad gamble at all.

DC: Robert created the *Battle Pope* concept, but you volunteered to draw it. What initially attracted you to the idea?

TM: Oooooh! Let's see . . . guns, sacrilege, what's not to love? Seriously though, when he pitched the idea to me, it sounded like Lobo with a big hat. I was hooked!

DC: What comics artists are your biggest influences? Non-comics artists?

TM: Well, like most comic geeks my age, I grew up on Jim Lee and McFarlane. They were my heroes growing up, and the driving force for my wanting to get into comics. Technically, their work was highly influential to me starting out, though now I try not to let their styles seep into mine. Personally, I love artists that are a little more off the beaten path. Simon Bisley, Dave McKean, Mike Mignola, David Mack, Dave Johnson, Bill Sienkiewicz, Frank Miller . . . those guys are amazing. Their work doesn't really so much reflect in mine, but they're my heroes now. That's what I want to be when I grow up. I'm also a huge fan of early illustrators, Alphonse Mucha and Edward Hopper.

As for non-comics artists, I love Jim Dine and Jerome Witkin; pop artists such as Warhol, Liechtenstein, and Jasper Johns; and classical masters like Da Vinci, Michelangelo, and Reubens (my personal fave).

DC: Let's discuss the technical aspects of drawing comics. What tools do you use to ink your work? How long does it take you to finish a page? Do you view penciling and inking as two separate procedures, or are they part of an organic whole?

TM: People are gonna ostracize me for this, but I ink a lot of stuff with Sharpies, pens, markers, whatever; I just love how they lay ink on the page. They'll fade to purple in a few years, but I can't help myself. I usually start off with a brush and some Windsor-Newton black ink to make sure I get good initial line weights, and then break out the really thin Pilot V5s for the details. A lot of black and white books are hard to read because they lack the depth that color and shade have to offer. I try to get past this handicap by doing quite a bit of crosshatching and stuff like that. Some people hate it because they prefer cleaner linework, but I think it works considering my intent and purpose. Besides, it kinda makes sure *Battle Pope* doesn't look exactly like everything else on the shelves. I like it.

When I'm in my zone, I can pencil sometimes up to three pages a day, though I usually weigh in at two. Inking a page usually takes me a whole day, though depending on the complexity of the work and what kinda day I'm having, I can sometimes squeeze out a second page. Inking's a bitch. For the most part, I wish I had someone else doing it, but in a way I love it, because I'm such a nitpicker when it comes to my work that doing it myself is the only way I can ensure that it'll come out the way I wanted it. So, I guess for me it is somewhat an organic whole at this stage of the game.

DC: *Battle Pope* has got to be offending people, especially with your portrayal of Jesus Christ. Any hate mail yet?

TM: Heh. Surprisingly, very little! We've only gotten one pissed-off letter, and that was the very day our solicitation for #1 hit shelves in *Previews*. Must've really touched a nerve or something. I like to think people who are initially offended by the premise of the book are buying it just so they can kinda "know the enemy," and by the time they've finished it, they like us so much they have to write us fan letters instead. Anyway, I'm amazed (and in a sick way, a little disappointed) at how few people have sent in fire and brimstone hate letters. C'mon, ya buncha pansies!

DC: In addition to drawing *Battle Pope*, you created and maintain the Funk-O-Tron website. How is that going?

TM: Well, I'm kinda lagging behind on this one. I've been spending so much time on the book that the website's not quite as smooth as I'd like. Generally speaking, it looks about right, but I'd like to iron out some of the kinks, beef up some of the content, and kinda retool the sections that are already there. Oh well, someday. Maybe.

DC: At the end of the letters page in the first issue, you wrote, "And as unlikely as it may sound after reading this book, I have to give proper respect to the Big Guy, yes, the Man Upstairs, for being so good to me." Would you

Controversy was nearly nonexistent despite a nerdy Jesus being described as "inca-pable" by God the father. From *Battle Pope: Genesis*, Volume 1, by Robert Kirkman and Tony Moore; Image Comics, 2006.

describe yourself as a religious person? Now that you're drawing this comic, do you think you might be going to Hell?

TM: Yeah, I guess I'd consider myself a fairly religious guy. That doesn't stop me from running my mouth like a sailor or thinking that dismemberment is funny, but overall, I'd say I lead my life in a pretty respectable manner. As a kid I was dragged to church every Sunday, where it seemed everyone was more interested in what everyone else was wearing than God's word, so I got turned off church for a while. But I started going back to church with my fiancée, and I really like how they go about things there, so I've become somewhat more of a wandering Methodist, probably more wandering than Methodist.

As for going to Hell, no. I don't think so. I know God has a sense of humor, and won't fry me because of that. Besides, I'm sure he digs how I draw him. That big floating Oz head thing is GOLD!

DC: What are you planning on doing after you finish *Battle Pope*?

TM: I'll take some time off, fine-tune the website, try to boost my GPA and get out of school, and attempt to patch up some of the miscellaneous holes punched by my rotten work ethic. And I'll be working on some more comics stuff, some of it even Battle Pope, for release in the not-so-distant future.

DC: You and your cocreator really gush about each other in the letters page. Come on, let's be honest here. What's one thing about Robert Kirkman that really annoys you?

TM: For some reason, he refuses to take any credit, insisting I refer to him only as "my letterer." I don't know what's up with that. No, seriously, when you work as closely as we do, most of your differences get put aside fairly quickly. He's 110-percent anal retentive and I need that, because it would all turn to shit if we were both slackers like me. So, actually, I've grown to appreciate his idiosyncrasies and recognize 'em as things that make this thing of ours run relatively smoothly.

If he wrote a bunch of shit about me on this, though, I'm gonna wring his neck.

Interview: Robert Kirkman

SEAN FAHEY / 2004

From *Thor's Comic Column* hosted by *CHUD.com*, March 22, 2004. Reprinted by permission of Sean Fahey

If you haven't heard of comic book writer Robert Kirkman, then you've been living under a rock and deserve your uncomfortable fate. With a diverse portfolio of extraordinary independent titles, Kirkman has quietly (and not so quietly) moved into the upper echelon of the up and coming. His dark comedy superhero title *Brit* is an "anything goes" romp about an indestructible senior citizen and his stripper girlfriend that is as hysterical as it is bone-crushing. Kirkman's *Invincible* has recast the mold with respect to teenage superhero comic books with its unique father-and-son superhero-team dynamics, and his zombie apocalypse survivalist adventure *The Walking Dead* is simply one of the finest ongoing series being published right now.

If you haven't heard of Robert Kirkman, you're about to get a second lease on life. The trade paperback collecting the first six issues of *The Walking Dead* is going to be released next month, and will get readers completely up to speed with this amazing series. The second trade for *Invincible* will also see print next month, and will also get readers up to speed with that series. I can't say enough about either title.

I recently had the pleasure of speaking with Robert Kirkman, and I can say with authority that he's a great guy. He deserves all the success coming his way. What's more, he has a terrific sense of humor, and this interview was a blast to do; and in case you didn't already know, Robert Kirkman is also a family man. In this interview we talk about his books, all things zombies, his approach to creating characters, his influences and finally his upcoming run on *Captain America*. This guy is clearly on his way. Tell Robert Kirkman that he is on the verge of becoming an A-list writer though, and he can only laugh . . .

Sean Fahey: I think it's safe to say that you're on the verge of becoming a household name among comic book readers . . .

Robert Kirkman: [*Laughter.*]

Fahey: . . . seriously, *The Walking Dead* is red hot, *Invincible* is on its way, *Brit* has been well received, you've got some diverse projects coming up. But it seems things really took off for you when *The Walking Dead* hit the stands. Could you talk about how important that book has been for you, and whether its had an effect on your other books as well.

Kirkman: I think if *The Walking Dead* has done anything, it really has told people that I can do more than the goofy superhero type stuff. I've gotten a lot of compliments on the range that *The Walking Dead* shows, because it's completely different than anything I've ever done. I think it shows people that I can do a serious drama, because everything that I've written before *The Walking Dead* had some level of comedy in it. I think *The Walking Dead* is not funny in the least.

As for effect, *The Walking Dead* sales figures started going up with issue 3, and we've gained sales on each issue after that. Just recently *Invincible* sales figures have gone up as well. I don't know if that's because people are reading *The Walking Dead* and come over to *Invincible*, or whether it's the word of mouth that's being generated from both books. But I can definitely see how the success of *The Walking Dead* is helping my other projects.

Fahey: You laughed when I said that you are on the verge of becoming a household name among comic book readers. You don't think so?

Kirkman: [*Laughter.*] I don't know, man. My books are selling a lot better than they used to, and that's really cool. But, I don't know. I would certainly not object to becoming a household name, but I don't think I'm there yet. I'm not completely convinced that it's going to happen soon, but I sure am working hard!

Fahey: [*Laughter.*] You are?

Kirkman: [*Laughter.*]

SF: Seriously though, household name or not, there are a lot of people who are now discovering Robert Kirkman that had never heard of you before *The Walking Dead*—and I'll freely admit I was one of them. But like myself, I think *The Walking Dead* has led people to *Invincible* and *Brit*.

Kirkman: Yeah, I think *The Walking Dead* is bringing in a lot of people. I think a lot of people that read comics also really enjoy zombie movies. So, *The Walking Dead* has a built-in audience that is coming on that book not caring what exactly it's about or who's doing it. They just want to see if it's actually a good zombie book. I get a lot of mail saying, "I've been waiting for a good zombie book! Here it is. I'm so happy." So, I think there's a few people just coming in on the basic content.

Fahey: Putting aside the basic content, what types of themes are you looking to explore with *The Walking Dead*?

Kirkman: I think the main theme about *The Walking Dead* is that deep down we really are all rotten people. The main character himself is genuinely a good guy, and he's really there to reflect off the other people in the book that are just going to slowly be losing it over the next few issues. But eventually even Rick, the main character, will be just . . . The object of the book is to show all the people in their introductions, and I want everybody from when they first appear to be completely different within ten issues. The whole book really is just based on me thinking, "Wow, this would be really screwed up if it happened to me." I can't help but think that having your life change overnight into something so completely different, so completely savage—that's really going to mess people up.

For me the whole book is about how Rick protects his family, so I wanted to bring them in as early as possible. So for the most part the book is about Rick Grimes, small town cop who has never shot his gun, waking up from a coma in a world that's completely different from everything he's ever known, and having to learn how to build fences and grow crops and be an expert marksman and fight off hordes of zombies, and learn the potential of his own mental strength—becoming a person he'd never thought he'd have to be, and at the same time we've got a group of characters around him that are trying to do the same thing to a certain degree. It's all about a guy expanding and growing and changing. It's very much a book about growth . . . [*laughter*] with, you know, flesh-eating zombies running around getting their brains blown out.

Fahey: You mention the inherent cruelty in all of us. I had a history professor in college that liked saying that the history of mankind was conflict, and that we would never unite, as a species, absent some external threat. But even then, people are still going to be petty. People are still going take advantage of the weak amidst all the chaos regardless of whether the survival of the species is at stake or not.

Kirkman: Even the nicest person, when the right buttons are pushed, is going to do what they have to do. Even the most mundane father figure, got three kids, works at a bank, is going to flip out and do some evil shit just to keep his kids safe. It's under the surface for everybody. I don't care who you are. There's something that will get you to do something violent and ugly.

Fahey: What kind of a man is Rick Grimes?

Kirkman: Rick Grimes will hurt you for the right reasons. But I think that his "right reasons" will be the right reasons of 90 percent of the readers. So, I think that ultimately everybody is going to root for Rick Grimes. Just like everybody else, you push his buttons and he's gonna flip. But ultimately he is a nice guy, and he is the pillar of morality that keeps the book together.

As we go on, we're going to see him take on a more active role in helping people. Making sure everybody's safe. Figuring out how they can survive, and where they're gonna get food, and where's the best place for shelter. Rick Grimes really takes charge.

Fahey: You said that it's important for you that every character be "completely different" from where they begin the series. We're five issues in and you're already developing an interesting cast. What's the most important thing for you as you create these characters, as you introduce them to the book and their journey?

Kirkman: With this book the main thing is to not get too attached to them. Because of the way this book is, I eventually have to kill . . . somebody. And it's going to have to be somebody that you've met in the book before and you care about, or there's just no point in the series. There's a few characters that I really like that are safe, but the readers aren't going to find out who those are. I have to be willing to let them go for the good of the book.

Fahey: I think the series works because of the characters. No offense, but while "zombie apocalypse" rocks in and of itself, it's not the most elaborate plot, and it's been done before. But this series transcends any genre label, because it's so character driven. It's not an action book. It's not a horror book. You yourself have said as much.

Kirkman: Yeah. I said that in the first issue in the text in the back. A lot of people look down on the horror genre, and unfortunately a lot of people read into that that I was somehow ashamed of the horror genre. That I didn't want this to be lumped into that, and this was above that somehow. That's not what I meant at all. I love horror movies, and if this could be counted among horror movies, I would be honored. I would be honored for this thing to be considered a horror book. If the book ends up scaring you, that is awesome.

But, in my opinion, horror is driven by motion and sound—and you cannot do motion and sound in comics. So, in the book I am not focusing on "Is this going to scare anybody?" I'm not doing anything in the book for the express purpose of shocking anybody. I'm just trying to explore how these people survive and how they live, and the relationships among them.

Just trying to keep it as plotless as possible. [*Laughter.*]

Fahey: [*Laughter.*] I didn't mean that the way it sounded.

Kirkman: Oh now, I'm kiddin' man. Come on. You're absolutely right. It's a character-driven piece. I mean, they're not setting out to do anything. There's no job for them to do. There's no goal other than . . .

Fahey: Just live.

Kirkman: Yeah. That's the whole point of the book. So, I don't take offense to you saying that it's character driven and there's no plot, because you're exactly right.

Fahey: Now, you just said that there's a general tendency to look down on the horror genre. Why do you think that is? Horror used to be an incredibly popular genre in comic books.

Kirkman: I'm not really saying people look down on horror comics. I think as far as the EC stuff goes, I don't think I could name one well known horror comic that wasn't from that time period. I think just about everybody considered that EC stuff to be classic. I was more referring to movies. It's like, the difference between *Dawn of the Dead* and *Return of the Living Dead*. If you respect *Return of the Living Dead* for what it is, it's a slapstick comedy . . . you know, "Let's have fun!" horror movie. *Dawn of the Dead*, while it has some comedic moments, is for the most part an exploratory high-end look at social situations. You know, all that kind artsy crap with gore thrown in there. It's a serious piece of fiction.

I think when most people think of horror movies, they would think of a *Return of the Living Dead*–type movie before they would think of a *Dawn of the Dead*–type movie, because there's just so much more of them out there. I think because of that, people are like, "Oh horror movies? That's just about showing a girl's breast, and having them run through the woods." It's like *Frailty* versus *Friday the 13th*, or Hitchcock versus *A Nightmare on Elm Street*.

Fahey: So you would say that if a horror comic is going to work, it has to be more "creepy" than "shocking," because at the end of the day they can't shock? More manipulating reader's expectations than anything else.

Kirkman: In my opinion, yeah. You're not going to have that irritating music and that loud noise when the guy busts through the wall. There's not going to be any kind of shock stuff. I just don't think it can be down.

Fahey: Turning back to *The Walking Dead*, are we ever going to find out what caused the apocalypse, or is that irrelevant? This happened; how it happened doesn't matter because the journey is about the character's dealing.

Kirkman: If it's going to piss you off, and you're going to stop reading the book, then I will eventually figure it out and let everybody know. If you don't like it when zombie movies tell you how everything happened, then don't worry I'm not gonna tell anybody. [*Laughter.*]

The thing about *The Walking Dead*, though, is that it is about normal people in Atlanta, and they're in the woods—in a camp—and they're stealing canned goods from grocery stores, and hanging out in the woods fighting zombies every now and then. Those people would never find out what happened. Unless the government came with tanks and said "Ho! Somebody dropped a dead rat in the water supply and some crazy shit happened, and it all went wrong. But we're fixing it now. Let's get you to a shelter, get you all cleaned and let's go." That's the only way they would be able to find out.

In *The Walking Dead*, barring things that hinder the story and slow it up, I'm trying to be as realistic as possible, and it's not realistic to think that people living in the woods are going to find out what happened. So, unless I absolutely have to—unless I hear about readers just pissed off that they're not finding out what's going on—I don't plan on ever telling anybody what happened.

Not knowing makes the book more realistic. If it's aliens that are attacking, and bringing the undead back to life so they can have an army to take over, then it becomes a ridiculous sci-fi thing. If it's a gamma bomb that goes off and contaminates the water supply. Stuff gets too hokey and science-fiction-y. But for some reason if it's just zombies walking around, people are like "Well, it's slightly more realistic." For me, it's just more realistic with them not finding out.

Fahey: This is a weird question, but I'm going to ask it anyway. Did the aftermath of the September 11th terrorist attacks affect the development of *The Walking Dead*? The book is essentially about surviving a catastrophe, the aftershock. This book is about rebuilding.

Kirkman: I was developing this book at a time when people were buying large rolls of plastic and duct tape, so they could bar up their windows in case of a chemical attack. I was developing this book within that first year after 9/11. I started thinking about . . . actually, it did kind of come from that. You know, we were living in times when someone could get anthrax in their mailbox, and at any time someone could get a hold of a big bomb and really mess us up. Just from a fiction writer's standpoint, seeing that kind of stuff does affect you. I guess I did start thinking, "Hey, what would I do if this stuff happened?"

Fahey: You've said in your letters page that you're personally committed to the long haul with this book if sales warrant it. Is there an end in mind? I think of *Y: The Last Man*, which is another apocalyptic journey book, but Vaughan has said that he has a definite story he wants to tell, that an ending is planned. How do you see this book?

Kirkman: Right now I don't have anything planned as an ending, but I also don't see this thing going on forever. I have not set out with a Point A and a Point B. I'm making up these peoples' lives. There's a lot of times when I writing something for the book, I'll reread an issue and say, "Hey, this is a natural progression from that event." A lot of things that are happening in the book are just building on things that I come up with on the fly. I think that it might make it a little more realistic that way—nobody really knows where they're going in life, and these characters don't know either because . . . I have no clue.

Fahey: That seems like an interesting way to write this type of book. It's more spontaneous. More organic.

Kirkman: Yeah. I mean, I've planned out up into the 20s with what I'm going to do in the book. I'm not making stuff up that bad as I go along. [*Laughter.*] But I don't know what the end is, and I don't even know if Rick's going to make it to the end.

Fahey: What about the immediate future of the series?

Kirkman: It is finally decided that living near Atlanta is too dangerous. What happened in the book is that the government saw these undead hordes roaming the countryside, and they said, "Hey everybody. Get to nearest city, and that's the only area we can protect." So basically they organized as much military as they could to protect large areas of population . . . and it kinda backfired on them, because you get a couple of zombies in a large area and it'll spread like wildfire.

So, what you got were these hot zones of zombies, where anywhere there was a populated area is where you got thousands upon thousands of zombies. Up until now, the idea has been, "When the military comes to save us, they're going to come to the cities first, and we need to be as close to the city as we can." Without giving too much away, after a few events happen, they decide that living next to Atlanta is too dangerous, and the next story arc is about them finding safer shelter . . . and winter comes, so they're all screwed.

Fahey: In general, why do you think zombies are such a hot pop-culture item right now? The *Resident Evil* games are insanely popular. Movies like *28 Days Later* and the new *Dawn of the Dead*, which is generating a lot of prerelease buzz. There's a couple of other comic properties, like Steve Niles's IDW series *Remains*. What do you think the appeal is?

Kirkman: I have no idea [*laughter*], but I thank God for it every morning when I wake up! As far as movie monsters go, I think zombies are the closest reflection to what we are. All the good zombies movies play up the whole, "Hey look at those guys, they're trying to attack us, and they're animalistic and savage, and . . . well, not very unlike us." They make you think about your-self. It's strange, because most zombies aren't threatening alone, but the idea of being surrounded by the things is so terrifying. But as far what the mass appeal is these days, I got no idea.

Fahey: I always thought the whole idea appealed to an adolescent desire in guys to just want to build forts and blow shit up.

Kirkman: [*Laughter.*] You know, I wish I thought of that. That's pretty good.

Fahey: The influence of the Romero films on *The Walking Dead* is obvious; anything not so obvious influence the book? Something people wouldn't nor-mally think of, or see in the book.

Kirkman: They definitely are Romero films. I've had a few pieces of hate mail referring to this as "Romero fan fiction." But I am using them as a basis for what the zombie rules are, because it seems that every time someone does a new zombie movie there's a new set of zombie rules. You know, "These zom-bies go fast. These zombies only eat brains. These zombies are slow." I think there was one movie where the zombie caused himself pain, and that made him not hunger for brains. There's just all these things going on. So, I figured I'd take the Romero model and just build off of that.

Fahey: Well, it is the most recognized model. So, it only makes sense.

Kirkman: Yeah. I think a lot of movies use the Romero model. It's just like someone coming along and doing a Dracula story and saying, "Okay, well, vampires suck blood, and crosses are bad, and holy water and sunlight . . . " Then someone comes along and says, "Well, that's what they did in Dracula! You can't do that!"

The thing that really inspired me to do this book though, and the thing that excites me the most, is that any story arc of this book is going to be a zombie movie—where it has a beginning and an end, and the end is always, "Well, we're done telling you about these people, and now they are going to do something else." Because that's how every zombie movie is, unless they all die. It's like, "We're done telling you about these people. Here come the credits. Go home." It's always, "Oh, we're on an island now. Bye!" or they hop on a helicopter and leave the mall.

I want to know what the hell happened to those people! I want to know where they go. I want to know what happens next. I want to know what they're doing. I want to know if they make it. I want to know if the girl has the baby and the guy helps her raise it. Where are they going to land the he-licopter, and what do they do next? That's what I want to find out. With *The*

Walking Dead, and sales pending . . . and right now the book is just kicking ass, so I'm tickled to death that we're getting to this. So, we're sticking with these characters, and we will find out what is going on. We will see what comes next. That to me is the most exciting aspect of the book.

Fahey: Just out of curiosity, which one of the three is your favorite?

Kirkman: I like 'em all a great deal. It kinda bounces back and forth between *Day of the Dead* and *Night of the Living Dead*. I think *Day of the Dead* has the best effects, and really is the most fun to watch. But you gotta recognize that *Night of the Living Dead* has a better story than the other two, and is so revolutionary and all that artsy stuff. A lot of times I'll say that's my favorite, but right now I'm going with *Day of the Dead* because I think it's a great movie.

Fahey: So you're a big fan of Bub?

Kirkman: I'm all about the Bub, and there's nothing more fun than watching a bunch of people in a cave going crazy.

Fahey: When the zombie apocalypse does come, what is your weapon of choice going to be?

Kirkman: My weapon of choice? Duct tape!

Fahey: Duct tape?

Kirkman: Yeah! You can do anything with that stuff!

Fahey: So, you're really counting on the zombies being the slow-moving type then.

Kirkman: Logically, when you think about it, these guys are rotting corpses. They don't know kung fu. Their brains aren't working too good. Some of 'em . . . they might not even have a foot! You know, they got a foot blown off, and they're walking around on the stump. These guys aren't in peak condition. [*Laughter.*] Rigor mortis is setting in. Their guts are rotting. They're falling apart by the day. If they were out in the sun, it'd be even worse. So, they're not gonna run! They're not gonna jump! They're not gonna climb! It's not gonna happen. Fast zombies just don't make any sense.

Fahey: What do you think of the upcoming *Dawn of the Dead* remake then, taking the *28 Days Later* slant of fast-moving zombies.

Kirkman: It worked in *28 Days Later*, because they weren't necessarily dead. It was a zombie movie. But it was people that were infected with a virus that were going crazy—those people, they can run. *Dawn of the Dead*? I'm actually looking forward to the movie. I know a lot of people who are big fans of the old movie, and they're going, "Oh, this is going to be crap!" and "Oh, I don't want to go see that." But I can't wait. I think it's going to be entertaining, and, that said, I think the fast-moving zombies are stupid. [*Laughter.*]

Fahey: [*Laughter.*]

Kirkman: It's something you have to accept. People in Hollywood don't think that zombies that move slow are threatening enough to be scary. I think they're wrong.

Fahey: While we're on the subject of Hollywood, any television or movie potential for *The Walking Dead*? I mean every comic book property under the sun is in "preproduction" right now, but anything serious going on?

Kirkman: A lot of people are announcing. A lot of people in comics are announcing that they have a producer, and that they're shopping their thing around as an option. If that's the case, then I've gotten at least that far. There actually is a director that's attached that wants to put it together as a television show. Whether or not that happens is up in the air. I mean, as far as I understand it and as far as my manager tells me, somebody has committed to fund it. A director is attached. A producer is attached. A writer is working on a story bible, and they are trying to talk to networks now. So, it's looking pretty good as far as I know. But I'm a guy from Kentucky who doesn't know shit about Hollywood, so what do I know. [*Laughter.*]

As far as I know, it looks good, it looks good. I'm excited. But, we'll see—and the people involved really like the comic. From what I've heard if the television show does happen, it's going to be very close to what the comic is.

Fahey: I'm going to change directions here. Looking at your work as a whole, your portfolio is somewhat diverse. *The Walking Dead* is a horror-survivalist tale. *Invincible* is more traditional superhero stuff. *Tech Jacket* is more science fiction. But all of your books seem to touch on family as a theme; in fact I'd say it seems to be a central theme in a lot of your work. Family. Whether it be Rick and his wife and kid in *The Walking Dead*. Jessica and Brit, and Jessica's family. The Graysons in *Invincible*. Zack and his father in *Tech Jacket*. Could you talk about why this is so central a theme in your work, or am I reading into something that's not there?

Kirkman: It seems to be there, doesn't it . . . but, it's not there on purpose. I don't know. In the case of *The Walking Dead*, I got a guy that I have to keep interesting. If he has to protect his family, I can take him more places emotionally. In *Invincible*, it was . . . in superhero comics the dad is always the guy that inspires the son to do something. I don't think there's ever been a superhero comic where the father has actually been there with the son together. They talk. They work together. They're good friends. They have a good relationship. *Brit* . . . I thought it was funny that an old man and a stripper could be hooking up. [*Laughter.*]

A dinner-table exchange that portrays the extraordinary ordinary life of father and son superheroes. From *Invincible*, Compendium 1, by Robert Kirkman and Corey Walker; Image Comics, 2015.

I definitely have a good relationship with my family. I don't know if it makes me a bad writer, but I'm always drawing on stuff in my life. That stuff always carries over. Eventually I'm going to do a book about some people that don't have a family or hate their family just to try something different. That doesn't answer your question does it?

Fahey: Sure it does. You said you draw on your life for your writing, and part of what's important to you is your family. Like I said, I could be reading something into this that's not there, but family as a theme, to me, just seems pervasive in your work.

Kirkman: Well if you want to get dramatic and have an Oprah moment in your interview . . .

Fahey: Why don't we have a Dr. Phil moment instead.

Kirkman: [*Laughter.*] Is there really any difference?

Fahey: No. But I would feel uncomfortable being Oprah.

Kirkman: [*Laughter.*]

Fahey: I'll be Dr. Phil if that's ok.

Kirkman: Sure. OK, just to let the readers in on a little personal Robert Kirkman fact. I have a younger brother and sister. My brother is five years younger than me. My sister is thirteen years younger than me. When I was nineteen, my dad came to me and said, "Hey son, we're moving to 'The Florida,' and you can either come with us or get a place of your own. Whatever you want to do. But I figured I'd let you know." So, I had a girlfriend at the time, and a job—cause I didn't go to "The College"—and I decided, "Hey, screw this. I'm staying in Kentucky," and my family up and moved to Florida. Now I see them—I talk to them on the phone—but I see them once or twice a year. So, maybe, just maybe, I write all that family stuff in my books to regain a little bit of what I lost.

[We joked a little bit about Dr. Phil and Barbara Walters, and I figured it'd be a good time to change directions again.]

Fahey: *Invincible.* It must have been an amazing challenge to create a superhero book when DC and Marvel have cornered the market, and they've got a lot of their own unconventional stuff. So, you can't really aim to be different for the sake of being different. But *Invincible* actually succeeds in being unconventional, in part, by tapping into older superhero sensibilities. It's not naïve, but it has a definite, and great, "gee-whiz, it's cool to be a superhero" quality to it. How do you approach a superhero book these days with the two towers ominously out there?

Kirkman: Yeah, well like you say about them doing their own unconventional superhero stuff—five years ago all you had to do for a superhero book to compete with Marvel and DC was something like *Astro City*. It was a different approach, and something you couldn't get from Marvel and DC. Now, you've got Marvel and DC doing *H-E-R-O* and *Alias* and *Runaways*, and all these unconventional superhero books that make it harder to do something unconventional and get noticed.

You can't just come out and say, "Well, this is your standard run-of-the-mill superhero book, and . . . I have no reason for you to buy this as opposed to *Superman*." One of the things you do have, with creating your own thing, is that I'm not answering to stockholders, and I am not perpetuating a property. I am not obligated to keep someone in the same costume because there's a lunchbox on the shelf, or keep him with his girlfriend because there's a movie coming out where they're together. So, I have a lot of leeway as far as, say, killing characters—or doing whatever I want. I don't answer to anybody. I can do something off the wall, and when you're buying *Invincible* you don't know what you're getting.

Based on other issues, you're pretty confident you're going to get something you like. But I could just up and kill *Invincible* one issue . . . and the book would tank. [*Laughter*.] It's definitely tough. When Cory (series artist Cory Walker) and I were coming up with the thing it was really tough, just sitting around wracking our brains just trying to figure out something where someone wouldn't immediately go, "Hey, that's just like this." And I'm up against that every time I try and create a book. As far as superhero stuff goes there's just not a lot of stuff left. But, I didn't see any father and son dynamic stuff going on. [*Laughter*.]

Fahey: [*Laughter*.]

Kirkman: I thought I'd [*laughter*] . . . I thought I'd hit that . . .

Fahey: [*Laughter*.]

Kirkman: What are you laughing at? Come on now, I'm being serious here. [*Laughter*.]

Fahey: [*Laughter*.]

Kirkman: Well seriously, are there any superhero books out there featuring a father and son character teaming up and stuff?

Fahey: No.

Kirkman: No. No, there's not, right? But seriously, with all my books, I'm trying to think of something that is not there in the industry that I can fill a gap with. When I did *Invincible*, and even *Tech Jacket*, I didn't notice a lot of teen superhero books coming out at that time. Now there are a lot of team superhero books coming out, and it feels kinda dumb for me to even say that at one time there wasn't. But, there was no *Teen Titans* and no *Runaways*.

In order to compete with the big boys, I have to do something completely different with my superhero title—and my superhero title is different because people change. Stuff happens. Bad stuff happens to good characters. People break up, people die, and the book keeps going. What goes on in *Invincible* is very much in the spirit of that.

Fahey: Is Invincible connecting with teen readers at all? What kind of feedback . . .

Kirkman: Are teenagers reading comic books these days? [*Laughter.*]

Fahey: That's the question behind the question.

Kirkman: I haven't heard exact stories of teens picking up the books, but I have heard stories of people giving the book to their nephew and younger kids actually reading and responding to the book. That's really good. Scott Kutrz, he's the guy who does PvP, he's a buddy of mine, and he's got a nine-year-old nephew who is hooked on the book. I send Scott Kurtz previews of the issue before it's printed. His little nephew runs over and hops on the computer and reads the e-preview on the computer because he likes the book so much. That stuff's really cool. It's nice to know that you're doing a book that kids actually enjoy.

Fahey: I like the book, and what I think is unique about it is that it doesn't have teens moping around, depressed and misunderstood. You've got active teens, excited about doing very cool things. In my opinion too much of teen pop culture is just this whole BS marketing thing of, "You're young. You're depressed and misunderstood. Your parents can never understand you, but Mountain Dew does. Buy our soft drink."

Kirkman: Yeah. [*Laughter.*] Just from my own personal experience, I wasn't a teenager too very much long ago, and I wasn't misunderstood and depressed. I had a lot of friends that, when they were teenagers, weren't misunderstood and depressed. I mean there certainly was acceptance and peer pressure, and all that stuff. But I wasn't walking around going, "Oh, my god! My arms are growing at rapid rates, and I've got acne. I'm going to go curl up in a corner and cry." I was breaking stuff. I couldn't do a book about teen angst, because Spider-Man wrote the book on that.

Fahey: You've mention a couple of times in this interview characters dying. Why is it important for you that characters be able to die? I think they should. I don't think it happens enough, and as a result some comics just aren't that suspenseful or credible. But I'm interested in why it's important to you.

Kirkman: I grew up reading *Savage Dragon*, and when that thing hit I was just freaking out. Most people hear *Savage Dragon* and they think, "Early '90s.

Image comic. Must have sucked." But *Savage Dragon*, way back in 1992, was doing everything that Warren Ellis and Mark Millar ended up doing much later in *The Authority*. Most people don't know that. Dragon was a superhero that had sex with his girlfriend, and got drunk in bars. If he couldn't find any other way out of the situation, he would kill the bad guy. Nobody in Dragon was safe.

Issue #7, I'm fourteen years old, and the first six issues have built up to this big battle between Savage Dragon and the Overlord. You're convinced Savage Dragon is just going to kick the Overlord's ass. I couldn't wait. *Savage Dragon* #7 was twenty-two splash pages, okay—and it's an issue where the Overlord beats the shit out of Dragon, blows his arm off, and throws him out of a fifty-story skyscraper. Page nineteen! Dragon is thrown out of the building. Page twenty is him falling. Page twenty-one? Page twenty-one, he falls on a spike and it impales him! Blood goes everywhere, and the last page is a close up of his hand with blood dripping down off of it, and that's it. You had a month to go, "What the fuck just happened?" [*Laughter.*]

This was 1992, nobody did that. There was *Watchmen* and *Dark Knight Returns*, but if you were just reading *Spider-Man* you weren't used to that. Up until that point you didn't know Dragon had a healing factor, and that he was going to be okay, and the arm was going to grow back. You didn't know these things, and that issue was the most shocking, defining moment of my comic-reading adventures in my entire life. If I could do just half of that in *Invincible*, then yay for me. But that's what I'm setting out to do.

I'm setting out to shock people. I'm setting out to surprise people, and death in comics does and the appeal to me is that you never know what's coming. No character in *Invincible* is safe.

Jimmy Olsen could get his head blown off tomorrow. I'm not going to show it on panel, and it's not going to be gratuitous, and I'm not trying to do a gritty and depressing superhero comic, but that guy could go tomorrow. So I want people that read Invincible to know that I am not going to keep Invincible the same. Five issues from now it's going to be completely different stuff.

Fahey: With *Invincible*, what was it like being asked by Image to help them launch a new superhero line of books? To be part of that? I know a lot of those books have . . . not met with a great deal of success to put it mildly, but what was it like to be a part of that process? Launching a new superhero line.

Kirkman: It was an exciting time. I just came off of *Battle Pope*, and Cory and I were trying to do a book called Science Dog, that Image decided was retarded. Eric Larsen asked us to do *The Super Patriot* miniseries, and while we were doing that series we pitched Science Dog, and Jim Valentino, Eric

Larsen, and Eric Stephenson were like "Whoa, Whoa, talking dog? No, that's not going to sell." They came to us and said, "We want a superhero thing."

It was really cool because all of a sudden all these people were going to be doing superhero books, Jim Krueger, Keith Giffen, Phil Hester, and all these guys, and we were doing *Invincible*. It was exciting being a part of that thing, and I wish the whole line had succeeded. Being an up-and-coming guy, coming from a book like *Battle Pope*, and all of a sudden I've got a character that's on the cover of *Previews*. It was surreal for a while.

Jim Valentino was really instrumental early on with the superhero line. He had a mandate where he wanted all these superhero books, but he told everyone that he didn't want antiheroes, and he didn't want guys running around with guns in the middle of the night. He really wanted to get away from '90s superhero stuff like . . .

Fahey: The stuff Image became famous for doing.

Kirkman: All the Image guys were doing books that reflected on the times in 1992, but all of those guys grew up reading books in the Silver Age. They recognized that stuff as being really cool. They were just trying to do something cool and different. So, Jim Valentino really helped shape the creation process of Invincible, because we had certain parameters and guidelines knowing what he wanted. It probably wouldn't have been that much different, because I'm not a moody and dark guy, but it was nice knowing what he was looking for.

Fahey: Your journey to Image seems to reinforce in my mind that there really only are two ways to break into the business. You either self-publish, as you did, or you make a mark in another medium and come in with credentials.

Kirkman: Well, there's some people that just plug away with the submissions. You know, they'll get a little fill-in story on a *Spider-Man* book and eventually build from that. But I think it's easier and more fun to go the self-publishing route because you really get to learn your chops without any outside influence. So you really either survive or fail on your raw talent. I didn't know what the hell I was doing when I started *Battle Pope*, and I think the first *Battle Pope* stuff was a little rotten. But it had some funny stuff in it, it was a lot of fun to do, and I learned a lot. Self-publishing is really fulfilling. But that said, I did it for three years and I will never do it again. [*Laughter.*]

Fahey: Let's talk about your future projects. Tell me about *Reaper*.

Kirkman: *Reaper* is a one-shot about an unkillable warlord, and an assassin that's sent to kill him. It has all kinds of gore in it, and I like to say that it's like *Hardboiled* with swords. But I only say that because I want people who like *Hardboiled* to pick up the book. Without trivializing what I do on the book, every page I wrote in *Reaper* is an excuse for me to see Cliff Rathburn cutting people all to shit. Anyone who enjoyed *Kill Bill* will enjoy *Reaper*. There's a lot of brains hitting the floor, and intestines going flying, and people getting heads chopped off. Nobody gets their head chopped off at the neck, let's just say that. [*Laughter*.] It's going through their eyes. It's going through their teeth.

Fahey: So, this is another one of those family books that you've become famous for right?

Kirkman: I don't think there's any family shit in *Reaper*. So there. [*Laughter*.]

Fahey: [*Laughter*.]

Kirkman: But yeah. Scott Kurtz's nine-year-old nephew will not be reading *Reaper*.

Fahey: Anything else planned with either Marvel or DC in the future?

Kirkman: I have an eleven-page Jubilee story coming up in *X-Men Unlimited* #2, and then I have a Spider-Man story coming up in *Spider-Man Unlimited* #4, which will be out in July. It's not Marvel or DC, but I've also got another *Brit* one-shot in July and another *Super Patriot* miniseries in the works.

Fahey: *Brit*. Let's get a plug in for *Brit*. This book rocks!

Kirkman: *Brit* is the wacky, mature, violent superhero stuff that gets the *Battle Pope* out of my system these days. Brit is an old, senior citizen who just happens to be invulnerable. He works for the government, and any times there's something really bad going down and they have no other option, they take Brit in a helicopter and kick him out on top of the thing, and he lands on it and beats the hell out of it. He's married to a stripper and they have a baby, so there's going to be a lot of family dynamic. [*Laughter*.]

Fahey: [*Laughter*.] What's interesting though is that he doesn't have superstrength.

Kirkman: Yeah. He's got no superstrength. No heat vision. His only superpower is that if you punch him it'll hurt your hand.

Fahey: I love it. He'll run to the top on a ten-story parking garage, hotwire a car, and drive it into a frost giant's eye to get the job done.

Kirkman: Yeah. [*Laughter*.] In the first issue, he's fighting a traditional superhero type that's taken over an entire country, and the way he beats him is he lets the guy beat on him for two days straight. At the end of the two days, the guy's hands are all mangled and bloodied, and Brit with his normal human strength leans over and snaps the guys neck and goes home.

Fahey: This is your "fun book."

Kirkman: Yeah. It's the "anything goes" book. My favorite scene in *Brit: Cold Death* is when Donald, Brit's government liaison—who was a pencil pusher, and always wore the suit and tie—goes on a mission with Brit. They're in a helicopter, the helicopter crashes, and Brit thinks that Donald died. Then Donald crawls out of the helicopter, and his skin is all melted, and he's got a robot body underneath, and Brit goes "Donald? You're alive! And you're an android!"—and Donald looks at him and goes, "Huh. So I am." [*Laughter.*]

It's anything goes. If I want to have a guy become a robot suddenly, that's funny stuff. And you know, he was always an android. We just didn't find out until it was the funniest. [*Laughter.*]

This last portion was done after the initial interview. At Wizard World LA, Brian Michael Bendis, who is leading Marvel's efforts to overhaul their Avengers line, announced that Robert Kirkman would be working on "Captain America." I thought this was very cool news. I called Robert, and he was nice enough to talk about the project to the extent that he could.

Fahey: How did *Captain America* come about?

Kirkman: The short of it, Tom Breevoort sent me an email that said, "You want to write the ol' *Captain America*," and I said sure. I don't know what the behind the scenes was, but I had done the *Spider-Man Unlimited* story, so I'm guessing based on that—he liked that and got me the Captain America gig. I think Bendis had something to do with it too, because he's been telling me that he's been trying to get me some work at Marvel. So, I'd definitely like to thank him. You gotta love ol' Mr. Bendis.

Fahey: How far are you along with the book?

Kirkman: I've already finished the first script. I've plotted all four issues, and I'm about to start the second script.

Fahey: So your run is limited to four issues?

Kirkman: Yeah, as far as I know.

Fahey: As I understand it this is part of the Avengers "Disassemble" event that's going to happen later this year.

Kirkman: Yeah. It all starts in July and runs until October. But I think the majority of that thing is just going to be in *Avengers*, with the three other books—*Captain America*, *Iron Man*, and *Thor*—touching on that stuff. I'm going to be reflecting on that in my story. But I don't think they want it to be an event where everyone feels they have to read all four books. My Captain America story should stand alone pretty easily without having to read the Avengers stuff.

Fahey: I know you're limited in what you can say, but can you say what the basic narrative is?

Kirkman: I think the basic narrative is a return to old school, action-packed Captain America fighting supervillains and all that cool stuff.

Fahey: Who's the artist on the series?

Kirkman: Scott Eaton (*Thor*).

Fahey: What attracts you to Captain America, or was it just the idea of doing a Marvel superhero comic book?

Kirkman: I'm a big fan of all the Marvel heroes, and Captain America is definitely up there. I've been a huge fan for years. *Captain America* was one of the first comics I started reading regularly when I started reading comics. I started buying comics when I was in the sixth grade, when Eric Larsen was on *Spider-Man* and Jim Lee was on *X-Men*, and *Captain America* was one of those first books. So, just the idea of getting to work on a character I enjoyed as a kid was great.

Fahey: You said a return to "old school" sensibilities. Are you going to try and push Cap in a new direction at all?

Kirkman: For the most part that's what I'm going to be doing. There is going to be a certain Robert Kirkman flavor that only I can bring to plate. [*Laughter.*] But it's Cap fighting supervillains. I'm bringing back HYDRA and the Red Skull and cool stuff like that.

Fahey: So it's going to embrace tradition.

Kirkman: Yeah. That was one of the mandates I was given when they told me to get started. It's going to be awesome.

Interview with Robert Kirkman

MARC-OLIVER FRISCH / 2005

From *Comicgate*, November, 2005. Reprinted by permission of Marc-Oliver Frisch

Robert Kirkman first entered the North American comics industry with his small-press outlet Funk-O-Tron. In addition to titles like *Double Take*, an anthology that included Joe Casey and Charlie Adlard's "Codeflesh," Funk-O-Tron also published Kirkman's own *Battle Pope* series.

In 2002, Kirkman moved his projects to Image Comics. Starting out with lukewarm initial sales, both of Kirkman's ongoing series—the superhero epic *Invincible* and the zombie saga *The Walking Dead*—began climbing the sales charts in 2003.

Following his success at Image, Kirkman soon found himself at Marvel, writing company-owned projects like "Sleepwalker" (in *Epic Anthology*), *Captain America*, the X-Men spin-off *Jubilee*, as well as a series of one-shot comic books titled *Marvel Knights 2099*. Most of these projects lacked the critical and financial success of his own creations, however.

On the occasion of the German release of *The Walking Dead*, Marc-Oliver Frisch had the opportunity to talk to the prolific author. The following interview was conducted via e-mail between October 11 and November 4, 2005.

(Disclosure: At the time of the interview, Frisch was the translator of the German edition of *The Walking Dead*. Versions of this interview were published in *The Walking Dead 1: Gute alte Zeit*, as well as at the German online magazine Comicgate, in 2005/2006.)

Frisch: When did the idea for *The Walking Dead* first occur to you? How long did it take from your initial inspiration to the start of the series at Image Comics?

Kirkman: The idea for *The Walking Dead* came from my love of zombie flicks. I used to watch those movies like they were going out of style, and I always wanted to know what happened after the movie. So I came up with the idea to do a comic that was basically a zombie movie that never ended. I wanted to do an open-ended exploration on the zombie holocaust and follow it all the way to its natural conclusion. That was the idea behind *The Walking Dead*. I came up with the idea probably in October of 2002. I asked Tony Moore to draw up some pages and I pitched the book to Image in December of 2002. Originally I was going to use the name "Night of the Living Dead" for the sake of recognizability, since I had heard that movie had fallen into public domain. Jim Valentino, then publisher of Image, suggested I just make up my own name, so that I would own the whole thing. I then came up with the title "The Walking Dead." I don't know if I've ever thanked Jim Valentino for making that suggestion. Anyway, I pitched the book and it was accepted aside from a name change. I wanted it to debut in March of 2003, but Image wanted to hold it for October 2003 so that it could ship around Halloween.

Frisch: Did you always want it to be a comic book series, or was there a point when you considered another medium for the story?

Kirkman: It was always a comic. It's what I do for a living. I don't write TV or novels or cereal boxes. I always wanted to do it as a comic.

Frisch: Can you walk us through the process of creating a typical issue of *The Walking Dead*, from gathering story ideas to sending the book to the printer?

Kirkman: Well, it starts with me getting ideas for the characters. I have a lot of stuff already planned out for specific characters, have for a while. But I don't know exactly when those events are going to take place in the book, so I have to figure that out and all the while I'm coming up with new stuff that happens before and after those events. So I'm always running through this stuff in my head, when I shower, when I drive, when I'm eating, when I'm supposed to be having a conversation with someone . . . it's taken over my life. When it's time to do any given issue, I try to organize my thoughts into a rough outline. I lay everything out on paper, organize it chronologically and scrawl out dialogue notes. What I end up with is a piece of paper numbered from one to twenty-two that has notes for what happens on every page. Then I sit down at the keyboard with that thing and use it as a guide to type up the script. I'm not bound to that plot outline; I veer from it quite a bit—I've even completely changed the last half of a couple issues at the last minute because I've changed my mind. I'll decide to kill off a character or I'll decide not to kill off a character; it's all up in the air until it's typed up.

From there I send the script off to Charlie [Adlard]. He usually spends a month or less on the book. He's a dream to work with, beautiful pages and on schedule every time. I'd marry him if we weren't both already married to someone else . . . and heterosexual. He usually roughs out the whole issue (unless I've only sent him a partial script, which we'll both admit happens more times than either of us would like) in pencils first. He breaks down the pages into panels, roughs in the people, details out any complicated items, and then jumps into inking. Once the pages are all inked up, he sends them off to me.

Back when I lettered the book myself, everything from issue #19 back, I would letter the book at this point. Now, I send the book off to the letterer, Rus Wooton, and the gray tone artist, Cliff Rathburn at the same time.

For Rus, I shrink the pages down to jpegs and I do balloon placements. I go into Photoshop and with a mouse I draw in crude little balloon shapes for where the balloons should go on the page. While I do this I do a final pass on the dialogue, changing things, lengthening and shortening dialogue, making things flow better and fit with the art perfectly . . . at least, that's what I'm trying to do. I've rewritten entire pages in this stage before. I frequently pull out lines of dialogue entirely if they're not needed. Once Rus has the script and balloon placements, he letters the whole book on the computer, using some program or another.

Meanwhile, Cliff Rathburn is toning the pages . . . doing his beautiful gray wash painting over Charlie's inks. He does this in Photoshop as well, I believe. I think the tones are very important to this book. It gives it a more finished look, closer to a color book than a black-and-white book that just runs flat line-art. Although, I must say, it's a shame that people rarely get to see Charlie's art in stark black and white. It's mesmerizing to look at. I've stated many times that it kills an entire day when he turns pages in, I just stare at them all day long when I get them. And then my schedule takes another hit when Cliff turns in the toned pages.

After the toning and the letters are done, Rus goes in and merges the lettering with the toned pages, to make them one final completed page. Then that's sent to Image Comics so they can send it off to the printer.

Frisch: *The Walking Dead*, like most of your other works, is serialized in monthly twenty-two-page issues (the standard format in North America) before being collected in trade paperbacks. What role do the two formats play in your approach to structuring and pacing a story?

Kirkman: To utilize the monthly format I always try to write to cliffhangers. I always try to end an issue with a moment that will make the readers hungry to come back for more, so to speak. Now, not every cliffhanger can be some startling event, or after a while they'll lose all effect, so from time to

An unconventional "cliffhanger" portrays Rick and Carl dealing with the trauma Carl experiences after killing Shane, his father's friend and attacker. From *The Walking Dead*, Book 1, by Robert Kirkman and Tony Moore; Image Comics, 2008.

time I have some pretty lame cliffhangers that are just, "Whoa, they found a generator," and stuff like that. But I always try to end on something at least interesting.

Since I know that these issues are going to eventually be collected into paperback volumes, I try to make sure that the first page of every issue fits well next to the last page of the previous issue. So that if they're read together without any interruption, the transition from one issue to the next isn't jarring.

I never write the story and plot it out with a six-issue break in mind. From time to time if I can, I try to end the sixth issue with a resolution of some kind, but only if the story is flowing to that around the time I'm writing that issue. I would never lengthen or shorten a story to make it fit in a trade paperback. Which is why the third volume ends with a cliffhanger.

Frisch: Are you happy with the monthly format?

Kirkman: Absolutely. I guess most of Europe is all about the graphic novels, and there's a lot of them here, in the US, also. But for my money, I enjoy the monthly installment plan. I dig buying monthly comics and getting a serialized story. It's not the perfect format for every book. And I'm told *The Walking Dead* does read better in collected form, but I love the single issues. I don't ever plan to abandon the format.

Frisch: Speaking of Europe, how familiar are you with the European comics scene? Are there any particular European creators or works that have influenced you?

Kirkman: I live in Kentucky, which I guess is considered one of the more rural states in America. That's not to say that that stuff is unavailable to me. It's just that I'd have to specifically special-order whatever I want. I'm just not that familiar with European stuff. I mean, I love Moebius as much as anything. He's probably one of the only guys I know by name. I see stuff like *Dylan Dog* and *Blacksad* and *Red Hand*, the thing Kurt Busiek did recently. I think that stuff all looks great. I'm a huge fan of the oversized, thinner graphic-novel format. So much so that I hope to do one myself someday soon. But I'm just not overly familiar with the stuff in general. It's certainly on my to-do list.

Frisch: I suppose you haven't seen the new *Astérix*, which came out last week, then. Is there any chance you're going to take *The Walking Dead* to Europe, or other parts of the world?

Kirkman: Haven't seen *Astérix*, no. *The Walking Dead* is already published in a few countries over there. I don't really keep track of where, since I let Image Comics handle all that stuff.

Frisch: I actually meant the story, but that's interesting, as well. Let me rephrase: are there any plans for showing other countries or continents in *The Walking Dead*, or do you want to keep the focus on the United States?

Kirkman: Well, I plan on staying with the same group of characters throughout the run of the book. The ones that live, of course. There may be times when the core group splits up and I follow both of them. But the only time I'd show what's going on in Europe for instance is if our characters took a boat over there to see what's up. For the time being at least, the book will only take place in America.

Frisch: Without revealing too much to German readers, *The Walking Dead* has touched upon several controversial social and political issues, including gun control and the death penalty. Now, the United States has been widely lambasted in Germany and Europe at large for many of its policies in those areas, and vocal critics like Michael Moore or Noam Chomsky are treated as pop stars for their opposition to the American administration. What are your thoughts on those reactions in Europe, as a writer and as an American?

Kirkman: I don't really see how relevant a political question is in the scheme of this interview. Is it okay if I decline to answer this question? I mean, it would be like asking me about religion. You divide the audience no matter what your opinion is.

Frisch: Fair enough, feel free to decline any question. The relevance of the question, to my mind, is that these subjects definitely come up in *The Walking Dead* in a prominent fashion. Given that they're fairly relevant political issues in the United States and elsewhere, I thought it would be interesting to have some insight into your thoughts. Would it help if I rephrased the question, e.g., by leaving out the international aspect?

Kirkman: I'm not really trying to make a statement along those lines in *The Walking Dead*. That stuff cropped up only because it's logical that it cropped up, not because I had something to say on the matter. I'm not a writer that tries to force-feed his views about anything on the public through his work. That could be my answer to the rephrased question.

Frisch: Fair enough. Let's move on, then. Early on in your career, you created and published a title called *Battle Pope*, featuring a rather idiosyncratic version of the pope, which is currently being reprinted at Image. Have the recent death of John Paul II and his replacement with Benedict XVI, a German (and a Bavarian, to boot), given you any ideas for a potential continuation of the title?

Kirkman: *Battle Pope* was never even remotely based on the real pope in any way. *Battle Pope* was basically a superhero comic, featuring a character who happened to be the Pope. I made little reference to Catholicism or anything like that. So no, a new pope wouldn't have any kind of bearing on what I would do in future *Battle Pope* stories. That book is way too silly to be based on anything remotely real. I would like to continue the title if the reprint series continues to do well.

Frisch: Your Image Comics series *Invincible* was recently promoted with a special #0 issue with a $0.50 cover price. Could you shed some light on the economics involved with this sort of promotion, and whether it's been successful so far?

Kirkman: *Invincible* 0 was an astounding success. We did a much shorter story, twelve pages, and lowered the price a great deal. As a result of the low price, *Invincible* 0 sold almost five times what the current issues were selling, and then afterwards the sales on the title abruptly shot up by 20 percent and have maintained a steady climb since. With the number of copies sold, the issue still broke even. So we didn't make money off the book, but it helped sales on the series as a whole, and it didn't cost us a dime to do. I was very pleased with how it all turned out.

Frisch: Were you worried at all that the issue could turn people off the first few collections of the series? After all, *Invincible* 0 basically reveals the plot of the first twenty-two issues, spoiling some fairly big surprises for potential new readers in the process.

Kirkman: No, the issue 0 was for people who more than likely wouldn't buy the trades, so they needed a little push. It spoiled things, yes, but if they liked it they could read the full story by going back and getting the trades or they could continue on with the book from that point on. I have no regrets.

Frisch: Except for *The Walking Dead*, all your current works are superhero titles, and *Marvel Zombies*, your upcoming limited series, seems to take this dichotomy to its logical conclusion, showing Marvel's superheroes as zombies. Are you concerned about being typecast as "the superhero guy," or "the zombie guy?"

Kirkman: I'm not concerned at all. I think there's enough variety inside my superhero work itself to keep things interesting. My zombie book is also just a character study—it could almost just be straight drama, so I don't really think I'm in any danger of being shoehorned into either category.

Frisch: In your Marvel titles and in your online column ("Buy My Books" at *Comic Book Resources*), you make no secret of your affection for some of the storytelling approaches (like the Michelinie/McFarlane/Larsen *Amazing Spider-Man* formula of structuring arcs and introducing subplots) and characters (such as Sleepwalker, Darkhawk, or Terror, Inc.) that were tremendously popular throughout the early 1990s but seem to have largely fallen out of favor since. What's the appeal of those styles and characters for you?

Kirkman: That's back when comics were fun for me . . . and I think the only reason for that is that I was at "that age" when I read those things. Everyone who reads comics always has a fondness for the books they read first, the books that got them into comics. They may not be the best comics, and I'll admit that, but they were what I was reading when I started reading when I was twelve or fourteen or whatever. They're special to me, flaws and all.

Frisch: Obviously, those books and characters must have made quite an impression on people back then, given that it was the most thriving period of American comics in recent history. Can you elaborate on what you think the strengths of those titles are? In particular, the way you set up subplots and the way you cut back and forth between Peter Parker's personal life and his exploits as a superhero in *Marvel Team-Up* reminds me of the approach creators like Michelinie and Larsen employed to great effect fifteen years ago. Would you say that's a fair comparison?

Kirkman: Absolutely. To me, that's just how comics are done. A core story for each issue or arc, something that's entertaining and fairly important . . . and subplots setting up future core stories. I don't like it when an entire story is self-contained in six issues, followed by another completely self-contained arc. I want things to build in my stories . . . and build up to payoff, so that people feel rewarded by reading long runs of the books. That's what I liked as a fan, about those books in particular, and that's what I like in the books I write. It keeps me interested.

Frisch: One of the first Spider-Man stories I read was that two-parter with the Punisher, by Michelinie and Larsen, which was followed by a two-parter involving Venom, and then the six-parter which brought back the Sinister Six, and so on—as you say, I liked the way those built on each other and never let you off the hook as a reader. At some point, however, this way of combining flashy "villain of the month" stories with ongoing soap-opera plots seems to have been abandoned, and is something of a lost art these days, a few exceptions like *Marvel Team-Up* or *Gødland* aside. Why do you think that's the case?

Kirkman: Things are always changing. I think really all it takes is for someone to get popular doing something else and then it begins to spread throughout the industry. I don't know where the current seemingly disconnected arc style came from, but I think it had a little to do with the rising popularity of trade paperbacks. It also probably had a little to do with the need to get new readers and to keep things light on continuity so anyone can pick up the book. Personally, I prefer comics the other way. I think dropping things in a story that reflect to old stories makes a new reader want to hunt down back issues. So that's how I do things, the way I prefer. That's really all I can do. I'm writing this stuff all day, every day. I'm the one that has to be kept happy.

Frisch: How personal are your stories? Especially in your longer, creator-owned works, *The Walking Dead* and *Invincible*, are there any characters or situations you particularly identify with?

Kirkman: All of them, really. I mean, 80 percent of the time I'm just trying to figure out how I would react to certain situations and writing that. In a lot of cases I try to have characters react in ways I think no one would, just to spice things up, but most of the time, it's me. So as far as that goes I identify with the characters very much. Now, the situations they're in and their interactions with other characters, that's all made up. Some people think writers only write stuff based on their lives and that all stories are thinly veiled retellings of things that happened to them. Not me. If that were the case my life would be way too stupid.

Frisch: So, to clarify, what you're saying is that there are no zombies in Kentucky, either?

Kirkman: Correct. Well, for the most part.

Frisch: What's your take on the current trend to legally or illegally distribute comics in digital formats, be it on DVDs or CDs, as simple downloads, or on platforms like the PSP, to read on iPods, cell phones, or handheld PCs?

Kirkman: I certainly don't support it. But I don't get pissed if someone who would never buy my book gets to read it for free, though. I think to a certain extent it can lead to more sales. But it could also, very easily, lead to much, much less sales. I think I'm on the fence with a wait and see on that one.

Frisch: There appears to be a widespread negative view of manga in the US comics industry which sees Japanese comics as a threat or, at best, as an entry drug for American comics. Do you have any thoughts on this particular debate?

Kirkman: I like manga. I don't view it as a threat at all. To see kids reading comics in any form is a good thing, I think.

Frisch: Which comics are you currently enjoying or looking forward to?

Kirkman: *Ultimate Spider-Man, Doc Frankenstein, Planetary, Savage Dragon, Shaolin Cowboy, Runaways, Captain America,* and countless others.

Frisch: In an old interview, you said, "I don't think I'll ever write a book I don't letter, because I don't think it would be as good. And I'm such a lettering geek, I don't think I could trust anyone." You've since changed your mind, right?

Kirkman: Well, times change. At the time I was doing only one or two books a month, if I recall. I actually enjoyed lettering back then. The thing about it is, I was so anal about lettering placement and whatnot I never really got that fast at it. So it took me almost an hour to do some pages and nearly an entire day or more to letter a book. I from time to time will still letter a page or two if it's easy and I don't feel like explaining to Rus Wooton (my letterer of choice) exactly what I want. I lettered a page in *Invincible* 23 and some pages in *The Walking Dead* 24 recently.

The reason I said what I said in this old interview is because I would often redialogue entire pages while I was lettering. I'd add lines, take lines away, I would make all kinds of changes. Now, I do the same thing, but when I do balloon placements for the letterer instead of when I'm actually lettering. Also, I like lettering to look a very specific way and Rus Wooton has been able to match my lettering almost seamlessly. Rus is a great letterer; he's a big part of why I feel comfortable working with someone else. He was a sort of understudy for Chris Eliopoulos, and Chris's lettering is kind of what I've based all my lettering on, his and John Workman's stuff. So Rus was the perfect choice.

Science Dog and Zombies: An Interview with Robert Kirkman

D. J. KIRKBRIDE / 2006

From *Silver Bullet Comics*, January 23, 2006. Reprinted by permission of D. J. Kirkbride

You know who **Robert Kirkman** is, right? He's one of the hottest writers in comics right now, what with the superhero fun of *Invincible* and zombie tales in *The Walking Dead* at Image, as well as *Marvel Team-Up*, *Marvel Zombies*, and *Ultimate X-Men* at Marvel, and the proverbial much much more. The guy's on a winning streak and is keeping very busy, but he still found time to answer some of *Silver Bullet Comics*' own **D. J. Kirkbride**'s email questions. Kirkman's the man. Read on to find out why . . .

D. J. Kirkbride: You grew up in Kentucky, so riddle me this: why is it called the "Bluegrass State?" I've been there . . . the grass is green.

Robert Kirkman: Bluegrass is a type of grass that grows only here in Kentucky. It got its name because when it grows near a stream or pond it actually contaminates the water to a small degree and gives the water mild hallucinogenic properties. The pioneers who originally traveled through Kentucky called the grass bluegrass because when you drank this water it made the grass look blue. "Bluegrass Water" is something you can buy in head shops and hippy stores around the area. Believe it or not it's completely legal to sell. It's more of a novelty than anything else.

Kirkbride: What book or character first really got you hooked on comic book crack?

Kirkman: Spider-Man was always my favorite. When I started reading Marvel was publishing *Web of Spider-Man*, *Spectacular Spider-Man*, *Amazing Spider-Man*, and *Spider-Man* along with *Marvel Tales Featuring Spider-Man* and of course his appearance in every other Marvel Comic every couple of months or so. It was a cool time for Spider-Man fans. In 1992 when Image Comics started, I followed those guys over there and immediately fell in love with *Savage Dragon*, that "anything goes" kind of storytelling is something I always try to incorporate in my work.

Kirkbride: I know that you've answered this question a lot, but how'd you break into the comics industry? (Feel free to make stuff up.) Was it something you'd always wanted, or did you imagine doing something else (screenwriting, firefighting, break dancing) and then happen into comics?

Kirkman: A lot of people don't know this, but before my family moved to Kentucky I lived in Cleveland, Ohio, and I actually lived up the street from the kid who would become Brian Michael Bendis. Our families were friends with each other and he actually used to babysit me from time to time. He was like an older brother to me. Our families kept in touch after the move. I was in high school when he started doing *Jinx* and his other books at Caliber. I wasn't planning on going to college or anything after high school, and he seemed to be having fun doing this comic stuff, and I had always LOVED comics so I figured I'd give it a shot. Brian ended up helping me out a little along the way and even ghostwrote much of *Battle Pope* (although that's not really common knowledge). He's a great guy.

Kirkbride: If you could be doing anything else as a career right now, what would it be?

Kirkman: I know this is going to sound like a bullshit answer, but I always kinda wanted to be an astronaut. I mean, going out into space and fighting aliens and meeting sexy space babes always seemed like a lot of fun when I watched those astronaut reality shows on TV. I think being up close to most of the aliens I've seen on TV would probably scare the crap out of me, so it's probably best that I did comics instead.

Kirkbride: Who'd win in a fight: Battle Pope or Jon Voight as Pope John Paul II?

Kirkman: See, that's hard to say. If it was the actual Pope John Paul II instead of Jon Voight posing as him, I'd give it to JP in a heartbeat, before he died I mean. You've got to look at it this way. JP has the power of GOD himself at his disposal; I mean that's his job, right? Talking to GOD and laying down the law and stuff. He'd be able to ask GOD for a flamethrower or a baseball bat and poof, it'd just BE there. So JP hands down. Jon Voight is an actor . . . so he's just got the power of Satan at his disposal, and we all know Satan ain't all that. So even though Battle Pope is totally imaginary, I'd have to give it to him if he were to fight Jon Voight, because dressing up like the POPE would probably piss Satan off and make him take away Jon Voight's powers.

Kirkbride: You inked some of the first *Battle Pope* stuff, right? Any desire to get back on the illustration side of comics?

Kirkman: I penciled some *Battle Pope* stuff too. It's in issue 5 of the new colored series. I inked a bunch of stuff toward the middle of that run . . . all in all, it was pretty bad, so I don't really think I'll be dipping my toe into the art side of things anytime soon.

Kirkbride: Arguably, Invincible is the character you're best known for. How long was he running around in your head before you got the book together?

Kirkman: Not very long at all. Cory Walker and I came up with the guy expressly because Image wanted us to do a superhero book for their new superhero line instead of *Science Dog*, the book we'd originally pitched to them. So he was invented in July or so of 2002, developed while Cory and I worked on *Super Patriot: America's Fighting Force* for Image and then on the shelves in January 2003. So he hasn't really existed all that long.

Kirkbride: Any word on the *Invincible* movie? Who's your "dream cast?"

Kirkman: It's still moving along at a snail's pace . . . nothing new to report. My dream cast? Mel Gibson as Omni-Man and Michael Cera from *Arrested Development* as Mark . . . if he could do the action stuff. Him or the kid from that movie *The Squid and the Whale* who kinda looks like him. That kid was a great actor.

Kirkbride: Is there an end in sight for *Invincible*? Or is it "from my cold dead hands?" Could you see the universe continuing on, sort of like a latter-day Batman or Superman? Kids in Invincible underroos? Invincible cereal and toothbrushes?

Kirkman: Who could say no to those things. In a perfect world *Invincible* 600 will be out in however long it takes and if I'm dead, someone else will be writing it. I like the idea of it just continuing on without me. Maybe my kids will want to do it . . . if they're not too busy being astronauts.

Kirkbride: What's cooler: superheroes or zombies? (Or zombie superheroes?) Seems like you've got your bases covered either way.

Kirkman: I do one zombie book (or one and a half if you count *Marvel Zombies*) and four or five superhero books (depending on what's been announced yet). What do you think? Very soon, though . . . I hope to branch out into comics that are neither zombie books . . . or superhero books.

Kirkbride: Do you write more monthly comics than Bendis right now? How is this possible? How do you have time for this dumbass interview? (Maybe . . . maybe don't answer that last part . . . or even think about it.)

Kirkman: Well, it's taken me over a month to get this back to you. Maybe that answers your question. I also work almost nonstop, taking breaks only to sleep. I'll take the occasional day off here and there so the wife doesn't leave me . . . but other than that, it's nose-to-the-grindstone comic making. But I don't write more books than Bendis . . . that guy is a machine.

Kirkbride: What's your work schedule like? Do you keep "regular" writing hours?

Kirkman: I usually wake up around 8:00 a.m. and work until I go to sleep, with long breaks throughout the day. I'll go see a movie with the wife or go grab a bit to eat, or if we have friends over, I'll stop, but for the most part, I'm working.

Kirkbride: How's your work for Marvel different than the Image work? Do you approach the writing differently?

Kirkman: Not really. I mean there are certain ground rules to follow, and I try to follow continuity as closely as possible when I'm writing for Marvel, but other than that it's all the same to me. My stuff, their stuff, whatever . . . it's all comics. I enjoy them all equally.

Kirkbride: With *Marvel Team Up*, you've been able to put your words in a lot of classic/mainstream superheroes' mouths. Any Marvel character you'd love to write that you haven't had a crack at yet?

Kirkman: I haven't had a chance to do anything with Ghost Rider . . . and Oeming killed Thor right when I started at Marvel, so the only time I've really had a chance to write him was in that recent *What If* book I did with Mike. I'd like to get a real crack at Thor. And I always liked Cyclops, but I've only used him in a small cameo so far . . . there's a LONG, LONG list . . . I could go on for days. US 1 . . . I can't leave out US 1.

Kirkbride: How'd this *Ultimate X-Men* deal come about? Is it for a set number of issues?

Kirkman: Right now I'm keeping the seat warm for Bryan Singer. I'm slated for nine issues but I'd love to do more. I've got a lot of big stuff planned; they're going to need somebody to come along and clean up this mess when I'm done and hopefully that'll be me. I'd been talking to Ultimate editor Ralph Macchio about other stuff, including *Marvel Zombies*, and when Brian K. Vaughan left the book I guess something fooled them into thinking I'd be good for the job. I couldn't be happier.

Kirkbride: Have you been approached by or approached DC about any work? I can see you doing a really fun Superman if given the chance.

Kirkman: I'm currently exclusive at Marvel. I'd love to one day get a crack at the DC icons, but I'm very happy where I am right now.

Kirkbride: You've worked with some really talented artists (Cory Walker, Tony Moore, Charlie Adlard, Paco Medina, Ryan Ottley—you know who they are). Do you write/format your scripts differently for each of them?

Kirkman: In some cases once I figure out what their weaknesses are I'll try to avoid that, but like you said, I've been lucky enough to work with some really great artists so half the time I'm trying to force them to draw really hard stuff so that I can be amazed when they pull it off.

Kirkbride: Who's your dream artist (that you haven't worked with yet)? Any specific project in mind?

Kirkman: I'd love to do a run on *The Incredible Hulk* with Ed McGuinness. I'd also like to do a book with Walt Simonson or Erik Larsen. There's a huge number of guys.

Kirkbride: *Science Dog*—tantalizing title. When will it happen? Any hints as to what this is about?

Kirkman: It'll happen someday. It may be a while, but Cory Walker and I will get around to producing at least a one-shot at some point.

Kirkbride: What books are you into right now?

Kirkman: *Desolation Jones, Y The Last Man, Fell, Girls, Godland, Noble Causes, PVP, Savage Dragon, Sea of Red, Ultimate Spider-Man, Ultimates, Daredevil, New Avengers, Runaways, Captain America, She-Hulk, Powers,* and tons of others. I think *Ex Machina* is my favorite book right now. It's really kick ass.

Kirkbride: Now that you're no longer an "up and coming" writer and in the big leagues, who's an "up and coming" writer nipping at your big-league heels? Who should readers be looking out for?

Kirkman: I'm no longer "up and coming," what the hell? When did THAT happen? I REALLY, REALLY don't think I'm in the big leagues or even close to it. I've got quite a few steps to go before I get to that point. If you want to see who readers should be looking out for though, look no further than Image Comics. From me, to the Luna Brothers, to Rick Remender—that's where all the talent is coming from these days . . . and they're not cutting their teeth there or learning the ropes, they're making some of the best comics on the market. Image Comics has one of the best lineups it's EVER had right now. I'm just thrilled to be a part of it.

Kirkbride: Okay, what haven't I asked you that I really should've?

Kirkman: Boxer briefs . . . but only half the time.

The Robert Kirkman Interview

SIMON ABRAMS / 2008

From *The Comics Journal*, April 2008. Reprinted by permission of Simon Abrams

Having transcribed my interview with Robert Kirkman, I couldn't help but be struck by the number of times he paraphrased other writers. It not so much that he was speaking for others while he was talking but he was speaking *as* others, incorporating their ideas, sentiments, and manner of expression into his vocabulary seamlessly. This carries over into his word balloons and is a large part of his writing's everyman appeal. What makes his voice distinct is that it's not trying to be. His heroes are amalgamations of what have come before them, continuations of a tradition that differ from their predecessors only in the time and the situations they face. Kirkman's breathless, dialogue-heavy melodramas appeal to his readers' need to see what happens next. By embracing the serialized nature of comics, he paces his characters' lives as an unfolding saga alongside the lives of his audience.

The fact that his characters are enduring the problems that come with our world's relentless sense of time endears them to us and allows us to track their progress, to see what might happen if we could keep watching their world change and them with it. When crisis strikes, it hits the community first and then ripples through individuals. In both *Invincible* and *The Walking Dead*, Kirkman's most popular creator-owned series, we see an exploration of what life would be like if his protagonists were to depart from the world they know to overcome their uncertainty and build a new one. Whether confronted by superpowers or zombies, their idea of home must adjust to the changes affecting them.

Spectacular changes destroy the foundation of their family and community and are the first and most salient sign that nothing is sacred. Even in *Marvel Zombies*, a title as brainless as its protagonists, Kirkman makes the loss of the superhero the loss of the familiar. Just because they're pulpy doesn't mean

Kirkman's heroes are allowed to be above the community that they protect. The rock-steady icons that we thought we could count on in times of crisis are dead, and with them the ability to translate their unwavering convictions into actions. Unlike other zombies, these zombies talk to taunt us with their weird need to feed on flesh and their uneasy coexistence with the personalities fans have become familiar with. Spider-Man still loves Mary Jane, but he can't stop himself from gorging on her brains.

I call it an approximation because that's just what Kirkman sells it as, a version of what could be from a writer who is very much a product of his time. Instead of drawing on the icons of Golden Age comics, Kirkman draws on the comics of the '90s, a time now considered to be one of the comics industry's darkest hours, both creatively and financially. Kirkman's stories prove the existence of the good through the gory, cataclysmic effects of the bad, a somewhat cynical, if well-intentioned, outlook that means that he doesn't flinch at the prospect of dousing his champions in buckets of blood so that they can become stronger for it later. *Invincible* is probably his best original series because it is his most optimistic, a testing ground for a budding force of good.

Kirkman's imagination is shaped by this optimism. Just as his superhero comics treat the protagonist's nickname and colorful costume as a gaudy but accurate reflection of the character's potential, his horror series subordinate the reality of social dynamics to the vocabulary of the genre, eschewing the affectation of "verité" style for a story populated by characters as flamboyant as they are genuine. Kirkman's stories rise or fall in relation to the believability of his characters, and while he's suffered a number of creative setbacks in his short career, he's also celebrated a number of remarkable commercial successes—*Marvel Zombies* just received its sixth printing, and both *The Walking Dead* and *Invincible* have enhanced Image's position on the sales charts, becoming two of the highest-selling independent ongoing series in the direct market.

Kirkman's experiences have provided him with a unique opportunity to see comics from all sides of production, from self-publishing his own brand of comics to lettering, inking and penciling, and writing his first series. Never wishing to stray too far into the kind of wild speculations that I wished he would, his sometimes-rambling responses proved him to be as unpretentious and verbose as his characters. Even in discussion, he seems to err on the side of caution, choosing not to mount his pulpit and preach his version of the gospel, but rather to talk as in his stories, with a voice that is one of many, one whose familiarity sustains it.

Simon Abrams: What kind of formal education did you have?

Robert Kirkman: None whatsoever. As far as formal education, I graduated high school, but it was pretty clear that I was finished with the whole "going to class and doing homework" thing—I think I went through my entire senior year without doing any homework but still managed to get fairly good grades. I was just sick of it and pretty much dove right into the workforce.

Around that time, my dad had owned his own business, so he'd decided to sell that business, retire, and move down to Florida to live with my grandmother, so they came to me and said, "Look, we're moving to Florida in a year. You're welcome to come with us, but if you don't want to move to Florida, you're going to have to move out." My brother and sister were still going to school, so they moved down to Florida and finished out school—well, my sister's still in high school. My whole family just up and moved. I was kind of given a time limit for moving out, getting my own place and finding a steady job, so that year, I had been saving up to get a place. I thought working and making money was more worthwhile than training myself to make it through college, because I really didn't have the heart to do any kind of work. I figured I have learned enough.

Abrams: What did you do for a living?

Kirkman: I was working at a comic shop at the time, and I was doing that my senior year and the year after that. At the same time, the wife of the guy that owned the comic shop worked at a lighting distributor. I worked in a warehouse, and they sold light fixtures to builders and construction stuff. I worked there for four years.

Abrams: Were your parents supportive of your decision to work in the comics business?

Kirkman: My parents were not of aware of my decision for a good long time. I guess it sounds kind of crazy, but it seems completely normal to me, but they did not know I was working in comics until I started working with Marvel. I was doing comics for a good three or four years before they ever knew. I didn't want them to worry about me because I ended up quitting my job rather quickly. I wound up publishing comics only for about a year before I quit my day job completely and started publishing full time. I started out as a warehouse person there and got promoted a few times so that I was eventually a purchasing agent. I had my own office and monitored their sales, and at the same time I was pretty much ignoring all my duties at my job, talking to Quebecor, my printer in Canada and various artists.

I was pretty much running my own publishing company from my office so for the last year I was working there. I was working on self-publishing stuff until 3:00 a.m., and I needed to get to work at 8:00 a.m. the next day. It was a pretty stressful time, and I ended up quitting even though I didn't have any kind of financial stability. I took a pretty big risk, and by the time I started making money in comics, I had about $50,000 worth of credit-card debts racked up. It was a lot of fun. Because of that, I didn't want to tell my parents, "Hey, I quit my job to do comics. Remember how I used to read comics? Now I make comics, but I don't really make any money at it."

Abrams: Were you considering any careers outside of comics seriously?

Kirkman: Well, before I started publishing comics, I wanted to sculpt statues. I actually sent in submissions to manufacturers: I did that a bit in high school. I don't think I was very good at it, but I enjoyed doing it. I thought about doing that for a while, but I was a big comic book fan, so I wanted to work in the field. I originally wanted to be an artist but again, I really wasn't good enough. Aside from that, I had no other real aspirations. I could've made do: I'm a fairly intelligent guy, so I could've started a sandwich shop or something.

Abrams: You grew up in a small town in Kentucky so what was your earliest exposure to comics?

Kirkman: My first exposure to comics was from a baseball-card shop that had had a comic book section. I was collecting baseball cards at the time, which was silly because I didn't really like baseball. I played baseball but I didn't really watch baseball at the time, so I was collecting cards where I didn't really know who anybody was. I talked my dad into taking me to this comic shop, so, while I was getting baseball cards, my dad was getting comic books. My dad read comics as a kid, but he ran a sheet-metal business later. He was a big fan of Metal Men, so when we went to the comic book shop, he bought a shitload of *Iron Man* comics because he thought Iron Man was one of the Metal Men from back in the day. He had bought twelve issues, which had stayed around the house for a while around the time when John Byrne and John Romita Jr. had a short run with "Armor Wars II," and it had a bunch of Fin Fang Foom stuff in it. I ended up really liking them, so from there, our local Walmart carried comics. In fact, I think that local baseball-card shop went out of business fairly quickly after that.

Abrams: How well stocked was the Walmart?

Kirkman: Surprisingly well stocked, actually. As far as DC stuff goes, they didn't really have much: They had an odd issue of *The Flash*, some *Action Comics*, just two or three DC titles. As far as Marvel stuff at the time, they had all the big stuff. They had all the X-Men titles and all the Spider-Man titles, but they wouldn't carry some of the lower-selling Marvel titles, like *New Mutants*.

They had *X-Factor* and *X-Force* when that came out, *New Warriors*, *Ghost Rider*, *The Punisher*—so it was a pretty big lineup of those titles you could buy off the rack that Marvel was putting out at the time at Walmart. There were some local gas stations that would carry a few odds and ends like *Alpha Flight*, *Darkhawk*, and *Sleepwalker*. For the first year or so that I collected comics, I got them strictly from Walmart.

There was a bigger city, the second largest in Kentucky, called Lexington that was about a half-hour drive away from my house. My mother was always going there because they had a mall and she had friends there, so we were driving though the town one day and I saw a sign that said, "Comic Interlude."

I flipped out because I didn't know comic shops existed, so I pointed it out and begged her to take me but she refused, so I kept hammering her about it and eventually she agreed to take me. It was funny because when you walked in the door at the store, there was a poster on the wall: "*Youngblood!* Coming from Malibu Comics!" I don't think there was any hint of Image Comics on there yet. I went in and asked what this *Youngblood* thing was, and he told me all about this new Image Comics line that was coming out: "Oh, these Marvel artists are going to form their own company." And he listed them all off and I said, "Shit, those are all my favorite books!" So I started a reserve list for all Image titles at that store.

Abrams: Your first work with a major distributor was with Image. What Image titles specifically appealed to you?

Kirkman: I liked them all early on. Like I said, my pull box at that time had all Image titles. I was getting Marvel books at Walmart and I would get Image books at this comic shop, so then eventually I only bought Image books.

Abrams: Which comics and which writers made you say to yourself, "I want to make this my career?"

Kirkman: David Michelinie was doing *Amazing Spider-Man* and I really liked the way that book was put together, and (Eric) Larsen was drawing it at the time, so I'm sure he had a little bit to do with the way the story was going, even though I don't think Larsen ever admitted to following the plot too closely. I really liked that stuff at the time and actually, Peter David's *Hulk*. Every now and then, when I get bitter at all about comics and think, "Oh, man, this is starting to feel like a job," and I'm not really enjoying stuff, I just dig into these comics and get jazzed up about reading comics again.

A lot of times, those old Dale Keown/Peter David issues of *The Hulk* really do it for me as well as Peter David's *X-Factor*. Peter David is probably the first writer whose writing made me think, "Huh, I really like this guy's stuff." Of course, I wasn't able to buy *Sachs & Violens*, because I was too young.

Abrams: You and [penciler and longtime collaborator] Tony Moore grew up together. How close were you?

Kirkman: Very close. We met in seventh grade. We were the only kids in school that were drawing X-Men characters. We met and became pretty good friends.

Abrams: Were there kids in your neighborhood that were into comics?

Kirkman: It was a small town, and I was aware of maybe six kids in the whole middle school that read comics. I could talk to them, but as far as neighborhood kids—I lived out in the country, so I maybe had two neighborhood friends who were within bike-riding distance. I would go over to their house to play (Mike Tyson's) *Punch Out* but probably no one around me collected comics at all.

Abrams: You went to high school with Moore and your future wife Sonia? How long did you know Sonia?

Kirkman: I met my wife in seventh grade, also. She had just moved to the school that year and I had a few classes with her so the seventh grade was a big year for me.

Abrams: What were you like in high school?

Kirkman: What was I like? [*Laughs.*] I don't know? Cool?! I wouldn't say I was a nerd. I wasn't the most popular kid in school. I wasn't a big player. I was on an academic team, but I don't know that I was necessarily smart. I was into comics. I lost most of the fights I was in. I mean, I wasn't unpopular or anything. I had friends and I was fine. It was school, y'know?

Abrams: What was the part of town you lived in like?

Kirkman: I lived in a small area of Harrison County called Leesburg that had an old general store right across the street from us. I mean, this old country store was right across the street from me. I could go in there, get my soda pop and maybe get my baseball cards but other than that, we were pretty much out in the wilderness. I was helping my mother plant trees one summer night when a pack of wolves walked through the gas station, so we had to run inside in a hurry. We were out there.

Abrams: Was moving away from Kentucky ever something you seriously considered?

Kirkman: No, not really. I was born here. I kinda like it here. I live in a different area now so I've moved around a bit. I was actually born in Lexington and moved to the country in the fourth grade and moved back after I graduated high school. I've traveled a lot in the last few years. I've seen a good portion of the country at least and it's all fine, it's all the same. I know where everything is here.

Abrams: What was it about Image as an independent publisher that you liked compared to Marvel or DC?

Kirkman: I published comics for about three years, and I was kind of used to doing everything myself, and Image by design was a company that could allow me to do as much or as little as I wanted, and so, being a bit of a control freak, it was possible for me to control how the covers look, how the letters pages look, whether or not there is a letters page, and I could have a very large hand in how the books are marketed. Image was the perfect fit for me. Of course, I was a big fan of Image growing up so being part of Image Comics was a big deal for me. When it started to look like the publishing would never pan out and when it was clear I was never going to able to make that work, Image was definitely what I set my sights on.

Abrams: What do superhero comics have that other comics or genres in comics don't?

Kirkman: I can't really explain that. I grew up reading American comics in the '90s, so comics to me are superheroes. I had very little experience reading anything other than superhero comics up until high school, when I was going to comic shops regularly and could pick up things like Fantagraphics titles. Oni was just starting up, and I had a more active interest in Dark Horse Comics and whatnot. For whatever reasons, that's what's popular in America: Superhero comics dominate the market. It's all male-power fantasy stuff, and that's fine. I vastly enjoy my non-superhero books, and in the future I hope to do more non-superhero books.

Abrams: What drew you to superheroes in general? Do you think you could've gotten away with anything other than that at Image?

Kirkman: I definitely could have and I have, but starting out, I just really enjoyed reading superhero comics, so doing my own was kind of a big deal. There's definitely a wealth of different subgenres you can do within the superhero genre: you can do "superhero horror," "superhero Western," "superhero romance," or "superhero superhero." Take *Invincible* for example. I can do pretty much anything with that book. I can have an issue where it's a soap opera, just a guy and a girl talking about romance stuff and kissing each other and whatnot. That's fine because some people are invested enough in the characters and that's OK, because I can also have them fighting some space monster. Within that series, I can do almost anything.

That's also the appeal of Image Comics in general. Within your series, you're controlling everything, You're the owner, you're the guy that makes decisions, and if you want to go back in time for an issue and be a cowboy because your artist wants to draw horses, you can totally do that.

Abrams: Your series are peppered with pop culture references—for instance, in *Battle Pope*, you refer to everything from *The Big Lebowski* to Bruce Lee. What kind of movies and music were you into as you grew up?

Kirkman: I refer to *The Big Lebowski* in *Battle Pope*?

Abrams: I thought so. The line, "Does the Pope shit in the woods?"

Kirkman: Oh, no, not really [*laughs*]. That was actually a dare that [AIT/ Planet Lar publisher] Larry Young coaxed me into. I've tried to steer clear of pop-culture references because they date me a great deal. Any pop culture reference that's slipped in is begrudgingly on my part. You read those old *Fantastic Four* issues and you think, "Holy shit! This stuff is really old!" You don't even realize it's the '60s until they're walking around on the moon and going into space shuttles, and then you remember that that was before man's first trip in a space shuttle and the Space Race. It's a marginally timeless comic until you say something about Clark Gable or Humphrey Bogart—do they mention Gary Cooper in there? I don't know. I really dislike pop culture references in comics.

But, lord, I don't know. I was a big fan of Sonic Youth music-wise. I liked grunge rock: Nirvana, Soundgarden, and Pearl Jam. As far as TV shows, I watched *The X-Files* pretty religiously. I was a big fan of *Melrose Place*, and I'm not ashamed to admit it. Anybody that laughs at me for that did not watch *Melrose Place*. That show had people driving cars into buildings, cutting people's heads off—all kinds of weird shit was going on in that show. People breaking their necks on swimming pools . . . and I'll be honest, I watched it for the romance, but that show was crazy! I watched all the shows that were on before *The X-Files* that were canceled every year: I like *Strange Love*, *VR5*, *Brisco County Jr.* There were others I can't really remember right now.

As for films, I was into the same things I'm into now: *Star Wars*, *Indiana Jones*, *Ghostbusters*, *Reservoir Dogs*—Tarantino movies in general, of which there were, what, two at the time? The normal stuff. I will say I inexplicably hated Stanley Kubrick for a while; I just thought his films were boring. I started forcing myself to watch them and now I'm a really big fan. My taste has changed a bit, but for the most part they've stayed the same. I watch the odd romantic comedy; I guess in high school I wouldn't.

Abrams: What kind of literature were you interested in?

Kirkman: I hate to admit it, but I was one of those kids who was never forced to read, so I kind of didn't enjoy it and I was never really into classes that made you read *Moby Dick* of any of the other "classics" like *Call of the Wild* or anything like that. I never really read books that much. There were a few titles like *The Chronicles of Narnia* series—I read most of it. I read a few books on my own, but mostly I read comics. I read some Stephen King because my dad was into that stuff; I don't think I ever got through with those either. Not because I didn't like it but because I was a kid.

FUNK-O-TRON

Abrams: For *Battle Pope*, you let loose your inner autodidact and did everything from the stories and character layouts to lettering and inking. Did you ever want to draw, or was writing comics your first career choice?

Kirkman: Well, *Battle Pope* wasn't the first book Funk-O-Tron did. Funk-O-Tron actually started when my friend Robert Sutton came to Red Rock at the time—Red Rock was the name of the comic book shop I worked at in high school. When he came by, he said, "Let's do some comics. You can do the art and I'll write it," because I drew all the time. I had wanted to be an artist and I had told him, "No, I work in a comic shop. I know how things are." It was the late '90s, so everything was gloom and doom, comics weren't selling, yadda yadda, yadda, so I said, "I'll never get into that." I wanted to get into the lucrative business of toy sculpting.

Six months went by, and there were people coming by the comic shop that were doing small-press books, and I was seeing a lot of minicomics. I was kind of doing stuff at the comic book shop that let me learn how comics are distributed: I learned that Diamond had become the big distributor recently; Heroes World had stopped distributing Marvel books, so there was a lot of talk about that. I kind of knew how comic shops got distributors to the stories, so I started to get back to Eric Sutton that I would do a comic with him, and wrestling was really popular at the time.

Abrams: And that [series] was *Between the Ropes*?

Kirkman: Yes, *Between the Ropes*! Wrestlers were really popular at the time, and I knew when that *Previews* catalogue came out, anything I did would be in the very back in those little postage stamp solicitations saying, "Hey, here's a book!" even though there were about five hundred other books back there with it. My idea was to do something unique. There were a few wrestling comics at the time where it would be like, "Hey, here's the Undertaker and he's fighting zombies!" but there weren't any wrestling comics that were about wrestling. It sounds really dumb now, but I wanted to do a comic with a fake wrestling federation where you would see the wrestler go to work and talk to their wives and wash the kids, and then you'd see some of the matches and see them planning stuff out and doing different things. That was my big idea: "Oh, I'll do a big wrestling comic about wrestling and it'll appeal to thousands upon thousands of wrestling fans, and I'll do a small-press book that actually does OK! And I'll draw it!"

I ended up cowriting it with my friend and wound up changing all that when I drew it. I did a thirty-seven-page one-shot that I cowrote and penciled and inked—poorly—and I submitted that to Diamond and they rejected it because, as a distributor, they actually look over everything they distribute and, if they deem it to be a book that wouldn't sell enough to make it worth distributing, they won't do it. I got my rejection letter and I was very depressed, but while I was working on that book, I came up with the idea for *Battle Pope*. I was going to do *Battle Pope* by myself after I did *Between the Ropes*, but now I had met someone who was a better artist than I was. I just thought that I could do *Battle Pope* with Tony. While I was working on *Between the Ropes*, we decided to start working on that. The first issue of *Battle Pope* was completed pretty close to after my rejection letter for *Between the Ropes*. That wound up being accepted and wound up being Funk-O-Tron's first published book.

With *Battle Pope* there was the same idea that I had to do something that would stick out in the back of the catalog. The book's not necessarily antireligious. It doesn't necessarily attack religion; it just pokes fun at it, which is fine, I think. It wasn't that I hated religion or wanted to do something that was that over the top out of necessity, but it was rather, "What can I do to get noticed? Oh look, if there's a book called *Battle Pope*, surely the readers will take notice of that!" That was the kind of idea behind that.

Abrams: Did you ever seriously consider penciling *Battle Pope*, or had you given up hope of the idea of drawing at that point?

Kirkman: The only reason I went to Tony to draw *Battle Pope* was I was working on *Between the Ropes*, and I was so excited to get going on *Battle Pope* that I didn't want to wait to get finished drawing *Between the Ropes* to then draw *Battle Pope*. I was very much prepared to do *Battle Pope* on my own. I did layouts for it because I had already done layouts for the series. I already knew what the book was going to look like and what the first story was going to be, and so I had already started laying out the pages when Tony came onboard. I was ready to pencil it myself, but it would've been terrible and it would've been an embarrassment and I wouldn't be here today. It was a good thing I brought that guy on.

Abrams: How was Funk-O-Tron originally conceived?

Kirkman: We had already started on *Between the Ropes* when Tony came on to do *Battle Pope*, I was thinking, "Hey, we already got two comics that we're publishing ourselves. What's this company going to be called?" I came up with the name and we filed an LLC in the state of Kentucky. The three of us went to the state capital and paid our $85 to start our company. Having a comic book company is nothing monumental; it was just that we had gone to the capital and gotten a piece of paper. The publishing company was my computer. All we did was design papers and send computer files to the printer for comments. It's not like we got an office or hired a staff or did any kind of work on it.

Abrams: For a company that basically operated from your computer, it expanded considerably. In your first entry of your Buy My Books column on Comicbookresources.com, you say you wrangled together "Joe Casey, Charlie Adlard, Andy Kuhn, and Matt Fraction." How did you contact them?

Kirkman: [*Laughs.*] Gosh, all four of them were doing work at my company because of Larry Young and Val Staples. Larry Young and Joe Casey were doing a book at Image called *Double Image*. Joe Casey and Charlie Adlard were doing a series called *Codeflesh* and Larry Young and John Heebink one called *The Bod*. It was one comic and two stories so that when you flipped it over, it would have a cover on the back. Val Staples, who was a colorist at the time for Hi-Fi and did a bunch of Grant Morrison's *New X-Men* run and a bunch of other stuff, went on to start MV Creations. Val decided that he wanted to produce some comics that he would have me publish because he was coloring *Battle Pope* at the time, so we were pretty good friends.

He came to me and said, "I've got these two friends that are really talented that I want to help get published, so if I pay for the printing, would you publish some color comics for me?" He put the books together and all I did was slap a logo on it and get it to stores. He shouldered all the debt because publishing color comics at that time at that level was crazy. The book was called *Double Take* because it was the exact same format where one guy would do a ten-page story and another guy would do another ten-page story, and it would publish as a flipbook. I don't know what happened, but *Double Take* didn't end up continuing after issue #5, so Larry Young was going to publish it himself, but he had published single issues, so he had come out at the time and said, "Single issues are dead, I'm only being asked to do trades." AIT/Planet Lar said that they only do trades, so he came to me and said, "Hey, you publish single issues. Do you want to publish *Double Take*?"

I think the reason he came to me was because I had *Double Take* and said, "Oh we can just do these and *Double Take* and that'll be exactly the same thing except that the Image part will be taken out." I don't know if he was worried about Image suing him or anything but *Double Image* #6. Seven and 8 came out as *Double Take*. That's how I ended up working with those guys because Larry stopped doing *The Bod*, and he was then putting out *Rex Mantooth: Kung Fu Gorilla*, which Matt Fraction and Andy Kuhn were doing together on one side of the book and the *Codeflesh* story on the other. I wasn't headhunting—that was Matt Fraction's first published work. I didn't know anything about him; he was just a friend of Larry Young's. It was a great book—I mean, he was too talented even back then. I had little to nothing to do with that.

Abrams: How well did those books sell?

Kirkman: Super poorly [*laughs*]. I think the last issue of *Double Take* sold . . . less than a thousand copies? I mean, it was a bit of a disaster because those books were supposed to be color, and the *Double Image* books were color, and you went from *Double Image* #5 to *Double Take* #6, was black and white because it sold fairly poorly, and I would've lost my shirt if I had published in color.

I told Larry, "I really want to help you guys end out your run but I cannot afford to publish in color" because it would have cost me $2,000–3,000 to publish each issue in color, and that's money I wouldn't have made back. I wasn't even making a living at the time, and my wife had decided to take a break from college, and she was managing a coffee shop. There was no way I could afford to take $3,000 to publish a color book. It was cool, because I met Charlie Adlard and Joe Casey—Joe Casey was doing *Uncanny X-Men* at the time and I stayed in contact with Andy Kuhn. The relationships won from that book were well worth it, but even as a black and white, I lost money on that book.

Abrams: How worried was Sonia about the business expenses you were incurring?

Kirkman: Oh, at the time, she was more concerned with the fact that she never saw me. I was in a room in our house working on comics all the time. I was doing far less than I was doing now, but I had lettering to do back then, which took me a while. I think she was more concerned by the fact that I was working so much. I guess it was one of those "trust me baby, it'll work out" kind of things. It was a little rough spending so much time away from her working and whatnot, but we were twenty, twenty-one—we were young. We would go out every now and then but for the most part, "Oh, honey, I love you but I gotta work. I gotta make this thing or else I won't be able to make a living."

Abrams: You paid for Funk-O-Tron mainly through credit cards. How hard was it to get a loan on credit?

Kirkman: I got a $10,000 business loan when I quit my job. I always had good credit because I bought a house when I was nineteen, and I had saved up money when I was living at home knowing that they were going to abandon me, and so my dad was really good when I was a teenager with teaching me the importance of paying the bills. Instead of buying me a car, he helped me to buy my own car with my own money. He helped me and he cosigned for the loan, so as far as the bank and credit stuff, I got the $10,000 business loan—I imagine it was a home-equity loan or something, but I call it a business loan because I spent it on the first annual Wizard World Convention in Chicago. I blew through that money in a year, and that money was supposed to last me until I started to make money on the business, but I got the loan pretty easy because my credit was good.

I guess because I had gotten that loan and was keeping it paid pretty well, I was getting credit-card offers because I was of the collegegoing age when credit-card people are hounding you to get credit cards so that you'll fuck up your life. I got—shit, I think twenty credit cards, ranging from $500 for the credit line to the one that was $10,000. I had a massive amount of credit cards and the more credit cards you have the more credit cards they want to give you and I would get every credit card I could. What I would do to live . . . because my wife had the job, but she wasn't making that much, so what I'd do was publish comic books, and it'd be something like. "Battle Pope: Whatever" and it made, oh, $200 or $500. I think the most we ever made on an issue of *Battle Pope* was $700.

Tony and I would split that and then the printing on the book would be $2,000 so I would get the Diamond check that would be $200–500 over what the printing would cost. I would get $2,000 checks and give $1,600 for printing, and what I would do was pay for the printing on the credit card so that I would be able to keep the Diamond money. It was almost like I was making money but not really at that time because I was so in debt. I was paying my bills with the Diamond money and the printing bills on the credit card. We were doing trades back then, too, so it would cost $7,000 to print a bunch of *Battle Pope* trades and I would max out one credit card to get a trade paperback printed.

Abrams: You printed seventy-five issues of the first *Battle Pope* preview. How much did you anticipate that it would sell?

Kirkman: I actually did submit *Battle Pope* to publishers just in case they were interested, so I submitted *Battle Pope* to Image and Oni and I think [Image publisher] Jim Valentino I heard back from. He wrote me back and said, "Not interested!" and that was all he said. I wrote him and said "well, can you tell me whether you're not interested because of the subject matter or if you're not interested because of the quality?" because I wanted to know: Did he think it was a shitty book or did he think it was a controversial book and that he didn't want to put up with it? He wrote back, "I cannot go into details at this time on this matter, because it's not my position as a publisher to say," and I thought, "In the time it took you to write all that out, you could've just written 'Quality' or 'Subject Matter.'" I found out later it was because of the subject matter, but those first *Battle Pope* pieces were pretty rough. We were both pretty young and inexperienced.

To get back to your question, I had talked to Diamond and my rep at the time was Chris Schaff, and he had told me that, if I got close to a thousand that I should be happy and that if you were selling eight hundred, nine hundred out of the gate as a complete unknown, you were doing great. I was expecting maybe six hundred, maybe seven hundred, but I was hoping for ten thousand, because I had my pie-in-the-sky dreams of the Catholic League hunting me down and getting me on CNN and people going into comic stores in droves to see what this thing was about. That was the purpose of the thing being what it was: "Gosh, if we could only have the Vatican pissed off at us! If we could only get some death threats, then we'd really sell some books!" And it never happened: We got two or three hate mail letters in the entire run of *Battle Pope* and we ended up selling 1,300 of our first issue, which was over a thousand, and we were happy. The bill kept going up on each of the issues, so that was pretty good, but you don't make a lot of money off of a book that sells 1,300 copies.

Abrams: What kind of advice did Schaff and Young give you about distributing?

Kirkman: Schaff was great. I know that eventually we were buddies, but I'm sure in the early days of me calling him up, he must've been thinking, "Why is this guy calling me with these goddamn questions all the time?!" He was so helpful telling me things. At the time, Diamond had a document that you download as a PDF off their website that was, "Everything You Need to Know to Be a Vendor," and there were all these little things in the document that even Chris Schaff wouldn't know. I had read the document from cover to cover a few times just to make sure I knew everything. There were things like, "If you produce a promotional poster for retailers that folds down to 8½ x 11," Diamond will distribute it to all the retailers for free as long as you provide enough for them to send it to every retailer.

I called him up one day and asked, "Well, you say it folds down to 8½ x 11 but what if it was just 8½ x 11?" It is infinitely cheaper to print a sheet of paper that's 8½ x 11 than a poster that pulls down to that length, and he looked into and said, "Oh yeah yeah, that works." We produced this shitty

More than an attack on religion, the series was an homage and spoof of '90s-era comic books with musclebound superhero action. From *Battle Pope: Genesis*, Volume 1, by Robert Kirkman and Tony Moore; Image Comics, 2006.

little *Battle Pope* mini-poster that was basically a slick piece of typing paper that was black and white and was a little advertisement for the book and that cost maybe $2,000. There was little stuff like that Chris helped me to do that I think got the word out, and people would tell me, "I was in the comic shop and there was this little piece of paper on the wall that said *Battle Pope*, and I totally had to get that book." I know that it was a bit effective so Chris Schaff was really instrumental in selling the books and making me look kinda professional.

Larry Young helped out just as much because I solicited *Battle Pope* through Diamond, while I was soliciting to other publishers because I was doing everything at the same time, and so if Image had come back and said, "Yes, we'll publish this," I would've had to pull that solicitation and not accept orders or cancel orders and had to solicit them again through Image. I had already decided to publish it while I was a separate company, but I had no idea how to print a comic or where to print a comic.

I had a buddy locally whose name was Mark Kidwell, who's working with Image now and, back then, he just ran a printing press in Lexington. I was just gonna print the book at his printing press. He had never printed a comic book before, but he said, "Yeah, we can print it down to five," and I didn't know anything about paper. I think it would've looked pretty crappy if I had printed it there, but that's the point, I was just going to print it at this local printing press and ship it to Diamond. I didn't know how to do anything. Larry Young contacted me after the book was solicited, because he was helping out at Comix Experience in San Francisco, and he was putting out a newsletter for them called *Onomatopoeia*, and he was writing that up with the new *Previews*, saying, "Hey, these are some cool books that you should buy."

He saw *Battle Pope* and wanted to feature it in their newsletter and wrote to let me know. He was doing *Astronauts in Trouble* at the time, so I started talking to him, figuring that he's a guy that could help me sell more books and he hooked me up with his contacts at Quebecor, the printer in Canada that put out about 70, 80 percent of the comics books at the time. I didn't even know where I was going to print the book until I started talking to Larry. He helped me out a great deal as far as dealing with Diamond; where to print, how to print, how to get files to the printer.

Abrams: What were the last few titles Funk-O-Tron put out before it shut down?

Kirkman: The last title was *Battle Pope: Wrath of God*, which was a three-issue miniseries with Tony Moore. He hadn't been doing much with the book, and he came back to do the miniseries. *Battle Pope: Wrath of God* was being published at the same time as *SuperPatriot: America's Fighting Forces*, so my last Funk-O-Tron book and my first Image book were being published at the same time.

Abrams: As a former distributor, what are some of the problems facing independent creators?

Kirkman: I don't really keep up with how things are going right now. I know there's a lot going on with different policies that Diamond is starting to institute with sales limits and whatnot, but while I know that stuff's going on, I don't know all the details. I'm sure that stuff is pretty terrible and making it harder for people. I don't have my head in that world anymore. The general stuff that is hindering people publishing at that level is just the number of products being put out, so standing out from the pack can be a big problem. When I was publishing there was Oni and Chaos! Comics, but there was not Devil's Due, there was no IDW, there was no Dynamite. There was Fantagraphics and stuff like that, but there are all those medium-level publishers now that are crowding the back of the catalogue, so that's hustling out the people that are publishing at the same level Funk-O-Tron was.

BATTLE POPE

Abrams: Where did the idea for *Battle Pope* come from?

Kirkman: I was in World Civilization class and I was sitting next to my future wife, and I don't know if we were talking about the papacy or the pope in general, but basically I would take notes on the right side of my notebook, because I was a terrible student. I drew this skinny little pope guy carrying a gun, and I'm not sure if I was going to do an animation because I was doing some animation stuff in art class, but I just had this idea of portraying the biblical fight between good and evil in a more literal sense, having the Pope toting these guns and fighting the devil.

I didn't have the name *Battle Pope* at the time. I did a few sketches and then it went away. While I was working on *Between the Ropes*, I have no idea why, but the name "Battle Pope" popped into my head as a funny juxtaposition of two words. That stuff that I had drawn in World Civilizations immediately came to mind. I still had that notebook because I was a bit of a packrat and had kept anything that I had drawn on, for the most part—I had created my own superheroes and stuff that would eventually appear in *Capes*, and a lot of those drawings were in my World Civilizations notebook because my teacher really didn't pay attention in that class.

Abrams: What kind of upbringing did you have?

Kirkman: Well, Pentecostal. My mother was on-again, off-again religious all the way throughout my childhood, and my father was very much an atheist. That was a little weird because my mother was going to a Pentecostal church while my father would stay at home and say, "Ah, it's just a bunch of nonsense!" He ended up going to church with my mom a lot, and then later on in high school, I was forced to go to Sunday school at a small church right around the corner from the convenience store that was across the street from me on the highway. I would go to Sunday school classes, but as far as religion goes, I would kind of lean towards my father, because my dad would go, "Eh, it's kind of nutty. I don't know why you're going to that." I would go to church with my mom and it all would seem kind of nutty to me. I was never really very religious growing up, and I'm not really religious now.

Abrams: There aren't too many, but there are a couple of biblical references in the characters of Balaam, St. Michael, and parts of the aspects of Lucifer. Where did that come from: was that from you or was that more from Moore?

Kirkman: St. Michael is all Tony because when I came up with *Battle Pope*, I had Jesus, Lucifer, and the Pope and he said, "Well, we gotta have St. Michael in there." He showed me this image of St. Michael he had done right after I had told him my idea for *Battle Pope*. That's kind of the crux of the first story, them saving St. Michael, but that story came about because Tony had created St. Michael. He was always pushing to have more biblical stuff in there—he wanted to put Pontius Pilate in there, and I think at one point, he mentioned bringing in Judas. I never wanted to do any biblical stuff in the book just because to me it was a superhero book that happened to be about Jesus and Battle Pope fighting demons and Lucifer. I didn't want to put any heavy religious stuff in it, because I wasn't out to spoof religion or attack religion, but I did want to do a really kickass superhero yarn that had some funny parts in it and that got noticed. I exploited the religious stuff for that.

Balaam was just me and Tony on the internet looking up demon names. There's a lot of neat names demons have in the Bible, and we came across Balaum and I though it looked better with two a's, so that's why it's spelled differently. And Lucifer—well, your bad guy's got to be Lucifer, right? The original idea was that every name for the devil would be a different identity, and together they made up the Lords of Hell and they would rule Hell together. We ended up introducing Mephistopheles, and I was going to introduce Beelzebub, Satan, and a bunch of other ones as the series progressed. I never really got past Mephistopheles, though. There was an origin-of-Lucifer story for *Battle Pope: Shorts* #1 but we never came back to that.

Abrams: Before Image colorized it, *Battle Pope* was published as a bunch of interconnected miniseries. Was the choice to make them miniseries a financial or creative decision?

Kirkman: Tony and I started working on *Battle Pope* in June of '99 and he was still drawing issue #3 in June of 2000 when the first issue came out. It took that long just to get two issues done, just because he was at college . . . and Tony was a real slacker. It was always planned to be four issues, but when I saw that, I thought, "Well, there's no way we can just roll on with #5 just like that." The original plan was to do #1–4 from June through September and then do *Battle Pope: Christmas Popetacular* in December because we figured if we kicked out #3 and #4 over summer, we could probably get another thirty pages or so done in time to ship in December. We barely got #4 out on time; I had *Battle Pope* scheduled really well. Every issue shipped at the last Wednesday of every other month we would post shipment. I was able to put the shipping date back to issue #1 saying, "Come back in July and buy #2," and it would ship on time. It's something I'm really proud of and wish I could do today.

For issue #4, when we were sending the actual art boards to the printer so that they could be shot and burned into plates, we had to FedEx the artboards over to the printer. We would be driving into a FedEx station, which would close at about 8:00 p.m. and I think Tony was inking in the car. That issue was such a headache to put out. There was no way we could put out the next issue that year, and solicitations were due the next week, and I just decided to put it off. It became clear that it was going to be a sporadic series of miniseries at that point.

Abrams: You said in *Buy My Books* that *Savage Dragon* was "one of the first superhero titles to feature real sweeping changes for its title character." By the time you got to the "Mayhem" story arc in *Battle Pope*, it seems like you're taking a similar approach in picking up the threads of the Pope's last encounters right where they left off. How interested were you in maintaining a semi-realistic continuity to the stories?

Kirkman: I come to all of my books as a reader and a writer at the same time, so with *Battle Pope*, I'm thinking if I had read the first four issues, how am I going to figure things out and what am I going to want the reader to see? Because *Savage Dragon* is one of my favorite stories, of course I want a continuing story that's going to pick up right where things left off and follow the characters down different paths into a long, continuous soap-opera story. That's what appeals to me most in comics: that's why *Invincible*'s like that, that's why *The Walking Dead*'s like that, that's why my *Ultimate X-Men*'s like that. Any kind of long run on a book I have is going to be like that because that's the way I think comics should be. Even though Battle Pope was a bunch of miniseries, and there were always gaps in the miniseries. We did that Hellboy thing where inside each front cover where Battle Pope: Shorts #1 was actually Battle Pope #5. After it was reprinted by Image, I think it still held together as a fourteen-issue run, where we had crammed everything into a regular monthly series and just got rid of the miniseries covers when we republished it.

Abrams: You may not have gotten the kind of hate mail you wanted, but was there any backlash against the series or the constant sex the Pope is having?

Kirkman: Really, none whatsoever. I got a lot of letters from Catholics and churchgoing folk that assumed we were getting a lot of hate mail and they'd write to say, "We just wanted to let you know that some of us out there love your series." We had a couple of scathing reviews: one in particular said something like, "The writer sucks. The art's OK, but the writing just sucks," and I don't know if he was saying that because of the content or because of the quality of it.

We got a few bad reviews, but they were mostly 95-percent positive. That's a sign that your book is selling poorly. People say that if you're getting nothing but glowing reviews and positive mail, not enough people are buying your book, because the only people looking at your book are the ones that are looking at it because they know they're going to like it. Nothing really comes to mind, but I think in Battle Pope #2, I wrote a letter as somebody else because I wanted to have at least one piece of negative mail. We got four [pieces of] hate mail if you count the one I wrote. It's OK to make up mail if it's negative mail, right?

I don't really have any issue with religion personally. I don't believe but I don't begrudge anyone. I live in the Bible Belt, so the majority of people I know are religious, so I'm very respectful of that and understand people's reasoning behind it. Tony Moore is a religious guy. He often talked about praying and making sure the Big Man was OK with us doing the Pope. He was there to make sure nothing was too offensive. The most outrageous stuff I did was probably the Virgin Mary.

Abrams: Oh, yeah. A Frank Cho-sized chest will do that for you.

Kirkman: [*Laughs.*] It's all in good fun.

Abrams: How did Moore react to that?

Kirkman: He didn't have too much of an objection at all. I pushed for the breast size because I thought it had good comedic effect. I told him she was going to have big knockers, and he said, "Oh, like this?" and I said, "No, no, no" and had to bump them up a couple of sizes while he was doing sketches. I think some of the misogyny aspects of *Battle Pope* are really funny. I got a kick out of how politically incorrect that is, having a Pope that, aside from having sex all the time, has no respect for women. That for me made it funnier.

Abrams: Was matching up your respective work schedules ever a major issue?

Kirkman: Tony was in college at the time, but I had my mortgage and my day job and those kinds of concerns, so I guess we both had our constraints. He had big art projects and his mom pushing him along, making sure that he wasn't completely wasting his time in college. The only time when it came up was when we were supposed to do that Christmas special, and instead I had the idea to do what became *Battle Pope: Shorts* #1. He did about twenty-two pages of work in it—he inked a five-page story that I penciled, and then he did a fourteen-page story on his own and a five-page story on his own and inked some of the other people's story, but I had a ton of three- or five-page stories because I had wanted to just keep the book going.

At that time from that January to that June, he had decided to take some time off to focus on college and that was a bummer for me, because *Battle Pope* #1–4 had done really well, and at the time when I wanted to build on that momentum, he said, "Ach, I'm going to go to college." When we did *Battle Pope: Mayhem*, we had a guy named Matthew Roberts—who I think Tony spotted first online and he had shown me his art—pencil them and Tony later on would ink them. It was almost as much inking Matt as it was penciling and inking himself because it's a slow part for him. We didn't end up gaining much time, but I will go on record as saying that Matt was a much better penciler than Tony at the time. I really liked how *Battle Pope: Mayhem* turned out. I'm not being mean or anything: in fact, I think Tony would admit to having learned a few things from Matt and you can see how Tony's art changed after those two issues. Our schedules were a push-and-pull thing. It's well documented that he was a pain in the ass.

Abrams: How open were you to the idea of using crossovers as a means to boost sales?

Kirkman: I would've done anything to boost sales on *Battle Pope*. I was basically a used-car salesman at that point. I would've done whatever it took. I would've crossed over with the book I hated the most if it would've got me sales. We never actually did a crossover, certainly not for lack of trying. I had met Erik Larsen because a friend of mine (Terry Bogard) was running a website called PencilJack.com where I found most of the artists that worked on *Battle Pope*. It was an art community forum and my friend was trying to put together a real Newsarama-style site that just happened to have a message board, and he put the message board up first when he was developing the site. He had scheduled a bunch of interviews, and I found out that he had gotten Erik Larsen's phone number and was going to have somebody interview him.

I said, "You know what? I'm working for your site now. I'm going to be interviewing Erik Larsen." I was a big fan and had never met the guy, and I figured I could finagle something out of him for using *Battle Pope* because I'm crafty like that. I interviewed him a good long time—it was, like, two hours or so, and I gave it to Terry and never saw it again.

Battle Chasers had just come back to Image for their final issue, so they had talked about *Savage Dragon* crossing over with *Battle Chasers*, and that never came out. One of the questions I had come up with for the interview was, "How is *Dragon* going to crossover with *Battle Chasers*? *Battle Chasers* is a medieval book, it's got monsters and *Dragon* clearly takes place in modern day."

He said, "Oh, I despise crossovers where they go through portals and do all kinds of wacky stuff to explain how the character got into that universe, so I think what Joe's going to do is just have Dragon be there and have Dragon be a different but similar Dragon in the *Battle Chasers* universe. I think that's cool. I wish that somebody would just have Dragon show up as a hot-dog vendor and say, "Hey, in this universe, I'm a hot-dog vendor. Lookit me, I'm a hot-dog vendor!"

I pounced on the opportunity and said, "I'll totally do that in my book." I think during the course of the interview, he found out that I published my own books, so he was like, "Yeah, um, OK, I guess?" He wasn't very enthusiastic, but I told him that I would be very enthusiastic to have Dragon in *Battle Pope* for two pages as a hot-dog vendor, and being the easygoing guy he is, he said, "Sure, whatever." It wasn't on the cover or anything, but I was hoping it would get us some readers.

Through Larsen, I had talked to Chris Eliopoulous because I had lettered *Battle Pope* and all of my early work and people told me that I was fairly good at it, so I contacted Chris because I was struggling for cash and wanted to ask him how I could become a letterer. Chris said, "Yeah, trust me, you don't want to be a letterer." I talked to him at cons a couple of times and he was doing his own book at the time called *Desperate Times*, which was a humor book starring two roommates and their high jinks with their talking sloth, so it was like a goofy '80s sitcom. I really liked the book and thought it was really funny, so I thought of this *Desperate Times/Battle Pope* crossover that I pitched to him where the boss character gets possessed by a demon and his roommates would team up and fight it. It was going to be pretty stupid, but it would've been a cool little book, and he said, "Yeah! Hell no! You are crazy!" He was not into the idea at all.

One crossover that I really wished had happened was with the guys that did *Sky Ape*, Phil Amara, Richard Jenkins, Tim McCarney, Michael Russo. Battle Pope actually ended up appearing in two pages, and Tony and I wrote and drew for a book called "All the Heroes," where Sky Ape got a bunch of superheroes together, and Sky Ape goes to recruit Battle Pope, but he's too busy having an orgy. We were then going to do a forty-eight-page crossover, and I forget why it didn't happen, because everyone had really wanted to do it. That crossover wouldn't have been to boost sales, because I don't think *Sky Ape* was doing that much better than *Battle Pope* in sales, but it's probably one of the coolest comic books ever put together.

Abrams: Before we talk about the pencilers you met on PencilJack, let me ask you about [*Invincible* cocreator] Cory Walker. Did you meet him on WizardWorld?

Kirkman: WizrdWorld.com, back when they had had it, used to have a school section that was run by Billy Scalera. Billy ran this thing called Wizard School, which was where comic artists would come in and do little tutorials and they would have a message board. That went under relatively quickly, and everybody went to PencilJack when it shut down. It's hard to remember which artists I met on which message boards, but I definitely saw Cory's work first on the *Wizard* message board and I may have contacted him when he was on PencilJack, but it was all basically the same message board. Guys like Cory Walker and Matt Roberts, Jon Boy Meyers, E. J. Su—

Abrams: And Mark Englert?

Kirkman: Yeah, but Mark Englert came much later. I don't actually find him until I was doing stuff at Image. There were a ton of people I got off the message board—even Terry Stephenson, who owns and operates PencilJack, I wound up working with on the *Battle Pope Presents: Saint Michael* miniseries.

Abrams: How hard is it to establish a connection or find people you genuinely want to work with?

Kirkman: It was easy for me because I had published comics before, and I was publishing them regularly, and I had a reputation as guy who could get a book out. I couldn't promise money, but I could promise them that they'd get published and they could use that for their portfolio—everybody wants to be able to show printed comics instead of just a portfolio. I could email someone like Cory and say, "How would you like to do a six-page *Battle Pope* story for

Shorts?" Because I was doing *Shorts*, I wasn't asking anybody to do twenty-two-pages or a miniseries, I was just asking for six, eight pages.

Of course, he said, "Oh yeah, sure. I've read *Battle Pope* and it seems pretty funny. You seem like a legitimate guy." A lot of times writers go on those message boards looking for artists, and they've never been published, and they say something like, "Hey, I'm Joe Blow and I've got this book together called *Johnny Nutsack*. How would you like to do seven issues?" That's not really going to work, but because I had a reputation, it was easy for me to wrangle people together.

Abrams: Is the internet the next best place to meet the people you want to work with compared to conventions or mailing samples to publishers?

Kirkman: I think the internet is the *best* place because what you lose in the face-to-face meet-up at a convention you gain in being able to peruse their artwork without their knowledge. When you think, "This guy sucks," you're not sitting in front of that guy and you don't have to say, "Oh, you're, yeah, no, not what I'm looking for. Sorry. But you're great." You can just click on the next thread and say, "Oh, that guy blows; not gonna look at him anymore." You can just blaze through a message board and find a new artist, flag them, and try to find more of their work. As far as artists go, if you're good, somebody will find you. Everyone that is good that posted on PencilJack, that was of professional caliber, was working in comics relatively soon. Travel Foreman posted on there, and he's working for Marvel now; Mark Brooks was posting there, and he's working for Marvel. Everybody that was good on PencilJack got snatched up and started work on comics.

The internet is great in that if you are talented, you will be found. It sucks because if you suck and you're going to conventions, you may be able to get some gigs based on your personality and your tenacity, but you can't really do that online. "My website was great, big flashing lights, so you're going to give me work" doesn't translate [as well].

I don't mean to talk specifically about artists, but I'm of the mind that writers are screwed as far as getting into comics. You cannot wrangle an artist into doing a book for you and producing a book that you can show to people. Getting writing samples is nearly impossible. I have stated publically in my column and other places that people do not read writing samples. You can send a twenty-two-page script to Marvel and say, "I sure would like to write a book for you," but they are not going to read it just because it takes some time to read a script, sometimes ten, twenty minutes or even longer. They just don't have that kind of time to devote to talent searching. You can flip through an artist's portfolio quickly and you can rule out an artist instantly and you can see if you need to take a closer look instantly.

I've gotten in trouble for saying that, but then I've had people at Marvel say, "Thanks for saying that because that's totally true. We don't have the time to read writing submissions." And aside from hunting down people to produce comics with you, PencilJack is useless for writers. Nobody is going to read your fan fiction, so nobody is going to read your script. I don't like reading scripts. I don't like reading my scripts.

Abrams: What about the relationship between aspiring and established creators?

Kirkman: Taking your work to me or someone else is not going to be that beneficial. You don't bring your writing submission to Brian Bendis; Brian Bendis isn't going to hire you. I'm not going to hire you; that's something that people need to keep in mind when they're showing their stuff around. It's a tough game. Everybody's getting-into-comics stuff is different. There's no one way or one thing you can do. You can try and be an editor, you can self-publish—you can do any number of things. There's no secret formula for it.

BREAKING INTO IMAGE

Abrams: Val Staples got you work writing titles like *Masters of the Universe*, *Space Ace* and *Tales of the Realm* with MV Creations. How did that happen and how was that in terms of balancing your Funk-O-Tron workload?

Kirkman: At this point, Val had been coloring *Battle Pope* covers for at least one year now. He had worked through a lot of transitions really quickly: He went from a guy looking for work to coloring covers for free to coloring for Hi Fi; he started going for licenses because the word on the street was that that G.I. Joe revival was happening with Devil's Due and that it had sold. They hadn't gotten the numbers in though or the numbers hadn't been made public, so nobody knew what kind of success '80s properties would be at the time. Val was a huge *Masters of the Universe* fan and he ran HeMan.org, so he had an in with (*He-Man*'s owner) Mattel. He had the largest running website for *He-Man*, and so he dealt with Mattel from there. He was putting together proposals and pin-ups and whatnot, and Tony did a few pieces, and E. J. Su did a few pieces, so I was helping him out with the proposal a little bit, putting him into contact with other people.

At the same time, we were going out for the Transformers license. If he had gotten the Transformers license, I would've gotten to write the books, so that was pretty exciting for me, because I was still just doing *Battle Pope* at the time and didn't have any kind of experience. He gave me a little side work because *He-Man* and all those '80s books did so well when they debuted that he was able to expand a little into spin-offs. I'm not going to say it wasn't because I was calling him up every now and then and saying, "I could totally do something with Merman. I'd love to do something with Merman. If you could just pay me some money to do something with Merman, I could do the best Merman stuff ever. I promise."

I ended up getting a miniseries that was series of one-shots called *Masters of the Universe: Icons of Evil* that focused on the four most popular bad guys in the series. I actually got to bring a lot of people that were drawing *Battle Pope* at the time along; I did Beast Man with Tony Moore, I did Merman with E. J. Su, I did Tri-Clops with Cory Walker, who I was working with on *Invincible* at the time. Val was using his newfound success as studio head, because he formed MV Creations. He was helping me out the way I was helping him out by coloring *Battle Pope* covers for free. As far as contributions, he had the license to *Dragon's Lair* and *Space Ace* books, and he ended up letting me write *Space Ace*, even though I didn't know anything about *Space Ace*. When we asked the (Don) Bluth Group, the people who do the licensing for *Space Ace*, for reference, they sent us the game on a DVD. The game was basically watching a cartoon and when Space Ace was about to get hit by some monster, you had to hit "left" with the joystick, and it paused the cartoon to get to the next frame, where he continues running after dodging the next blast. If you don't push left at the right time, the game goes to a "Game Over" screen. The game was just a cartoon that was about eight minutes long. They sent us that for reference, and it's basically Space Ace going, "Ah! Oh! Ah! Ah!" dodging monsters and jumping around—little to no story content at all.

I wrote the first script based on that, and when I sent it in to the Bluth Group, they came back with corrections like, "Yeah, he works for the Space Squad, and this is what his boss is like, and this is reference for him, and here are some character profiles on everybody." It was tough sometimes working on that book, but I needed the money pretty bad at that point.

As far as *Tales of the Realm* goes, a lot of people think that's creator-owned but that was something Val Staples and Matt Tyree came up with. They came to me, because back when all three of us were doing *Double Take*, they were doing a *Tales of the Realm* story for the series. It was guys-looking-for-gold, fighting-trolls kind of thing, and then after that was published, Val came up with the idea that that kind of standard fairy-tale knights-and-dragon story was actually a television show that those people were working on. They had lived in the realm, but it was a little more modern. I thought that was a really interesting take, so when he offered it to me, I took it. I wrote that *Tales of the Realm* series as a tradeoff, Val having colored *SuperPatriot: America's Fighting*

Force because I had just started working with Image by the time I was working on *Tales of the Realm*. I wrote that for free, and he colored *SuperPatriot* for free. It was like doing a creator-owned thing, because it didn't have many restrictions.

Abrams: In *Buy My Books*, you've said that your work in *Tales of the Realm* is some of your favorite. What did you get out of that you couldn't get while working on established characters with other MV titles?

Kirkman: I guess I have more fun working on original characters. I could do more with them. Working on the *Icons of Evil* and *Space Ace*—and I heard this from everyone so it's not anything unique, but those characters are owned and protected by people who look over stuff and approve it. We got a lot of notes back on the *He-Man* stuff. From the Bluth Group, I got weird notes like, "How did he get to that planet?" and I would have to write them back and say, "Well, if you read page five, you'll see that he has a spaceship and he took that spaceship to that planet." It seemed like they were skimming the scripts and asking for all kinds of changes to make things make sense and there were little tweaks and comments like, "Oh, Space Ace would never do that!" With *He-Man*, I had to rewrite all those scripts at least once almost entirely. It was really a tough gig, but that's pretty much par for the course with those licensed books.

Abrams: When did you think of Image as a place to pitch your material to? Was it right after you finished up with Funk-O-Tron?

Kirkman: There was a book I was putting together called *Science Dog* that there were a lot of advertisements for in *Battle Pope*, and there was even a three or four-page preview in *Battle Pope: Shorts* #3. After Cory and I did a few stories in *Battle Pope: Shorts* #2 and #3, we really hit it off and I had this idea, which was about a talking, super-evolved dog that fought things with science. He was a super smart guy that outthinks his way out of situations. It would've been difficult for me, but I looked forward to the challenge. I was writing the first script for the first issue, and Cory started working on it. I really wanted to do it in color, but I couldn't do it considering the kind of numbers I was getting at Funk-O-Tron, and it seemed like we were good enough to be published by a larger company because it certainly looked polished enough, and Cory was definitely talented enough, and I started pitching that around to different people, but I knew the writing was on the wall for publishing.

I was publishing other people's books at the time: the *Double Take* stuff and an anthology called *Ink Punks* that was a bunch of people from PencilJack, like Matt Roberts and E. J. Su and a lot of artists I knew as well, such as Bruce Brown, the guy who's doing *Brit* for me now. I was having trouble finding time to put the books together, and I just wasn't enjoying the publishing side of things and started to realize that maybe I was a bad publisher because my heart wasn't as much in it as it was in writing comics, so I decided to hang it up and try doing comics for other publishers. *Science Dog* was of that wave— I think I pitched to Oni? I know I pitched it to Dark Horse, because Phillip Amara was working at Dark Horse at the time, and I had thought, "Oh, my buddy Phil will get me hooked up at Dark Horse, great!"

At the same time, I had pitched *Science Dog* to Image, I had been talking to Erik Larsen. I knew that Image was the best deal in town just because I knew what their deal was, and I knew what other publishers offered. Image was my first choice, but I didn't know if I could get in at all. Dark Horse never even responded. Phil told me, "Dark Horse is like a novel publisher: They can take up to a year to get back to you on a submission." I was so used to self-publishing where we could do a *Battle Pope* issue in the next three months, so that really frustrated me. I thought, "A year?! I could be dead in a year! We gotta get this book out."

I was talking to Erik Larsen and told him that I sent in a submission for a series called *Science Dog*, and Cory just did a drawing of SuperPatriot for fun, which Larsen ended up liking after I showed it to him. He said he'd publish it, and he did in *Savage Dragon* #93. When that book came in from the printer in the office, Larsen called me up and said, "Look, man, Eric Stephenson and Jim Valentino were over in the Image office and saw the *SuperPatriot* pin-up and thought, 'Man, this guy is really good. This guy should be doing a *Super-Patriot* miniseries!' I told them that that guy and another guy I was working with had pitched a series to them called *Science Dog*, and they said, '*Science Dog* is a stupid idea. These guys should be doing a *SuperPatriot* miniseries instead.'"

Larsen offered me a *SuperPatriot* miniseries over the phone and I have Cory to thank for that, I got to call him up on the phone and say, "Hey, you know how much fun we're having working on *Science Dog* and how much we're hoping a publisher will pull through with that? We have to do a *SuperPatriot* miniseries, we'll totally be able to get this *Science Dog* thing going."

Cory was actually very fond of *Science Dog*. He loved drawing him and was having a great time on the book, and he said, "I love *SuperPatriot*. This'll be a good opportunity for us. Let's definitely do this. But Robert, you have to promise me that as soon as we get done doing *SuperPatriot*, we're not going to get sidetracked, and we're going to jump back on *Science Dog*."

I told him, "I promise, Cory. Nothing well keep us from doing *Science Dog*." [*Laughter*.]

Abrams: What kind of interest did you have in the *SuperPatriot* character before you were offered it?

Kirkman: *Savage Dragon* was my favorite book, so the fact that I was talking on the phone with Erik Larsen was a big deal, and then the idea that he was going to let me write four issues of *SuperPatriot* was a huge deal. *SuperPatriot* already had had two spin-off series, which were written by Keith Giffen and drawn by Dave Johnson, and I had read those and loved them. I was actually excited to do a *SuperPatriot* miniseries.

Abrams: What kind of support did you get from Larsen as you developed your series?

Kirkman: On *SuperPatriot*, as far as the plot goes, he let me run wild. There were a few things I suggested early on, and he steered me away from that, but after that he really let me do whatever I wanted. If I hadn't been so self-sufficient by that point, I don't think he would've had a good time doing that at all. I would call him up and ask, "Can I use this character?" and he'd say, "Yep," and then I would get the whole comic done. When the first issue was done, because I was lettering myself, Val was coloring for me, Cory was doing the pencils and the inks, Larsen didn't have too much of a hand in it.

When the first issue would come on, Larsen would come in and say different things that you wouldn't really think about and were a little tedious but were good things to know, like, "You don't want to put a tall panel on right because you read the tall panel first." He was teaching me a lot of the fundamental information about putting balloons on a page that make the story flow a little better. He ended up having a lot of pointers for Cory too, so I think that helped us out a great deal.

Abrams: Was working under Larsen intimidating, after you had been working under your own brand for so long?

Kirkman: I don't intimidate easily, sir. I don't know if it was intimidating, because I called him from time to time and thought, "What could I possibly need to talk to Larsen about today? Oh, that's a good excuse!" At the time, I was doing a lot of lettering and layouts, and I had gotten to the point where I could call him at the same time and we would shoot the shit, and he would tell me funny stories about the Image days, like who inked what page uncredited while they were at an Image meeting. "Well, if you look at this face on this page in *Spawn*, you can tell that Rob Liefeld inked that panel." By the time I was working on *SuperPatriot*, we knew each other to a certain extent. We weren't best friends or anything, but I could hang out with that guy at a convention. Plus, Larsen's a real mellow, down-to-earth guy, so he doesn't really come off as an intimidating guy.

Abrams: Before Larsen was head publisher at Image, Jim Valentino had looked at your submissions, but as he said in his introduction to the first volume, he had only really gotten enthusiastic about *Tech Jacket*. Was this in any way due to the boom in manga and manga-esque titles?

Kirkman: That was part of the reason I wanted to do *Tech Jacket*, because that was a big deal at the time and still is. I figured if I did something that was flavored like manga it might do OK. I wouldn't say I was a sell-out, but I did try to think of commercial ways to make my books appeal to a broader audience at the creation stage. I was working with E. J. Su, who was from Taiwan and who drew in a manga-inspired style. I think Jim liked *Tech Jacket* a lot because his son did. The proposal for *Tech Jacket* was actually the last three pages of the first issue, where Zach finds the spaceship and it blows up and he gets the tech jacket. It should've been the first three pages of the first issue, but that was one of my many missteps back in those days.

Abrams: In *Pillow Talk*, the third volume of *Battle Pope*, the manga dream sequence you did with E. J. Su seems like a precursor to your work with *Tech Jacket*. Was this before or after you had gotten the idea to do *Tech Jacket* together?

Kirkman: It was pretty far before. I came up with *Tech Jacket* very early on, right before working on *SuperPatriot*. When *Between the Ropes* was not accepted at Diamond, I still tried to do that book. When Terry Stephens was doing the *Battle Pope Presents: Saint Michael* miniseries, I had asked him to do *Between the Ropes*, and he had done some character designs and was going to draw that book but ended up not being able to. Later on, I got the idea to do it as a superhero book because I had taken my superhero characters from high school and turned them into wrestler characters, which is a fairly easy transition, and created a few new characters that were just wrestlers. I ended up taking those characters and turning them back into superheroes and taking some of the wrestler characters and turning them into superheroes.

I was going to change *Between the Ropes* to *Behind the Capes*, and it was the same concept except that instead of being behind the scenes at a wrestling organization, it would be behind the scenes of a corporate superhero organization. I was going to draw that because I still hadn't gotten the idea that that was never going to work out for me. In the *Capes* trade, there are a lot of sketches of that. I guess while I was doing doodles for *Capes*, I came up with the idea for *Tech Jacket*. I think my first doodle for *Tech Jacket* is on a *Capes* drawing. I guess I liked it better at the time and contacted E. J. Su immediately because E. J. and I had not only worked on *Battle Pope*, but also on the *Transformers* proposal. I wrote an entire sample script for Val to show to

(*Transformers'* owners) Hasbro, and they ended up liking it, and we were really close to getting that license until Dreamwave snuck in at the last moment and got it. E. J. did loads and loads of pages, so we had been working together a lot more than people realized because most everything wasn't published.

I wrote a *Transformers* children's story, which wasn't published, where Bumblebee rescued a kid from a construction site that E. J. Su drew. E. J. did a five-page opening sequence of the script that I wrote; he did a short story with a bunch of Transformers fighting on Cybertron that I wrote—just a ton of stuff. Around the time that fell through was when I thought, "Well, if we're not doing *Transformers*, let's do *Tech Jacket*." I think I pitched *Tech Jacket* in June 2002, and the first issue of *SuperPatriot* came out in July 2002.

Abrams: What kind of anime or manga titles influenced *Tech Jacket*?

Kirkman: I worked in a comics shop for a while, and I read a bit of manga there. I don't think I bought it. I read it at the store. I definitely read a bit of *Akira* and a bit of other stuff, but mostly my exposure was through anime. I was really into anime in the later part of my high-school career. I had gotten *Ninja Scroll*, and *Macross Plus* was really popular at the time. *Vampire Humter D*, I thought was really cool. I liked that stuff quite a lot. I don't really watch it much anymore but back then . . .

Abrams: Most of the titles you just mentioned seem more adult-oriented than *Tech Jacket* was. Did you make a conscious decision to make it a kids' book?

Kirkman: *Tech Jacket* wasn't necessarily a kid's book, but at the time, Jim Valentino was very anti-grim-and-gritty, and pro-all-ages. I don't think I knew he was putting together a superhero line, but it's been so long, about four, five years now. I don't remember exactly how it happened, but it had something to do with Jim Valentino pushing people to do more all-ages stuff, stuff that would reach a broader audience. I was coming off *Battle Pope*, and I just wanted to do something that was a little more light, acceptable, and appropriate than what I had been doing, to prove to retailers that that's not all that that guy who did *Battle Pope* can do. That was a big worry at the time, because there were retailers who refused to carry *Battle Pope* at the time—some said that they would put it in their pull folders, but they wouldn't put it in the rack. It was a concern of mine that I wouldn't be able to shake the *Battle Pope* stigma.

Abrams: You've done a number of adult and all-ages titles, but would you say that comics are more for kids or adults?

Kirkman: Unfortunately, I think my comics are more for adults. Even *Invincible* would lean into the realm of mature themes. Mostly things I've done haven't been for a very young audience, which is sad but to a certain extent. I think Marvel and DC should handle young readers and once those readers get old enough to go, "Well, what the hell? Spider-Man just fights Doctor Octopus over and over?!" that's what Image and Dark Horse and Oni are for. I don't think there's a lot of young readers to be had right now. *Tech Jacket* was a bit of a failure for me, so when I was doing my Image stuff, if I was viewed as mature, things could be a bit better. My most mature book, which I think is *The Walking Dead*—at least, mature in that it's deemed for older readers—is my biggest success at Image. I think that just being able to do stuff at Image, you have to cater to the more mature, seasoned comic book reader.

Abrams: In *Tech Jacket*, the dialogue between Zack and his father seems like the first time you devoted a large amount of space to relating exposition through dialogue from one family member to another and depictions of family as a unifying place. How important is establishing these positive depictions of family in your work to you?

Kirkman: When I was putting *Invincible* and *Tech Jacket* together, I was thinking that most superheroes seem to come from a broken home. Their parents are dead or their father beat them or somebody wasn't around or their father ended up a bad guy, which happened in *Invincible*. The idea was to have superheroes that had a good home life, because I was always looking for ways to relate to the audience more. I had a good childhood, and there wasn't anything too traumatic going on in my life, and I figured that ideally the majority of people would have a normal childhood, so why not try to appeal to those guys for once? Let's show a book about a family that, for the most part, gets along.

Abrams: I mention the dialogue also because you don't really ever use flashbacks to show events, but prefer to describe them. Why is that?

Kirkman: I've had writer friends of mine ask me why I do that, and I honestly don't know. I just don't like flashbacks. If I were to sit here and try to tell a story, there wouldn't be any wavy lines and you wouldn't suddenly be seeing what I was telling you. I try to make it as short as possible: I don't try to make it go on for four pages about a story that you can't see, just seeing faces talking about this interesting stuff. Maybe I suck? Maybe I shouldn't do that? I've only done flashbacks a couple of times, but I only do it when it's absolutely necessary because of personal preference. Maybe that's because it seems more real to me, being able to put your own spin on things, being able to picture it yourself almost makes it like a novel. I'm putting the hard work on the reader instead of having the artist draw all the cool stuff.

Abrams: How do you pace your scripts in terms of how it's divided up between action and discussion?

Kirkman: I don't really look at it that way. If I don't have a fight scene in an issue, I'm very conscious of that, and that's done on purpose. I've only done it a few times. For the most part, I have fight scenes once or twice an issue, and I try to give the people some splash pages and some cool stuff to look at as much as I possibly can. I start by taking a piece of printing paper and numbering it one to twenty-two and block things out. A lot of times, the first thing I'll write is the last page when I'm at that plotting stage, and I'll work my way back through the book and think of an opening scene that flows forward. I try to make sure there's a balance between talking about stuff and doing stuff.

Abrams: What kind of difference can you see between Valentino's administration and Larsen's as a reader and creator?

Kirkman: As a creator, it's easier to get my book accepted, but I really haven't had many books accepted since Larsen took over. Valentino was doing a fine job. There were definitely some books that I think shouldn't have been accepted into Image and I don't think Larsen would have accepted some of the books [Valentino] did accept, but at the same time there are some books that Larsen accepted that I don't think Valentino would have. There are definitely differences but I don't really see that many big differences.

I am closer to Larsen because there were a few instances where Jim turned down a book and I went to Larsen and said, "Well, Jim turned this down. What do you think?"

Larsen would go, "Oh, I think it's a pretty good book," and he'd call up Jim and ask, "Why didn't you accept this?" and he say, "All right! Shit!" In that way, it's easier for me to work with Larsen. I've become closer to Jim since he was a publisher. I talk to him at conventions. Jim Valentino's a great guy, I don't think anyone would dispute that. I was sorry to see him go as a publisher. I feel like my friend replaced him so that's OK.

Abrams: Is there a difference in the kind of titles that the two put out?

Kirkman: I think Valentino leaned more toward artsy series, more black and white. I think Jim comes from a more independent world. He was doing *normalman* before anyone that formed Image with him was doing [anything]. I think he has a taste for that side of the comics industry in his publishing decisions. Larsen is more of a superhero guy. He certainly doesn't turn down fantastic independent-flavored books, but I think I can see more of a commercial approach.

Abrams: Tell me a little bit about your involvement in getting Rob Liefeld to return to Image?

Kirkman: [*Laughs.*] We're taking quite a leap. Frankly, Liefeld was talking to a publisher about bringing back *Youngblood* and licensing it from him. He was talking to me on the phone and said, "Yeah, they contacted me and I'm thinking about it and they're good guys, but I really don't know if I want to go that route. I don't know if I want to license the thing." I told him, "If you want to make a big splash, if you want to do a new *Youngblood* series, you should have an Image eye on it. That'll be a big deal." He said, "Yeah, I think you're right. That would be totally awesome." He got excited about it, but I guess he was unsure if the partners would be OK with that, because there had been some bad blood in the past.

I contacted them on his behalf and talked to Larsen and said, "Look, I think *Youngblood* should be a welcome addition to the Image line of books. Historically, that past that it's had with Image as Image's first book will turn some heads. What do you think about it?" Larsen was very open to the idea and went to the partners—Jim Valentino, Todd McFarlane, and Marc Silvestri, and they all agreed, and I told him, "Yeah, it looks like they're in." it was basically just a few phone calls on my part, but I really wanted to see that *Youngblood* hardcover come out with the Image logo on it. That was my involvement as a fan.

Abrams: Can you talk a little about what happened between you and Todd McFarlane at a panel you two were at during Comic-Con in 2006?

Kirkman: Sure. [*Pause.*]

Abrams: Did you two have a fight or a disagreement?

Kirkman: [*Laughs.*] Not really. People want to play it that way but it really wasn't. I attended this panel at San Diego, and when it opened up to questions . . . well, I have a bit of insider knowledge in that I know he's very hands-on in his own toy-production company and that he's somewhat still hand-on with *Spawn* and still looks over plot and approves art, but at the time, it looked like he focused more on toys than he did on comics. I stood up and . . . a lot of people misunderstand that I wasn't saying, "Hey, Todd! Why don't you draw books?" I basically stood up and said, "You do good toys and you keep your head in the toy industry and I know you're very hands-on with the way toys are produced, but you came from comics. If comics made you who you are, why stop with *Spawn*? Why can't you create another comic and be as hands-on with that as you are with the toys? If you aren't necessarily drawing it, why can't you create another Todd McFarlane character." I think Todd has a unique voice and that it sucks that there's not any new Todd stuff coming out.

He went off on some rigmarole about how if I were Walt Disney and I created Mickey Mouse, I would stop. There's no need to have Goofy or Donald Duck, but history dictates that it's pretty cool to have Goofy and Donald. That was basically the discussion, and through that argument it became known that I was Robert Kirkman, but he knew my books, so I jokingly said, "And I should put that book together!" Todd's a real cool guy. He's open to about anything. If I had said, "And why not make me CEO of your corporation?" he would've asked to see my resume. He's open to stuff. So after the panel, he had me give my contact information to Brian Haberline, who is editor-in-chief on his comic side of things. Things went from there, and Brian contacted me and put me in touch with Todd, and I've been working with Todd for over a year, almost two years now putting together a new comic book. And I think it's going to debut in summer 2008. It's funny how it all came together.

Abrams: What's the series called?

Kirkman: It's called *Haunt*. It's very early on, but it's about two brothers, one of them is a CIA agent and the other is a priest. One of the brothers ends up getting killed and haunting the other brother. Through the haunting, there's some kind of mystical ghost business that goes on, and the two together can form a superhero.

Abrams: Is Image a good place for creative risk-taking?

Kirkman: I think so, yeah. If anything, the company is stronger than when I started doing books there: You've got Warren Ellis doing a book there, the *Mice Templar*, whatever book the Luna brothers are working on, *Mad Men*. Things like that do really well now. As a company, I think it's stronger than it has been in a long time. The environment at Image has never changed. It's always been devoted to creative risk-taking and Image as a company is whatever you put into it. If you turn your script in and say, "I don't have time to oversee this book and make sure it gets put out or be hands-on," I don't think you're using the full potential of Image. Image is really set up to support self-starters and was founded in order to give creators an alternative outlet from Marvel and DC, and that I think has never changed. Anyone who had the talent can go and do that, and that's a special thing for the comics industry to have.

INVINCIBLE, BRIT AND CAPES

Abrams: *Invincible*, *Brit*, and *Capes* all came out within a relatively short period of time. How long had you been thinking about these characters?

Kirkman: *Invincible* came about while Cory and I were working on *SuperPatriot*. When we were putting that book together, I found out that Jim Valentino was putting together a superhero line. Like I said, he was putting together mostly independent, black-and-white books that weren't superheroes and weren't too commercial, and he had been getting criticism from fans saying, "Why doesn't Image publish more superhero books?" The fact was that he wasn't getting that many superhero submissions, and he decided to consciously go out and get some people to do superhero books. I think Eric Stephenson had told me about it at the time, and so I said, "All right, I want me a piece of that!" Cory and I were working on *SuperPatriot*, and I'm not sure who I contacted, but I think it was Jim Valentino, and I said, "You seem to like what we're doing on *SuperPatiot*. If we came up with a superhero comic, would you like to publish it with your superhero line?"

He said, "Yeah, I'm open to whatever you've got. *SuperPatiot*'s a good-looking book, you guys seem to be doing a good job on that, so if you have any superhero ideas, let's talk about it."

Cory was actually living with me at the time, because when we had decided to do *SuperPatriot* together, the lease on his apartment had just come up and he was willing to quit his job so that he could focus on getting *SuperPatriot* out, so that we could hopefully make a boatload of money on *SuperPatriot* and then focus on *Science Dog*. I said, "Well, shit, man. Why don't you move on up here to Kentucky and live with my wife and I? You wouldn't have to pay rent, and you could work with me in my studio." We had a small house with two bedrooms, and I made the extra bedroom my studio, and so Cory just slept in my studio, worked in my studio, and cried in my studio.

While we were working shoulder-to-shoulder on *SuperPatriot* together, I told him about some superhero concepts, but first I had to come to him and say, "Yeah, you know that *Science Dog* thing? They're not interested in that. But they would like to see a superhero idea from us."

I think I did ask, "Hey, what about *Science Dog* for the superhero line?" and they had said, "Nope, nope, nobody wants a talking dog." I guess we were both upset at the idea of not being able to do *Science Dog* yet, but *Invincible* was created on the spot. It wasn't a character I had from high school or even based on any idea I had for a character. Everything in *Invincible*, every character in *Invincible*, was created during that time we were working on *SuperPatriot*. Every character created recently was created as we working on the series, but we said to ourselves that we had to do a cool superhero comic, and that's what we came up with.

We were pitching *Invincible* by the time we were working on the third issue [of *SuperPatriot*], and I would send designs and drawings off to Valentino. We went back and forth: The character was originally called Bullet Proof, and they didn't like that too much. The Omni-Man character was originally Supra-Man, which I thought was brilliant, because it's a perfectly cool superhero name, and if you say it out loud, it sounds like another superhero name. They said, "That's a dumb idea, and you will get your pants sued off," so we did not do that. It was all created for Valentino's superhero lineup, which included *Clockmaker*, *Dominion*, and *Venture*—all books that we outlasted. [*Laughs.*]

With *Brit*, Tony lived locally, so he would come over and work with Cory and I. We were doing *Battle Pope: Wrath of God* at the same time Cory and I were doing *SuperPatriot*, so I felt bad because Tony would come over and work on this black-and-white book that wasn't really selling that well, while Cory and I were working on *SuperPatriot*, which didn't end up being a huge success but was a full-color Image book and was kind of a big deal for us. At the time, I didn't think *Wrath of God* was going to be the last miniseries. We were making no money on the book, so I don't know why I ever thought that, but at some point I thought, "Screw this. I am just going to put *Battle Pope* on hiatus and come back to it later and do something at Image with Tony."

I ended up pitching a few things with Tony, including something like a "zombies in space" book that we did a few pages for and pitched to Image. When *Dead Planet* wasn't approved, that's when I got the idea to do *The Walking Dead*, which was a zombie book that was a straight zombie story, and I really liked that, because I wasn't very familiar with *Dead Planet* and feel like it would've had more sci-fi elements to take into account. No one had really done something like a Romero movie on paper. I also came up with the idea of starting where Romero movies leave off, continuing until infinity, and that was the concept. That got accepted, but Valentino wanted to launch it in October, and I had pitched it for November of 2002. He said, "Nah, let's wait 'til October." He ended up launching it as part of a mini-horror line of three books along with *Dracula* and some other stuff. Because we wouldn't be able to launch until October, I figured Tony and I had to come up with something, so we came up with *Brit* and decided to do that while we were waiting to work on *The Walking Dead*.

Abrams: How much time did you devote to each series in terms of plotting and writing?

Kirkman: As much as I needed. I found the more work I was doing, the more work I was able to do, which has a limit somewhere, but the more work

I did, the faster I was able to work. If I had *Invincible* pages that needed to be lettered that day, and E .J. Su needed script for the next issue of *Tech Jacket*, and I needed to put together some text for the pitch for *The Walking Dead* at the same time, it seemed like it was easier for me to do that than just work on the *Tech Jacket* script all day, because anytime I would hit a low, I'd switch gears. I've been working at that pace ever since. Comics are hard work, but they're not really work; there's not really any other word for it, though. I'm not down here having a party or anything, but I've worked for a living and this does not seem like the same thing. It's fun to make comics all day long and easy to just let that get away from you and find yourself divorced, but luckily enough, I've been able to avoid that.

Abrams: How do you normally approach writing a script for an issue or story arc?

Kirkman: I find that I'm constantly laying tracks in front of a train that's moving really fast. When I write a script, I've already thought of what's going to happen in the next five, six, seven issues I'm working on and so I just pool all of my notes together. I'm thinking of what comes from that stuff. I think pretty far in advance so by the time I get to the script stage, it's just tying together different threads that I've got in notebooks and floating around in my head into a script.

Abrams: Are the scripts included in the hardcovers what a typical script looks like?

Kirkman: They're pretty standard. The scripts that are included in hardcover are pretty much like every single script I've written. First-issue scripts are usually pretty dense because I'm normally always stopping and writing descriptions. For something like *Marvel Zombies*, I had a lot of stuff going on then, because I think I started writing *Marvel Zombies* around the holidays or close to it. I had a lot of stuff going on, and I was working with Sean Phillips, and Sean Phillips is Sean Phillips, so it would be really insulting to write a bunch of stuff in the script because I didn't really need to give him the bare bones of what's on the page.

The cool thing about *Marvel Zombies* was that it took place in a burnt-out New York City, so there were very few descriptions aside from on the first page where it said what New York City looked like: full of burnt-out cars and demolished buildings. For the rest of the book, it was mostly, "You're looking at Giant Man," or "Wolverine and Giant Man do this while Captain America's doing that." It was one of the lightest scripts that I'd written for all those issues.

I definitely don't write Alan-Moore-length scripts. I think on the other end of that spectrum are Warren-Ellis-length scripts, which are basically one-sentence panel descriptions: "So-and-so sips tea." At least all the ones I've seen are like that. I'm a little more dense than that. I'd say something like, "So-and-so sits in a chair, and he's in the foreground, and you're looking past him in a swimming pool sipping tea." Also, my scripts are really stupid. Anytime my artists get together, they like to poke fun at me: "Did he do this in one of your scripts?" "Oh my God, he did that in one of my scripts, too! That's hilarious!"

It'll be because I say things like, "This guy's got a brick and he's getting ready to throw it through a window. I don't know, maybe he should have a crowbar to throw through the window because that might look cooler. Really, it's up to you." I do that to give them my thought process, so they can think, "Well, maybe it should be a brick." I think I should probably use the backspace button every now and then and get rid of things when I change my mind. I do that sometimes, but I like the free-flowing, I'm-having-a-discussion-with-the-artist style, and hopefully that's a little more fun to read than just a dry, "This guy is moving this way and fighting this thing. He's saying this . . ." It should be a little more fun.

I also get great pleasure from ending panel descriptions with, "Make it look good," or "This looks really cool." "Make it look good" is my favorite because it implies that before I typed that, they were thinking about making it look bad. I was joking about it with [*Invincible* penciler] Ryan Ottley, and he said it actually helps because he reads the panel descriptions and says that he has it pictured in his mind, and then when it says, "Make it look good," he goes "Oh! Oh! I really need to rethink what I did and make it look better than what I was just thinking!" [*Laughter.*] Maybe that's the key. Maybe if every writer ended every description with "Make it look good," the artist would be just a little bit better.

Abrams: The three *Brit* specials did fairly well and the character now has its own ongoing series. *Tech Jacket*, however, was cancelled after six issues. What happened there?

Kirkman: *Tech Jacket* debuted before *Invincible*, so it was my maiden voyage. I was under the wing of Larsen on *SuperPatriot* but when I did *Tech Jacket*, it was just E. J. and I. *Tech Jacket* followed an almost identical sales curve as *Invincible*, but it debuted a little higher than *Invincible* and it fell a little faster. While *Invincible* #1 didn't sell as well as *Tech Jacket* #1, *Invincible* #4 was selling a little better than *Tech Jacket*. I'm a numbers junkie when it comes to that so I meticulously map out sales with all sorts of pie charts and flow charts so I monitor how far an issue dropped and it looked like *Tech Jacket* was falling faster.

In hindsight, *Tech Jacket* was very close to how well *Invincible* was doing, and I kept *Invincible* going past the point where I kept *Tech Jacket* going. When we got back the numbers on issue #6, I showed the numbers to E. J. and told him that we weren't going to be making any money on this book, sales were pretty low, and it was the end of a story arc. I knew we would cap this off as issue #6 and do a trade, and I knew we could probably do issues #7–9, but I don't know if we can make it to another endpoint as cleanly. I was thinking we could go back to it if I gained any notoriety at all, and I still might. If I had *Tech Jacket* going, it might still be going today because *Invincible* continued to drop until #11, and it's been climbing in sales ever since. I had a lot of plans for *Tech Jacket* that I'm upset I never got to do.

Abrams: Did you ever feel hemmed in by the genres you were working in?

Kirkman: Not really. Back then, I was doing a lot of interviews and reading a lot of reviews where people were saying, "The diversity in Kirkman's books is remarkable," and they were all superhero books when you get right down to it. *Tech Jacket* was a science-fiction superhero book, *Invincible* is more typical, *Capes* was a humor book, *Brit* was an ultraviolent, ultramodern mature superhero book. I was running the whole gamut of what you could do with a superhero title. I was just trying to keep everything different. When I was sitting down to do these books, I thought that I wanted to do a new creator-owned Image book, and I would just sit and think, "What's not really coming out these days?" I didn't want to do anything that was being done at the time.

Abrams: Why do you think *Capes* was cancelled after three issues?

Kirkman: *Capes* did really, really poorly. *Capes* had word balloons on the covers and they were funny word balloons. Comedy has historically not done very well in comics, I think. Sales came in so poorly on *Capes* that I think the first issue of *Capes* sold two thousand copies less than the last issue of *Tech Jacket*. It debuted at the point where I thought *Tech Jacket* was a waste, so when it was approved by Jim Valentino, he said, "I like this, but why don't we do a miniseries?" I don't know how he came up with the idea of a three-issue miniseries, because I don't think anybody wanted to do a miniseries so short that you couldn't even do a full trade. Maybe it was my idea. In any case, when the numbers came in so badly, I was thankful that it was a three-issue miniseries. It was also solicited as a miniseries, which I think hurt it. At the time, and still today, when people see a miniseries solicited from Image, they say, "Well, it's not like it's a continuing series so I'll wait for the trade." For *Capes*, they waited quite a bit.

Sales came in so bad that I contemplated doing it as black-and-white book at the last minute. Instead, I ended up raising the price after we had solicited it. I had to make other adjustments and let Diamond and other retailers know, "The book you just ordered—poorly, but you ordered it—that was supposed to be $2.99 is now $3.50, so I hope you're okay with that." It was a disaster.

Abrams: When fans wait for the trade, does it affect Image titles as much as it affects Marvel and DC titles?

Kirkman: I think it hurts things across the board, but I think that the trade paperback is such a good thing for the industry on the whole that the successes greatly outweigh the failures. I don't know that there's necessarily any hard evidence that indicates that anyway. There're some people that think maybe *Invincible* or *The Walking Dead* would sell even better if we didn't put out trades constantly, but at the same time I think there's a pretty strong part of our readership that only buys trades, and there's also a strong part that only buys issues. I'd like to think that there are different audiences and cater to both equally and have a regular trade-shipping schedule, as well as for issues. You hear all kinds of stuff from fans, and you don't know how accurate it is or how much of the readership that actually represents. I think about 5 percent of the readers are vocal on the internet so who knows? I'm no expert.

Abrams: *Invincible* has of a Silver Age dynamic to it in the sense that it revolves around Mark's suburban high-school life and his superhero career. How do you break up the characters' personal lives so that it doesn't stray too far into soap-opera clichés during an ongoing series?

Kirkman: I'm a firm believer that all guys that read comics are sissies that wish they could watch soap operas, but instead they have this medium called "comics" that wraps soap operas into fight books. I think the more soap opera-y stuff you put in, the more you relate to the characters. That appeals on a personal level to comic book fans. I like fights as much as the next guy, but having two characters establish a personal connection, discussing important aspects of their lives . . . if you can make characters real enough that people care, you can never have too much of that stuff in the book. One of my favorite issues of Invincible is issue #22, where it's just Mark and his girlfriend talking. That's fun to read. You need to keep people awake, so it's good to have fights every now and then, but I think the core has always been personal relationships. The fighting just moves the plot along.

Abrams: Cory Walker couldn't keep up with the schedule of a monthly series. Tony Moore also wasn't available for the third of the three *Brit* specials

In contrast to most superhero comics, splash-page images are often reserved for human, not superhuman, drama (like a pregnancy test). From *Invincible*, Compendium 2, by Robert Kirkman and Ryan Ottley; Image Comics, 2015.

you did with Cliff Rathburn. How hard was it for you to sync up your schedule with these guys?

Kirkman: It wasn't a matter of syncing up my schedule with those guys; it was just a matter of their physical ability to keep up and the necessity at that time to keep the book in stores. *SuperPatirot* did OK, but it wasn't a big hit. *Tech Jacket* had been canceled, *Invincible* was struggling, *Brit* had just debuted, and *The Walking Dead* was just a blip on the horizon at that point. If I did a book that didn't ship for six months, people would just forget about it. *Invincible* did struggle pretty early on—we only put out six issues in our first year, even though it was a monthly book. We hit a point where if the book kept going like it was, we'd be gone at issue #10. There was no way we could get momentum if it wasn't coming out. Cory and I made the decision together that he would step back: If the book kept shipping sporadically, it'd be cancelled, and if we got someone else on the book, at least it'd still be coming out. Cory was the cocreator of the book and was very much involved and still does character designs—he, Ryan, and I are still good friends and we work over stuff.

Abrams: How did you end up meeting Ryan Ottley, Walker's successor on *Invincible*?

Somebody on PencilJack posted a link to something he was doing called *Ted Noodleman: Bicycle Delivery Boy*, and it was in Kevin Smith's website Moviepoopshoot.com. I think I had seen Ryan's stuff before on PencilJack. I had tried to get Ryan to do this book called *President: USA*, which I won't really go into, but he thought was a stupid idea. Ryan was brought on to do issue #8 as a fill-in issue for *Invincible*, and Cory would jump back on with issue #9. I had suggested Ryan for *Noble Causes*. Eric had suggested some guy named Fran Bueno. I liked his work, and because I thought Jay Faerber was going to use Ryan [on *Noble Causes*], I was going to get Fran to do issue #8 of *Invincible* just to see how it did, but when I want to get Fran, Jay said, "I actually like Fran's stuff better than Ryan's. I'm not going to use Ryan, you can." I actually prefer Ryan's work to Fran's. Ryan finished issue #8 before Cory finished #7, and that's when Cory and I had our discussion about Ryan just staying on the book.

THE SUPER CRISIS AND THE INDUSTRY

Abrams: What kind of creative and aesthetic impact do the "Infinite Crises" and "Civil Wars" of the '00s have?

Kirkman: They definitely have an impact on sales. It's a different audience reading comic books today than [was reading] *Crisis on Infinite Earths* or even *Secret Wars*. Right now, I think you have readers that have more of an income, because it's an older audience and it's also an audience that's more aware of continuity, probably reads more books than the average kid did and with more regularity, and also can afford to buy fifty tie-in issues. The significance is that it tells those people, "If you're reading a Marvel book, this is the Marvel universe, and you need to read all this stuff to keep up." That's cool for those guys because it's cool to feel like every book is important and you're in the know, and that's well they sell so well. The fan base today isn't just buying the books they like, they're buying the books that are important to the universe they like. When they have those crossovers, they highlight what's most important, and that's why they do well.

Abrams: As a writer, do you think the crisis-heavy universe is one that you look forward to? Does it hold as much appeal as doing your own creator-owned, continuity-based series?

Kirkman: As a writer, I try to avoid it, which is usually pretty foolish. When I was writing *Marvel Team-Up*, *House of M* was going on. I could have done a *House of M* issue; I could have done three *House of M* issues. I just kept thinking, "I'm going to have a long run on this book and when I look back on my run, I don't want to have to look back on my run and think, 'Well, issues #18–20 are *House of M*, so in order to understand those issues in my run, you have to go back and find those *House of M* trades and figure out what that stuff is about.'" I just wanted the reader to be able to sit down with #1–25 and think, "I picked up issues #1–25 and it all makes sense." As a reader, I still enjoy them. I enjoyed the hell out of *World War Hulk* and wound up tying into it with my *Irredeemable Ant-Man* series.

For me, as a reader, the veil has been lifted. I read *Infinity Gauntlet* thinking, "Oh my God! Sweeping change and nothing will ever be the same!" I know now that that's not how things work. I know that *Civil War* being what it is, Captain America will be alive again soon and Iron Man and he will be best friends and the Registration Act will be long forgotten and all the consequences of Civil War will be undone, if not under the current regime of Marvel, somewhere down the line. That's how it works: Some guy says, "I'm going to shake things up and make things cool," and that makes books sell, and when that starts to fade, someone comes along and says, "This was a mistake and I'm going to make books classic again!" And that's what makes them sell and then someone shakes things up again, and then someone turns it classic again. That's just how things work. That's still enjoyable and worth following, but as a liner story, it's a bit silly.

Something like *Savage Dragon* is my favorite book because Larsen is steering the ship, so he's not going to come along and say, "This isn't working. Let's shake things up." Or, "This isn't working. Let's make things classic again." It's just going to keep going, follow a direction and be one man's vision. That's the stuff that appeals to me personally, but I don't begrudge anyone else for enjoying other stuff.

Abrams: Two of the most striking scenes in *Invincible* are when Mark is taking a step back and looking at the Earth from above and when Atom Eve says to Invincible, "You'd be surprised how rarely people ever look up." Do you think we've somehow lost our ability to stop and put our lives in perspective? Have we lost a bit of our collective imagination as readers?

Kirkman: That's a big question, sir. Um, yeah, definitely. If you look at what kids had growing up in the '60s and '70s and at the excitement in the world at the time . . . I mean, we don't have a Space Race or the interest in politics they did then. There's not a concern with the world or an excitement in being an American that we had back then, so yeah, there are all kinds of things that are not making the imagination as it was back then. Now we live in a bitter society that's not very optimistic, and familiar with Silver Age books, but it does have an optimism and a sense of wonder that those books had more than books today.

Cory was kinda slow at the time, so doing a two-page spread that was mostly a star field seemed like a great idea, and it made for a really cool image. You never really see Superman land on the moon and declare, "I can't believe the Sun is over there and I am looking at the Earth. That's insane!" Invincible's a very different character and that's just another thing that allowed readers to get closer to the character early on, that he would sometimes step back and wonder at the stuff he's been doing.

Abrams: You said in the second hardcover that you didn't want to reuse Guardians of the Globe because they were "pretty derivative" of the Justice League.

Kirkman: Exactly! Who knows?!

Abrams: [*Laughs.*] At the same time, many of the other characters are riffs on comic and pop-culture figures, like how Atom Eve and Amber are Mary Jane Parker and Gwen Stacy to Mark's Peter Parker, or my personal favorite: D. A. Sinclair, who is a very loose and very funny take on H. P. Lovecraft's "Herbert West: Re-Animator." Is there a difference between one kind of tribute and another?

Kirkman: Yeah, saying that D. A. Sinclair is similar to Herbert West is one thing, but the Guardians of the Globe were cookie-cutter standards. I grew up with Alan Moore's *Supreme* and *Astro City*, which were such revolutionary, groundbreaking, fantastic series that were using analogs. Also, a lot of Warren Ellis' work used analogs. The late '90s were a time when analogs were everywhere. It got to the point where everybody was doing it and most people were doing it poorly because it had been so popular. I consciously try to stay away from analogs but the Guardians of the Globe were going to appear in one issue and they were going to be dead in that issue. I knew that going into it and I didn't want to create a lot of cool characters I was going to kill off because 1) I didn't want to have to bring them back and I didn't want to have to waste that time and 2) you only had two or three pages to get to know these characters and have their deaths have an impact. By doing analogs, which are completely legal, you play on the reader's knowledge of the characters you're analogging.

It worked because people saw it as a big deal, and it was a big deal because people saw that they were analogs of characters, and I had mentioned Guardians of the Globe a few times before so they knew it was a big deal. They were completely derivative and half of them are borderline completely lame—Immortal was the only one I thought wasn't derivative at all and was a fairly original character I could do stuff with. It was always written in the plot that he'd come back—I mean, he's called Immortal so that was always part of the plan. I did end up doing stuff with Darkwing—just because I like the name Darkwing—but for the most part, it's not something I wanted to do. As far as Atom Eve and Amber being Mary Jane and Gwen Stacy to Mark's Peter Parker, that was completely accidental. When we introduced Amber into the book, I would have never made her hair blonde if we had realized that. If you take away the hair colors, there's not that much similarities in their personalities and how they interact.

Abrams: So she's not going to die on the Brooklyn Bridge later on?

Kirkman: No, no. [*Laughs.*] Early on, there was an anything goes attitude to the book and we had characters like The Elephant and Damien Darkblood. I know there was an issue where we spoofed *Star Trek: The Next Generation* in the opening sequence to issue #9. I did fun stuff like that because I enjoyed it, but I realized early on that it's hard to take a book seriously when it's filled with analogs like that. From an early point in *Invincible*, I made a decision not to do that at all for the rest of the series.

Abrams: Are superhero comics just pastiche at this point? Can it ever move beyond where it's gone already?

Kirkman: I think there's a lot of life left in the superhero medium. I don't think these days you can nail that down to one kind of thing, but I definitely think you'll continue to see new ground being broken. It takes people with new ideas to do that, and I think, right now, the industry doesn't really support new ideas like it should. With our aging comic book audience that has decided what it wants in a comic book, they just want more of that. Publishers are shoehorned into giving them what they want to survive and, because of that, new ideas struggle to take off. Every series that Marvel is publishing right now is a series they've been publishing for a long time or a revival of a series they've published before. You don't really see a lot of new characters being introduced. If you look at the '70s, '80s, or even '90s, you don't really have any Iron Fists or Blades or Wolverines or Sleepwalkers or Darkhawks or New Warriors. I think *Runaways* is all that's started up and featured new characters that have stuck around and lasted long enough to make a foothold. It's an uphill battle to do new things these days, but that's what makes it fun. If it were easy, what would be the point?

FAMILY TIES

Abrams: All the pivotal plot points in *Brit* revolve around Brit and Donald's respective personal lives, making it seem like you've grounded their superhuman feats in a family-oriented reality. How much does that world mirror ours?

Kirkman: Definitely. I think that's a very important thing to have in order to have people interested. I watch a lot of sci-fi, and *The Terminator* is a super interesting idea for a movie, but if it had been a comic book series, at some point you have to ask, "How are these people surviving?" To a certain extent, *The Walking Dead* is an exploration of that, how you raise kids and whatnot. You have to keep an eye on a superhero book because you don't want to do anything too outlandish or not grounded in reality. If aliens were to invade and enslave everyone and started drilling earth's core—if that were what *Invincible* was about, it would be cool for about six months, but then you'd lose most of your readers, because you would lose the heart of the book; you'd lose the relatable aspect. I hate to say that this book is relatable, because I despise the idea that you have to like the characters you read, but to certain extent there's some truth to that. Comics are based on male power fantasies, so to a certain extent, it is imagining, "If I were in that situation, I could see myself doing this." That's the thought you want to play off in a comic book. That's what gets the reader to come back, I suppose.

Abrams: You've used the death of a child in *Brit* and *Invincible* as a means of pushing the heroes into uncomfortable territory, forcing them to see that even their villains are human and have families. Are you writing from a personal standpoint as you're developing those themes of family and loss?

Kirkman: To a certain extent I have to be, but I haven't lost a child, and I haven't lost a childhood friend or anything like that. I'm largely making this stuff up. I think I've put my character through a lot worse stuff than I've had to endure. I think it's all about setting up drama, and I agree with this quote Brian K. Vaughn told me: "The good writer always kills his babies." You take the character you like and put them through the worst shit. That's good drama.

Abrams: To what extent has your family life influenced or even changed your writing?

Kirkman: I don't know, there's got to some psychological scarring from the fact that my family moved a thousand miles away from me—I don't know how many miles away Florida is from Kentucky. I certainly don't dwell on it. People used to say *Invincible* is an accurate portrayal of high school and how high-school kids think and behave, and I think that's horseshit. It's certainly a nice thing to say and I'll take the compliment but I was just thinking back to some of the things I did in high school, making stuff up as I went along and I don't think it's an accurate portrayal of high school today. Maybe it matched how things were when I was in high school or when the reader was in high school. I take great pride in making this stuff up as I go along. There's not much basis in my life and experience. There has to be some level of realism, but at the same time, it's fun to put people in fairly unrealistic situations and have cool things happen to them.

Abrams: The death of the Guardians of the Globe in *Invincible* is a major turning point in the series. Up until that point the series was pretty much an all-ages title. How did you decide to make that step?

Kirkman: There were people blowing up in the first four issues, so there was always a slight level of maturity to *Invincible*. I liked the idea that the more sporadic the gory scenes were, the more impact they had. To have six issues that were gore-free and fairly light—I wouldn't say kid-friendly but to a certain extent all-ages—to follow that with a seventh issue that has extreme graphic violence and gore would have much more impact. If they were all bloodbaths, they would have no impact at all. I did risk alienating some people, because there were retailers that said, "It's nice to have a superhero book I can give to kids." The events of issue #7 were always planned, and I wanted to do that to shock people.

Abrams: How much did you hesitate about increasing the visible violence in the series?

Kirkman: You gotta top yourself. You gotta keep moving forward, so if you hit the point where you have visible intestines, that's just how things work. It's not just shock tactics, which people frown on for some reason. Allen the Alien getting eviscerated by the Viltrumites proves who the Viltrumites are, and is a pretty shocking thing to have a character that's well-liked get ripped apart. He healed from that, and that again was part of the story, just showing how powerful Allen is and there are three or four story reasons why that gory scene had to happen. That issue was designed to be a Golden Age, wordy, Stan Lee comic book. Anytime the Viltrumites show up, there's going to be gore because that's how they operate. I want to show those guys as being very vicious, and you can't make a guy tougher than making him kick a guy's ass while holding his intestines. That's pretty much the pinnacle of the tough guy. If he's holding his own beating heart in his hands so that he can keep beating someone up, that's not the kind of guy you want to mess with.

I think by now people reading the book accept that, and people who don't like the gore scenes see that there's a purpose to it in the book, and the people that love it, love it. I'm a pretty big fan of graphic violence in fiction. I was a huge fan of [Konami's violent fighting video game series] *Mortal Kombat* growing up. I didn't get into any fights or try to freeze people and smash their heads in. I don't really buy into the whole "corruption of youth" aspect. There are disturbed people and there are disturbed people, but that's not something to blame on fiction or entertainment.

Abrams: Putting aside the idea of corrupting the reader, did you ever think that the violence of issue #7 was a little exploitative of what you'd set up till that point regarding the expectations of the series?

Kirkman: Well, it was because it was done that way on purpose. That was something that I'd always planned. I did exploit what had come before it, but that was the purpose of the whole thing. The scene doesn't have the impact without the six issues before it.

Abrams: I know you are or were working on a film adaptation of *Invincible*. How did you get approached, and how did you secure the job as a screenwriter?

Kirkman: I have a pretty good manager. My Hollywood representative is a pretty kick-ass dude named David Alpert, who I met at the same Chicago Convention that I met Val Staples at a year before. I met him very early on when I was doing *Battle Pope*, and he came to my booth with a Dreamwave badge on, because at the time we were going after the *Transformers* license, and I was going to try to press him for information. I asked him what he did for Dreamwave, and he said that he was their Hollywood representation. I said, "Well, I'm going to need your business card, sir."

He gave it to me and I said, "Let me talk to you: I got this thing called *Battle Pope* and this thing called *Science Dog*, and you could totally make a movie out of them."

I think he rolled his eyes and thought, "Those are dumb ideas, and we could never do anything with that in Hollywood. But you know what, keep my card."

I kept in contact with him, and when *Tech Jacket* was solicited, I got contacted by a solicitor who said, "I was thinking about a science fiction take on Green Lantern, but then I saw you're already doing it, so let's do a movie." I didn't know what to do, because that scares somebody that doesn't know anything about that stuff. I called the only other guy out there I knew and said, "Hey, what do I do? He seems interested in that."

He said, "Well, this does seem like a cool idea. I think I'd like to manage you now." Before you couldn't do a movie with a talking-human-dog character, and *Battle Pope* would never fly, so I think I just seemed like a crackpot to the guy. When I had *Tech Jacket* and *Invisible* and *Brit*, I had some fairly sound concepts that he was interested in.

He became my representation and out of sheer luck, his management firm also represented Brian Michael Bendis, David Mack, Michael Oeming, Ed Brubaker—all those guys and the Wachowski brothers and a lot of Hollywood people, but I really lucked into getting the same representation as a bunch of cool comic book guys.

Abrams: How far along is the script?

Kirkman: The movie is technically in turnaround now, so that means that at this time, the studio has decided not to make it. That whole roller coaster ride is officially over, and we're back to the drawing board, which happens all the time. That's not a big deal at all; it can always be optioned by someone else. I wrote two drafts of a screenplay, and I don't know exactly what's going on with it. I think Paramount at this time had passed on the project. There was a big switchover at Paramount where the executive that decided to option the project had lost, and when that happens, things usually tend to fall apart because the new executives come in with their projects, and they don't want to take over outgoing executives' old projects. I got in the Writer's Guild through it and got to write my screenplay, and now I get all kinds of DVD screeners. And now I have screenwriting experience, so when I want to write another screenplay, I'll be able to.

Abrams: What's working as a screenwriter like compared to working on comic scripts?

Kirkman: Crappy. Incredibly difficult. I'll use this as an analogy, but it's like riding a bike, and you're really good at riding a bike, and that's comic book writing for me. I've been riding bikes for a long time, I know exactly how to do it and then someone came along and said, "All right, now you gotta learn to drive a car." They're basically the same thing—there are wheels, there's steering, you're moving forward—but completely different ways of doing it. I basically had to learn to drive a car while I was on a roadtrip. I had to learn how to write a screenplay while writing a screenplay. I grew up reading comics, so I know the basic function of the page and how things worked—didn't read a lot of movie scripts in my day. Writing a screenplay is pretty difficult for me. There was a learning curve though—I think my second draft ended up being much better than my first draft. I'm a visual thinker, so, to a certain extent, I know more than your average amateur screenwriter, but there's nothing like getting paid by Paramount Pictures to learn how to write a screenplay.

Abrams: Had you ever considered trying your hand at other media like screenplays or prose?

Kirkman: Screenwriting didn't ever seem like a possibility to me, the same with prose. Recently, I've had the option to do both. I may someday do prose, but then again, it's learning a completely different way of writing and I think I made a pretty decent living writing comics, and it's easy for me. If I enjoy digging ditches and make a good living digging ditches, I don't see why I would learn how to pour cement all of a sudden just for the sake of pouring cement. Writing prose might be fun, but at this time it's not something I want to pursue yet. As far as screenwriting goes, screenwriting ended up being really fun after I learned how to do it. If I get a break in my comic book career, I'll write another screenplay at some point. I'd like to be able to write some spec screenplays because I have a lot of ideas I want to put on paper, but finding the time . . . I write a lot of comic books. That does take up a lot of my time.

LIVE FLESH: *THE WALKING DEAD* AND *MARVEL ZOMBIES*

Abrams: When was the first time you saw *Night of the Living Dead*?

Kirkman: I know it was late night, I think when I was in middle school or my first year or two in high school. I had a TV in my room for the first time ever and I would stay up late watching whatever stupid shit was on late-night television. One night I was flipping channels and I saw it being announced, so while it was a school night I stayed up watching it until 2 or 3 a.m.

Abrams: Were you a horror junkie or was *Night of the Living Dead* an exception?

Kirkman: I wouldn't say I was a horror movie junkie. I wasn't really allowed to watch horror movies until about the sixth or seventh grade. I never watched *Friday the 13th* or *Nightmare on Elm Street*—I think the *Nightmare on Elm Street* film I saw was *Freddy's Dead* with Tony Moore. I was able to rent one horror movie every Halloween from a pretty young age and I really liked Pinhead on the cover of the *Hellraiser* video boxes I saw at the local Blockbuster, so I basically alternated between *Hellraiser* and *Hellraiser 2* every year.

Abrams: Considering how important the success of *Invincible* was in being able to establish *The Walking Dead*, the series may have seemed like a major departure from your superhero titles. How difficult was the transition between the two titles?

Kirkman: I get that question a lot, and it doesn't really seem like an issue to me. The situations are different, but it doesn't seem that different to me when it's on paper. I imagine, when the books come out, they seem pretty different, but I'm just typing words, so it's not like when I'm writing *The Walking Dead* and I think to myself, "I'm writing zombies, it's very scary and I'm writing zombies." I think, "What's happening to Rick today?"

Abrams: In your introduction to the trade paperback, you said, "We will NEVER wonder what happens to Rick next, we will see it. *The Walking Dead* will be the zombie movie that never ends." How important was the concept of keeping an eye on Rick the whole time for you?

Kirkman: I think it was very important. Rick is the main character of the book and he's the one people identify with. I still maintain that I can kill him at any point and make the book about somebody else—actually, I almost did that at the end of issue #6 but, thankfully, I decided not to. It would've been a very different book had I decided to so that. With *Walking Dead*, the concept is a zombie movie that never ends. I was referring more to the fact that, if they don't all die, they ride off into the sunset, mostly in a helicopter, and you never hear from them again. In *Walking Dead*, it starts off with them riding in a helicopter and keeps going forever or until everybody dies off. I just wanted to explore a natural progression of events in that type of society. I want to show everything that happens to Rick. I hate it when the movies end.

Abrams: Do you think you lose any tension by keeping the focus on Rick all the time?

Kirkman: It's not like he's on every single page of every issue. There are definitely different things that happen with different characters that I can cut to. There are other characters that have stepped up and become secondary main characters like Andrea, Dawn, and Tyrese.

Abrams: Even though Rick isn't always in the forefront, he seems like the moral compass of the series. How much should we sympathize with him, considering what he winds up doing as the series gets along? As the creator, do you like him all the time?

Kirkman: I'm indifferent; I don't like or dislike him. One of the things I wanted to show with Rick is how far people can go and what limits they can be pushed to and how much they can change over time. Over the course of *The Walking Dead*, Rick has gone from being an optimistic small-town cop to beating people to death with his bare hands when he feels his family is threatened. To a certain extent, he's a vicious killer, but he's still fairly likable and he has a reason for everything he does. If this was the kind of book where he could be rescued and taken to some kind of utopia, I seriously doubt he'd be able to adjust to that kind of society after everything he's been through.

Abrams: The world is definitely a darker place in the series, which is something you made explicitly clear in the characters of Michonne and the Governer. What do these two characters bring to the social dynamic of the book?

Kirkman: With Michonne, I wanted to bring a really unrealistically tough character, just because I think that's cool. I say unrealistically tough, but she's not doing anything that's impossible. It's just a little far-fetched that she would be so adept at killing zombies and that able to handle tough situations. I just wanted to put a little more flavor into the book. With the Governor, I wanted a bad guy that you could identify with—well, maybe not identify with. We had some bad guys that were one-dimensional, and then there are zombies that are an unknowing force that doesn't have much of a personality. With the Governor, I wanted to get some guy in there that could be a twisted mirror image of Rick because he's also been driven crazy by the world he's in now but he's gone a little bit further a little bit faster than Rick has.

Abrams: You've said you always wanted to steer the series away from the humor of *Return of the Living Dead* in favor of a more serious tone. What do you think is lost by poking fun at zombies?

Kirkman: You definitely lose some of the threat, and now they won't be taken as seriously as the Romero and the Fulci and the other serious zombie flicks. *Shaun of the Dead* is the only example where it pokes fun of zombies while being a compelling, dramatic zombie story. *Shaun of the Dead* is unique, because it's as heart-wrenching and dramatic as any Romero flick, and yet it's funny as hell. It definitely could be done but for *The Walking Dead*, I wanted to do a book that could be taken seriously.

Abrams: *Marvel Zombies* has a significant amount of black comedy scattered throughout it. How did you come up with the idea? Was it always a humor book?

Kirkman: To this day, I don't consider it a humor book. The people who are sadistic and messed-up think it's a humor book, but people who are level-headed and straight-laced think it's serious. There's definitely some comedy there, such as when Bruce Banner's stomach is popping or when Daredevil is discussing how his leg is filling up with blood because all of his lower extremities are filling with blood and his heart's not pumping. I was just trying to do disgusting, slightly disturbing, off-the-wall stuff to Marvel characters. It wasn't necessarily intended to be funny. It was always supposed to be bizarre to see Spider-Man do those things and Captain America's head lopped off and for him to be running around with his brains hanging out. It's odd to me but I guess if I were reading it, it probably is kind of funny.

Abrams: You've said a couple of times that you wanted the series to be taken seriously, but the parts that should scare readers are moments like when Captain America is beheaded by his own shield or when Hulk takes a bite out of the Silver Surfer. Is that really supposed to be taken seriously?

Kirkman: It never occurred to me that that would be considered laugh-out-loud funny. Someone biting off anyone's head could be portrayed as funny, but the Hulk biting off the Silver Surfer's head just seemed bizarre. I certainly didn't think people would think, "Oh my God, they bit off the Silver Surfer's head: It's so sad!" But I didn't think people would say, "Wahahah! The head is in his mouth and that's totally hilarious!" I thought it would be more like, "I cannot believe I'm seeing this. This is the craziest shit I've ever seen. I cannot believe the Incredible Hulk just ate some guy's head, and it's in a Marvel comic with a Marvel logo on the cover!"

In that scene in particular, Hercules pries his mouth open because he says, "I think it's still in his mouth! I don't think he swallowed it!" so I put the camera in Hulk's mouth looking up as the Hulk smashes Hercules' hands. I guess that's kind of hard to portray in a way that doesn't look silly.

Abrams: Did you come up with *Marvel Zombies* all at once or in stages?

Kirkman: *Marvel Zombies* is actually a spin-off series from *Ultimate Fantastic Four.* Mark Millar and Greg Land did a story where the zombie Reed Richards tricked the Ultimate Fantastic Four's Reed Richards into coming to that dimension so that [Zombie Reed] could eat everyone in the Ultimate universe. Reed ended up outsmarting him, and [Zombie Reed] wound up being trapped in the Ultimate universe and [starting] the Frightful Four, which is a really cool idea. While they were working on that series, they came up with the idea of a spin-off series that takes place in that universe called *Marvel Zombies.*

In *Ultimate Fantastic Four*, zombies are very different. They don't do enough to stand out aside from yelling, "I'm going to eat you." The Fantastic Four acts very sinister and evil and so when we were coming up with *Marvel Zombies*, it

The series uses zombie horror to revise superheroism into something antiheroic and strangely funny. From *Marvel Zombies* by Robert Kirkman and Sean Phillips; Marvel Comics, 2006.

was very hard to come up with what the book would be. When *Marvel Zombies* starts, all the humans are dead and the zombies are starving and there's nothing to eat. I couldn't have a bunch of Marvel heroes looking for food for five issues. I tried to figure out who would be alive and thought that Luke Cage has unbreakable skin, so logically he wouldn't end up being a zombie.

They told me, "We like this idea but we have a problem: Luke Cage is drawn in the background of *Ultimate Fantastic Four* as a zombie." When I was given the assignment, I was just given the scripts and in them, Mark would say, "The Human Torch is being chased by Marvel zombies," so while when zombie Hulk arrived he'd write, "Zombie Hulk's coming," for the most part he'd say, "The Marvel zombies are coming atcha: big splash page!" Greg Land would just pick who he wanted to draw, which I think is why everybody is '70s-themed, because he likes to draw '70s costumes.

It's a good thing that that happened, because I don't think it would've been as good a book. I eventually hit on making the zombies the main characters instead of the antagonists. I pitched that to them, and they liked it and came up with the idea of Magneto, being the last survivor of the Fantastic Four arc, to move him in from there. If the main characters are zombies, it's going to be really nasty stuff because you can't follow these characters around as the main characters without seeing the kind of things they'd be doing and talking about. I was told that we had a lot of leeway with what we can do with them, because they're zombies. Once it was clear that they were going to the main characters, I had to give them personalities they had before. Spider-Man is still Spider-Man after he's eaten, but as he gets hungrier, he becomes more of a raving, lunatic monster that's just trying to get flesh. Once he eats, he thinks, "Oh my God, I can't believe I'm doing this!"

Abrams: Did you ever imagine them not talking coherently?

Kirkman: Once they became the characters, they definitely had to be talking or it would be a completely silent book. It is *Marvel Zombies* so the non-zombie characters are few and far between until I started picking out which characters hadn't been shown before and put them in the book. I think the thing that makes *Marvel Zombies* unique is that those were the characters we followed and everything they encountered was a side story. I wouldn't be able to do that had they not been able to talk.

Abrams: *Marvel Zombies* is very different in tone and themes from the regular Marvel line. How did you think you would be able to get away with it?

Kirkman: I honestly didn't think I was going to get away with it. I turned in the first script and I thought I was going to get fired right away. Joe Casey called me up and asked, "What're you doing?" and I told him that I'd just turned in a script for *Marvel Zombies #1*.

I gotta say, most of the time when I finish a script, I think, "Oof, they're going to find me out, that I'm not really big on that one," just because I'm not a good judge of my own work. With the script for *Marvel Zombies*, I thought that it had turned out really well, so when Joe and I were talking about the script I thought, "Man, it's going to be crazy! They rip Magneto apart and eat him, and Spider-Man breaks his leg and rips it off, and Daredevil is popping his leg to drain the blood, and Captain America gets the top of his head lopped off, and it's going to be the coolest Marvel comic ever."

Casey said, "You . . . did you turn that script in?!"

I said, "Yeah!"

He said, "You can't get that all into one comic!" and I had never even thought about that.

When I got off the phone with him, I thought, "Man, this is crazy! What was I thinking?! I'm going to get fired!" They're not going to let me write this book—they're going to be pissed! They're going to think I wrote all those things as a joke to show them that I'm pissed that I can't do things at Marvel Comics, and they're going to think I'm some kind of troublemaker.

I then got a phone call from [*Marvel Zombies* editor] Ralph Macchio and I asked him, "Hi. Did you read the script?"

He said, "Yeah, we sent it off the shop."

I asked, "The gore? Not a problem?"

He said, "Nah, they're zombies. It'll be fine!"

I swear as soon as the art came in I thought that they were going to fire me again: "Whoa! We read on paper that his head was being ripped off, but we didn't think we'd actually see it! Now that we see it, we want to take it out"—which happens a lot. The page came in and everything was fine. We were being careful on the original miniseries and "Dead Days," its one-shot follow-up, and now that the thing is a success, we've got intestines hanging out . . . we tried to keep some things in shadows in the first miniseries, but now we're just getting away with murder.

Abrams: Did you ever think that it would be so popular that you would have to think of sequel ideas?

Kirkman: No, never in a million years did I think it was going to be a high-selling book. Bendis thought it was going to be a hit, because I was talking to him on the phone about it one day and he'd asked what I was going to call it. It was always called *Marvel Zombies*, but I think it was always assumed that wouldn't be the final title, so I said, "Well, we're calling it *Marvel Zombies* now, but I don't really know about the title: It seems kind of silly."

It seemed like something to do with a Marvel fan club, but he said, "Oh my God, that has to be the final title! If that's the final title, you're going to sell tons of copies of that thing. A book called *Marvel Zombies*! That'll do great!" I still was pretty skeptical but I didn't think anyone at Marvel was expecting it to be a huge hit. I was pretty shocked, but Brian Bendis knew all along.

Abrams: Arthur Suydam's covers for the series have been collected into a separate volume due to their popularity. Who had the idea to "zombify" classic Marvel covers?

Kirkman: I think it was the talent coordinator Chris Allo, but it certainly wasn't my idea. When I saw the first cover to *Marvel Zombies* as a riff on the *Amazing Fantasy* #15 cover, I thought, "That has nothing to do with the interiors and it makes *Marvel Zombies* look like a joke." I thought it was a great piece of art and Arthur Suydam is a fantastic painter, so I didn't complain about it. That was another reason why I didn't think it would be a success. As it turns out, I think those covers are a huge part of the success, especially the multiple printings. It went into multiple printings because everyone wanted to buy the new Arthur Suydam covers. They liked the book, and it certainly wouldn't have worked it they hadn't liked what was on the inside, but you're not buying a fourth copy of the same book because the covers aren't selling it.

Abrams: Undoubtedly, there was a cult following surrounding zombies at the time you saw *Night of the Living Dead*, particularly considering how many sequels *Return of the Living Dead* spawned. Since you started writing *The Walking Dead*, there's been a big revival thanks to *The Walking Dead* and your later *Marvel Zombies* and other homages like [director] Zack Snyder's *Dawn of the Dead*. Why do you think we're so fascinated by zombies?

Kirkman: I think zombies were popular during the Cold War and zombies are popular again because of the threat of terrorism and how we all live in fear right now. I think when we're living in an environment where we're told to go out and buy plastic sheets and duct tape like we're building nuclear bunkers in our backyard, we start to think about the end of the world, and that's become popular in fiction. *The Walking Dead* had the good fortune of being launched at a time when *28 Days Later* had just come out in theaters right before. It was a huge hit, so that spawned all kinds of zombie movies that were huge hits and we rode that wave. I guess it could be argued that there wouldn't be as many comic books without the success of *The Walking Dead*, but I really don't think we started the zombie craze.

Abrams: Does this type of literal deconstruction of the Marvel universe suggest that we secretly want to see those characters hurt?

Kirkman: I think [the main reason for] the success of the series—which relies on ten different things happening—is that it's the first time we've seen these characters in this light. That uniqueness is a big deal, and the fact that they've never really had Spider-Man eat Mary Jane is a big shock that drives the series forward. I don't think people are out to see these characters dismembered, but they're out to see new things done with them and I think this is definitely new.

Abrams: George Romero always made a point of emphasizing the clash and homogenization of social dynamics after the zombie crisis struck. What role do you think that plays in *The Walking Dead* or *Marvel Zombies*?

Kirkman: In *Marvel Zombies*, society has been completely destroyed. I've said a few times that I wanted it to be taken seriously, but I made a very conscious decision to make something different from *The Walking Dead*. While I didn't expect it to be funny, I thought it would be fun in a bizarre way. I didn't want people to think *The Walking Dead* and *Marvel Zombies* are two books but are the same thing except in *Marvel Zombies* with the Marvel characters. As far as how society breaks down, in the superhero world, it breaks down a lot quicker. Mark Millar said the zombie outbreak occurred and in two days, everyone was dead. *The Walking Dead* is about society tricking itself into thinking that there is still a society and that there is still civilization.

Abrams: One of the things you've caught a lot of flack for is the treatment and characterization of women in the series. Earlier *Capes* features Knockout as a character conforming to norms established by a male-dominated society after having significantly enlarged her chest to secure work. Is the devoted female/male dynamic in *The Walking Dead* a matter of unspoken taboos coming to the surface, because there's no society to be afraid of anymore?

Kirkman: I guess to a certain extent. Michonne was introduced later in the series. She's one of the strongest characters in the book, so I don't think I did too terribly bad with the portrayal of women in the series. In the beginning, even the male characters were weak. I wanted everyone to grow and change, so I purposefully portrayed everyone as not being prepared and going through their surroundings not really knowing what they're doing and just in general weak. When you do that with women, you notice. Just because Glenn was stumbling around and not doing a good job and Rick was not really pulling things off in the first few issues—nobody notices that, that's fine, but when you put a woman handling a gun, you get comments. In that situation, there were more men in that group that had handled guns—police officers, hunters—so demographically they are the ones that handle guns the most all over the nation. If you take twenty people, if one person would be able to handle a gun in that group, I can almost guarantee you that that person would be a man.

I've only held a gun once, and I've never shot a gun. I'm not saying, "Men carry guns" and stuff, but I'm just trying to be realistic. I think the main thing that pissed people off was that we had a very liberal, man-hating woman, and that was her character in the book and all the other women were taking clothes to wash down to the stream with her. She remarks, "We're going to wash the clothes, while they go to hunt? That's bullshit!"

One of the other women says, "I don't know, I've never used a gun. Do you know how to use a gun? They're police officers. I don't trust them to wash my clothes." That's just realistic, the other woman telling the first woman to shut up. She was just complaining, because that's what society had dictated, but when society is stripped down to necessity, there are certain people who are better at certain tasks than others.

Andrea became the best marksman in the group, and a lot of the male characters fell apart. Andrea is one the strongest people in the book right now, and she's been training people in recent issues to shoot guns and helping them prepare for the upcoming battle that they've got. Hopefully, the people that are upset with all that stuff are no longer upset to see that there's purpose to that stuff.

Abrams: In terms of the book's sentiments of upholding a community and family dynamic, is there a bit of you in these characters?

Kirkman: There are definitely aspects of the characters that mirror my view on things in a positive way. I guess I am a strong believer in family values, but I think it's more Rick trying to establish what is normal society. That's where he comes from. He, Lori and Carl represent the standard American family of 2.5 kids, and they're just trying to make things right again. A lot of times, I force myself to do things in comics that I really don't agree with. I would never have an open relationship with a girl, but when I was writing *Brit*, I thought, "This is bizarre, but I'm going to have Brit date a stripper and be in an open relationship where they can screw around."

Abrams: Do you feel like you're being pigeonholed as "the zombie guy" after the enormous success of *The Walking Dead* and *Marvel Zombies*?

Kirkman: My zombie stuff is definitely more popular than anything else I've done. My most successful book at Marvel is *Marvel Zombies*, and my most successful book at Image is *The Walking Dead*. At the same time, I think there are a number of comic book creators that would kill to have the success of either of those books. I can't really complain, but at the same time, I'm thinking, "Oh, man, Zombies? Really?! Is that for me? Is that the only thing of mine to catch on?" Certainly, *Ultimate X-Men* sells great, and *Invincible* sells remarkably well comparatively, it just doesn't sell as well as *The Walking Dead*. I'm doing OK, but there are people who think I'm the zombie guy. I'm not quitting anytime soon, so hopefully my pirate book will take off soon, and I'll become "the pirate guy."

MARVEL AND THE RETURN OF THE '90S

Abrams: On a post you did for the *Comic Book Resources* column *The Hot Seat*, you emphasized that any fledgling writers should "stop sending submissions to Marvel" and just go out there and make mistakes on their own creator-owned titles. What kind of experience did you have with Marvel initially?

Kirkman: I had an insanely, incredibly bad experience with Marvel originally. My first experience with them was with the now-defunct, immediately failed Epic line. I guess they had come up with a business model where they would pay people less to do different comics, and they started farming out people that had worked in the small press on lower-selling books and got them to do new books for them. They were announcing that they were accepting submissions from everybody, but at the same time, they mainly contacted me and some other people and said, "We want some people who have some name recognition to be doing some of these books." Before they started accepting submissions, they contacted me and said, "Could you pitch us a few books?"

I pitched them *Darkhawk* and *Sleepwalker*, and they accepted *Sleepwalker*, and I got to work on it. They had guaranteed me six issues so I got excited to be able to work for a while on it. My wife was managing a coffee shop for a while, and then she ended up managing a CD store, so we were living off of her income mostly. She had left college so that she could do that, and she'd been doing that for a year and a half or maybe two years, so when I got this *Sleepwalker* gig, I had a set amount of money I'd be making for six months, *Walking Dead* debuted and sales on that were going up, and *Invincible* hadn't been optioned, but things were looking up. I thought, "I have the eyes of Marvel on me. I can totally make this work and turn this into more work."

My wife was saying, "I really want to go back to school."

I said, "You know what? Go back to school. Everything will be fine."

The day after I turned in the third issue, they told me, "Oh yeah, so, um, the Epic Line isn't working out, so we're canceling the whole thing. Sorry." I told them, "Oh, wow, I don't understand. I thought I was guaranteed six issues," to which they replied, "Oh yeah, well, that's not . . . we're sorry. We're not publishing those books." As an added bonus, they said they weren't going to pay me for issue #3. It turns out Epic wasn't necessarily Marvel, it was Bill Jemas and a few other editors working under him to get a bunch of stuff, and I guess the Epic line failure happened right when Jemas left the company.

They ended up taking my *Sleepwalker* series—and we had pages for the second issue and were moving along with it quite a bit. Of the Epic books that were coming out, we were the last people to come out, and we had more work done than other people when they pulled the plug, so we were really kicking ass for them, damn it. They published the one issue of *Sleepwalker* we had completed in the *Epic Anthology* book, and this was right after she had quit her job and signed up for classes and everything was changing. It was literally three weeks after that when I was with my wife's family celebrating Christmas in Tennessee when I got a letter from Tom Brevoort saying, "I really like your work and would love to talk to you about doing stuff with Marvel." It was cool because it was like the Epic line had wrecked my life and two weeks later, Tom Brevoort was a light shining through storm clouds. I was originally going to drive my car off a bridge on Christmas Eve. Tom Brevoort saved my life. [*Pause.*] That part was a joke.

Abrams: Oh! OK. [*Kirkman laughs.*] When you started, were there characters that you wanted to work with, or did you feel like there were some titles that you wanted to but couldn't work with because it was your first time at Marvel?

Kirkman: They would ask me questions like, "Who's your favorite character at Marvel? What character do you really want to do?" and I would say, "I want to do all of them," because if I had said, "I really want to write *Namor*," they would've said, "Oh! I'm sorry! The correct answer was *Iron Man*. If you had said *Iron Man*, you would've gotten the book, but because you said *Namor*, you don't get anything." I told them, "I love all Marvel comic books, and I would love to write any Marvel characters you guys have." That's what led to me writing *Jubilee*. [*Laughter.*]

I did that with one of the editors of the Epic line, and when Epic went under, I believe she went into the X-office. They were getting together all kinds of miniseries—they had a Gambit series, a Jubilee series, and another one they were trying to put together. I was struggling for work, and I hadn't had any work offered from him yet, so I was pounding my ex-Epic editor saying, "Well, you guys really screwed me. You should make things right. Gimme some work." They wanted little twelve-page stories of characters, and she sent me a character list and asked which characters I wanted. I said, "There's forty characters on the list. Is there anyone you're really looking for a story about? I like the X-Men and I am fairly familiar with every character. What do you want?

She said, "You know what? I'd really like a story about Jubilee causing some trouble in a mall."

I said, "Well, I've been dying to tell that story all my life. Let's get going on that." I ended up writing a twelve-page story of Jubilee in a mall skateboarding that appeared in *X-Men Unlimited*. When I handed in the script, I jokingly sent an email that said, "I really enjoyed writing this script, and if you ever had a *Jubilee* series in the works, I would love to write that." I was joking, because never in a million years did I believe they'd be doing a series about Jubilee. I got an email back saying, "I'm accepting pitches for a Jubilee series. Send me a pitch and I'll totally put you in the running." I thought, "Wow, that's the silliest pitch I ever heard, but I'm writing a pitch right now." I sent in a pitch and I won. I won the Jubilee series.

That's about when Tom Brevoot had contacted me, and that's when he came to me about the whole "Avengers: Disassembled" thing. He said, "Brian's taking over *Avengers*, and we're doing things in *Captain America, Iron Man*, and *Thor* all at the same time. How would you like to write *Captain America*?" which was like winning the lottery. I said, "Yes, I'd love to write *Captain America*. I'm writing *Jubilee* right now!" [*Laughs.*]

Abrams: What were your editors like compared to Erik Larsen?

Kirkman: Tom, I think, is one of the best editors Marvel has ever had; he's definitely one of the best editors now. To be able to come into Marvel and be working for him was pretty good. My ex-Epic editor ended up leaving to do something else, but it was clear that she had no power and no say whatsoever because she would tell me things and the next day she would say, "Yeah, sorry, I shouldn't have said that." It's really frustrating to hear one day, "Jubilee can wear a blue hat," and then the next day, "Blue hats? Not allowed here at Marvel." To go from that to working with Tom was a breath of fresh air. Tom would say, "You're right Robert. It's all blue hats from now on," and if anyone had said, "No, no blue hats," Tom would say, "Fuck you, I'm Tom Brevoort! Blue hats it is."

Abrams: Sleepwalker has never been taken as seriously as other characters like Spider-Man or Wolverine. Along with Darkhawk and Speedball, whom you also brought back with your run on *Marvel Team-Up*, he's become marginalized as a jokey Z-grade character. What attracted you to them?

Kirkman: The fact that they're not taken seriously or well respected is bullshit. That pisses me off that people do that, because the only difference between Luke Cage and Darkhawk is that Luke Cage debuted in the '70s and Darkhawk debuted in 1992. I think that because we have an aging comic book audience, the majority of the people that read *Darkhawk* were older than I was. I don't think that I'm in the younger section of comic book readers, but anyone that was thirty when Luke Cage was created thought he was silly, while anyone that was fourteen thought that Luke Cage was the coolest character ever created. It's the same thing with *Darkhawk*. Anyone who read *Darkhawk* when they were thirty thought he was silly, and anyone who read him at fourteen thought he was great. What it really comes down to is when you were in that sweet spot, that twelve-to-sixteen age range.

Anyone who was between twelve and sixteen [in the '60s] will tell you Stan Lee and Jack Kirby were the greatest comics ever created, and they'd be right. Anyone who grew up in the '70s that any comic in the '70s was the greatest, and they'd be wrong; same with the '80s and same with the '90s. I have an affinity for those characters, while other people have an affinity for Luke Cage and Iron Fist. I think Iron Fist is the stupidest-looking character ever created. C'mon, he's got the giant collar, the slippers, he's wearing a bandana—he's a terrible-looking character. That's because I wasn't at an age when I was reading the original John Byrne *Iron Fist* issues.

I think the editor at the time said, "*Sleepwalker* is *The Sandman* done right," which is like saying *Spider-Man* is *The Sandman* done right. It's ridiculous and a very odd comparison because *Sandman* is a very serious work of fiction and *Sleepwalker* . . . isn't bad just because he fought a guy in the second issue with an eightball as a head and he flew around in a pool rack and his weapon was a cue stick—that's comics! There are odd things in every era. In *Fantastic Four* #2 or #3, there's a nuclear missile in New York City, and they detonate it in the Hudson River and everyone's fine. If I see one more [character] in a classic *Fantastic Four* issue turn into an asbestos flame retardant to cut through the Human Torch's flames . . . You can't say one era of comics is sillier than another.

Abrams: The original *Marvel Team-Up* was a fairly continuity-less series but, with the Titannus and the Iron Maniac characters, you seemed pretty eager to provide a story for the good guys' otherwise random encounters to take place around. How important was it for you to establish an overarching story for the characters?

Kirkman: I'd like to point out that my run on *Marvel Team-Up* was the longest run since the original series. They had relaunched *Marvel Team-Up* three or four times—I think *Ultimate Marvel Team-Up* ran to #18 [#16 plus an annual], *Spider-Man Team-Up* ran till #7, and I think there was another *Marvel Team-Up* that ran for eleven issues. When Tom Brevoort offered me *Marvel Team-Up* after my *Captain America* run, I asked if I could use Rick Jones. When Spider-Man and Wolverine are in the book, people who like Spider-Man and Wolverine buy it. The next week, when it's Reed Richards and Dr. Strange, nobody picks that book up. In issue #4 when Spider-Man comes back, the fans will come back. There's no consistent sales level to that series whatsoever. As a result, what they'd do in the past is call it *Spider-Man Team-Up*, and he'd be in every issue.

I don't know why I didn't do that. I probably should have done that and been able to sell every issue. Instead of just having an arbitrary, secondary Spider-Man series that just happens to tell the stories of when he met other people, I wanted to do a monthly series about the Marvel universe with continuity within the series. The main characters would change but there were always different threats and events that would continue throughout. I just thought I should make it a continuous story that you would continue reading whether you liked the characters or not.

Abrams: How many characters did you have in mind?

Kirkman: I was making up stories as I went along. By the time I was working at Marvel, I was well aware of the fact that everything could end at any moment, especially after the *Sleepwalker* debacle. I had my Titannus arc, and when I got to issue #3 or #4, they told me we were going up to #12, so I started planning up until issue #12. I thought for a long time that issue #13 would be the last issue, and then around #11, they said, "Things are going OK. Sales are looking all right so we're going to keep going until #18." I had to come up with a new idea for issue #13, and that's how the *Invincible* crossover issue came about. I had no idea what I was going to do, so I did that for #14. I sent them a list of things I could do as a joke, or I did a list with the fourth item being a joke, saying, "Or we could do a crossover with Spider-Man and Invincible. How cool would that be? I know the guy that does the book, I could probably make that happen."

Tom Brevoort wrote back, "That sounds really cool. Let's make it happen," and it happened. For issues #15–18, I used the idea I had for the second arc of *Sleepwalker* where he would team up with all different people that nobody expected much from, and it would be called "The League of Losers." I had the whole thing planned out down to the fact that they do save the world, but because of how time travel works out, nobody knows about it. I had that all worked out for *Sleepwalker*, because I was a fool, but then I brought it back.

They then told me, "You know what? We can talk it up to #24!" For #19, I wanted to do Freedom Ring as a series, and I wanted to bring back the Mandarin's ring from earlier in the series. I was going to do it as a series, but I think *Gravity* had just come out at Marvel and was doing really poorly, and because *Jubilee* had been canceled and *Captain America* was a short-time thing, I didn't want to do something that would be doomed from the start. I scrapped the idea to do a Freedom Ring series, and when I found out about going up to until #24, I asked Tom Brevoort if I could do what I planned for Freedom Ring's series in *Marvel Team-Up*. The idea of the Freedom ring was it was a book about a character who would get superpowers but is so terribly bad at it that it's the worst thing that happened to him. Every superhero had been about a hero who gets power and becomes a kickass superhero. Invincible and Spider-Man were both like that.

Issue #24 was the last issue, but I talked them into letting me do #25. I told them, "We're so close. Can we just do #25 so I can keep this series off?" They said, "Fine. #25. Last issue." And then they told me it was approved until #30. I had extended stuff so much that I had to do so much research for different characters that I said, "You know what? I'm so happy the book is continuing until #30, but I'm going to have to quit at #25. If you want to take #25 and give it to a new team, that's fine." It would be a good idea to let a new creative team on and start with that. Because *Civil War* had just started and they were starting so many series for that, and because I was quitting anyway, they decided to wrap it with #24 again, so I said, "No, no, I'll do #25."

Abrams: Considering that Curtis Doyle, Freedom Ring's alias, is a gay character, how did you plan on setting him up in a mainstream series?

Kirkman: There were a lot of things about that that were interesting. Freedom Ring was designed to be a terrible superhero, and at the same time, anytime anyone did a gay character in comics, it was a hyped-up, odd thing because everyone wanted to beat their chests and say, "I'm doing a gay character! I'm doing a gay character! I'm giving him AIDS and it's going to be a momentous, life-changing event." Nobody has done a gay character that wasn't supposed to be a stand-out event, and I just thought arbitrarily of making him a gay guy and not make it a big deal. It would be cool to have him just be a normal guy that asks another dude out and not show that as being anything unusual or noteworthy. I wanted to show him going out on that date, because I just wanted to have a guy go to the park with another guy and have lunch. I ended up getting a lot of positive responses to that from the gay community.

They told me, "It's great to see a character that is a character first and then happens to be gay," and I was glad to do that.

At the same time, it was probably the worst misstep I had in my career because I kept to my idea of him being a horrible superhero and winding up being killed. In the first three issues, it's "Oh my God! This guy is doing a down-to-earth portrayal of a gay guy going out on a date and it's completely downplayed and has nothing to do with the story. It's like Peter Parker—he's a superhero and he also happens to go out with women." I did this cool thing for the first three issues and then it became, "Oh, and then he got crippled. Oh, he's the worst superhero ever. Here's a realistic gay character and he's the worst superhero that ever lived and he just got killed." You could argue that heterosexual characters get killed all the time and that you can't get mad when he gets treated like every other character in comics and that was the thinking I had while I was writing it.

After I turned in the scripts, Joe Quesada was talking to me and he said, "I think you're not realizing how people might perceive this. People could perceive this as being really offensive."

I thought, "Well, that's crazy! Just because he's a gay character doesn't mean I shouldn't be able to kill him." I was inclined to think that it would be OK because it was done on purpose. There wasn't enough thought put into it. I thought, "I'm leaving the book, and he's my character and I'll kill him if I want to." I never even took into consideration the gay community's reaction and they were mighty angry.

It happened at a strange time at Marvel when there were a lot of coincidences. I guess there was something where the writer of some Marvel handbook made some series where the Rawhide Kid was gay part of continuity. He basically tried to say because it was in continuity, he wasn't really gay in the miniseries but was only acting gay to throw his villains off the trail. That was just trying to piece things together from a bunch of Marvel comics that didn't make sense, and what that was read as was, "Marvel is making that guy not gay now! That's offensive." It all came together in this perfect storm of a gay-hating Marvel, which was never the case.

Abrams: Is it difficult to get away from just recycling older characters or is that part of the appeal?

Kirkman: I don't really look at it like I'm recycling characters as much as continuing their story. I'm a big fan of continuing stories, so that's why *Invincible* and *Walking Dead* will continue for as long as sales will allow. If I could get to issue #300 on those books, I totally would, because I'm into showing a character's life and all the things they encounter. I love sequels and

I'll sometimes like a movie better when a sequel is made. For me, working at Marvel doesn't seem like I'm trotting out the same old guys but rather like I'm furthering their adventures.

Abrams: Many creators have decided not to create new characters they don't own. Do you prefer to save your new characters for Image?

Kirkman: I think that's a slippery slope. Once you start treating everything like it's gold and like it's something to be protected . . . I'm constantly creating new characters, and it's really not that difficult. There were about twenty seconds where I thought, "Titannus is a really cool character. Maybe I should make him a villain in *Invincible*." At the same time, it's cool to participate in the furthering of the Marvel universe. Sure, they're a corporation that takes new ideas and uses them as their own but at the same time, it's kinda neat to see something you've created punching Spider-Man in the face. I ended up making his origin that he was a Skrull, and I never could've done that in my regular series, and Iron Maniac is just a play on Tony Stark.

Once you start holding back, that makes things seem more important than they really are. The more you create, the easier it is to create, so I've never had a problem creating characters for Marvel. They're not the greatest guys that will be in Marvel comics for years and years, but it's a fun, easy thing to do and it's probably the most enjoyable thing I do in comics. Sitting down and creating a book is probably the best part of doing comics. Doing the actual work is a lot of fun, too, but those additional moments when you're sitting down and brainstorming on different aspects of the character and what they could lead to, it's so much fun that I have no real problem giving a few to Marvel.

Abrams: Why didn't *Marvel Team-Up* last? Was the "League of Losers" story arc a problem considering it didn't feature any headlining characters?

Kirkman: I think the "League of Losers" storyline was the most popular story of my run. Saleswise, there wasn't a huge spike for it, but I don't think it hurt the series at all. It's the story, of the run, that I hear people still talking about online. It didn't last because it didn't have a core cast. Marvel succeeds, because everyone's invested in the universe. They have the best universe, they have the best characters, and everyone is invested in seeing what happens to those characters and the world around them, so any book invested in that world is a better seller.

If they tell people, *Punisher: War Journal* is an integral part of "Civil War," which is an integral part of the Marvel Universe, it will sell well. *Marvel Team-Up* was peripheral: There was no main character and no dramatic change. Spider-Man appears, but he doesn't get a new haircut or become a vegetarian or get his foot cut off in this issue, so it's not an integral part of the universe people are invested in.

Abrams: *Terror Inc.*, a series whose title character you use in "The League of Losers," just got revived by David Lapham under the Max imprint with a particularly dark slant to it. Do you feel that that signals a need to make Marvel's '90s characters darker to make them popular again? Is this just another example of a logical extension of the character?

Kirkman: I don't think so. He's just an immortal that uses other people's body parts to sustain his life, and that lends itself to a dark take. I don't think a crime-noir *Sleepwalker* series would do any better than a superhero *Sleepwalker* series. The '90s characters by design don't need a dark take to be relevant, nor does any superhero concept. That's the trap created by the success of *The Dark Knight Returns* and *Watchmen* that still affects things to this day.

Abrams: Is the early demise of Epic indicative of a failure on Marvel's part to capitalize on a market outside of their already established ones?

Kirkman: Epic was participating in the Marvel universe and there were a few things that were original ideas, but Marvel plays off of the nostalgia of people that have been reading their books for years. That's what sells their comics. Epic was a fundamentally flawed idea from start to finish.

Abrams: Is there a place on the market for earnest, modern, light-hearted superhero series?

Kirkman: Right now, the audience doesn't want to feel that they're reading children's material, and the main demographic reading comics is eighteen to forty because we haven't been getting as many new readers and we haven't been losing all the readers we were losing, because comics are technically more sophisticated. Because of that sophistication and the urge to keep readers around as they grow up, it's harder to keep books light. Even *Invincible* has a dark tone; that's just something that appealed to me. I don't want to sound critical of older comic readers because I am an older comic reader, but those kind of books will always be a hard sell until somebody comes along and finds a way to get kids to start reading comics and bring a younger audience into the medium.

CONTINUING THE STORY

Abrams: How does your deal with Image work: Do you own your Image properties outright or share them with artists or with Image?

Kirkman: Everything done at Image is completely creator-owned. On the book where the artists helped me create them, the artist co-owns, and on the books where I created everything myself and brought an artist on to do the book . . . The creators of the book own the book. Image is a completely creator-owned company, Image doesn't own any trademarks other the Image "I" logo.

Abrams: What do you wish were different, if anything, about your working conditions with Marvel?

Kirkman: I'd love to be able to walk in and say "I'm writing Spider-Man and this guy is drawing it." That's definitely something I would change, if I had the power, but at the same time, I understand why I don't have that power. There are certainly things within the structure of how things work. I think things could be more efficient. I guess that sounds a little arrogant, but I come from a position where I've done every job that can be done on a comic; I've been an editor, I've been an inker, I've been a letterer, I've penciled comics before, I've worked at a comic book store, I've opened comic boxes and stocked shelves. I've done everything you can do with a comic book; I read comic books, I've smoked comic books, I've slept on comic books, I've turned comic books into a giant boat and ridden it down the stream—I've done it all.

There are certain times I'm thinking, "Why did you tell an artist this? Why did you tell me that? Why did you have me do this when I could've done that? What is going on?!" A lot of times I think that there are too many cooks in the kitchen. I just got a script where an editor went through and fixed all my typos, and while doing that, he underlined all my emboldened words. When I write a script, I make words bold instead of typing them in all caps, because when a letterer goes in to letter a book and the book is typed in all caps, he has to go in and find all the caps words to embolden, because when you're doing it in a lettering program, the text has to be emboldened. All caps doesn't translate.

When he was fixing my typos, he took out all the words I had emboldened and underlined them. That's frankly stupid because now the letterer has to take all the underlined words and embolden them. I know this and the editor doesn't, so he makes it underlined. There's a lot of times when the editors do little shit like that where if that editor were not doing that it would not slow things down. There are more serious examples, but there are thousands of instances of my time working at Marvel where I'm slapping my head saying, "That was unnecessary."

Abrams: You pitched *The Irredeemable Ant-Man* as an ongoing series, but it was turned into a twelve-issue miniseries.

Kirkman: It was turned into a twelve-issue cancelled series. I don't think anybody would like to pretend it was a miniseries.

Abrams: Do you feel that now *Marvel Zombies* has gone into its sixth printing and now that there's a sequel that you can get your projects out there more readily?

Kirkman: Um, no. [*Both laugh.*] *Ant-Man* debuted after *Marvel Zombies* and that success didn't seem to translate. I get people reading *Invincible* because of *Walking Dead* but it's really hard to translate the success of one book to another one. *Wanted* didn't sell as well as *Ultimate X-Men* or anything else Mark Millar did. There are so many things that contribute to the success of a book. It could be argued that because of *Marvel Zombies*, there are five thousand that bought *Marvel Zombies* that will now buy every single thing I now do and that means *Ant-Man* would've sold only ten thousand copies instead of fifteen thousand otherwise, but it's hard to see that for sure. To answer your question: no! If only it did.

Abrams: Do you think you can get back to *Science Dog* finally?

Kirkman: I could do *Science Dog* tomorrow, if I wanted to. I think it would sell pretty well and it would be fine. I've gotten to the point at Image where I've had enough success with them that they know I'm responsible enough to pick my own projects. The approval process between Image Comics and myself is I say, "I would like to do this book," and they say, "That's OK." I could do *Science Dog* anytime I wanted, it's just that I don't want to do *Science Dog* without Cory. Cory and I want *Science Dog* to be perfect when we're both in a position to do *Science Dog* for a long time. We're doing twelve-page *Science Dog* back-up stories in every twenty-fifth issue of *Invincible*, just because that's silly and hilarious, and right now that's pretty much all you're going to see from that.

Abrams: What other genres are you interested in tackling?

Kirkman: I want to eventually do more creator-owned work, because I've had my fun at Marvel and have gotten to do a lot of things I've wanted to do, but at the time I've spent at Marvel and been exclusive to Marvel, I haven't done a new creator-owned series. I've got a pile of creator-owned series ideas I've accumulated over the past four years. I went from doing *Tech Jacket, Invincible, Walking Dead, Capes, Brit, Cloudfall,* and whatever I forgot in there in a year and a half to just doing *Invincible* and *Walking Dead*. I was able to do *The Astounding Wolf-Man* also, but for the most part I've had to hold back and there's been a pretty big backlog of ideas I'd like to do. I'd like to do science-fiction books, Westerns—I wouldn't mind doing a romance book. I have a lot of ideas for new superhero books. I'm not ashamed that I enjoy superhero comics and enjoy doing them. At the same time, I enjoy doing *The Walking Dead*, and so I'd like to eventually do more comics for the audience that reads *The Walking Dead* and doesn't necessarily like superhero comics.

Nine Questions with Robert Kirkman

MARC-OLIVER FRISCH / 2010

From *Der Tagesspiegel*, March 2010. Reprinted by permission of Marc-Oliver Frisch

In February 2010, on the occasion of the German release of the tenth volume of *The Walking Dead*, Marc-Oliver Frisch had the opportunity to ask Robert Kirkman a series of questions.

(Disclosure: At the time of the interview, Frisch was the translator of the German edition of *The Walking Dead*. Versions of this interview were published in *The Walking Dead 10: Dämonen*, as well as at Berlin's *Der Tagesspiegel*, in 2010.)

Frisch: Looking back at the last six years' worth of *The Walking Dead*, are you happy with the way things have gone, in terms of the story and in terms of how it's been realized? Is there anything in particular that you'd want to do differently with the gift of hindsight?

Kirkman: Maybe . . . *maybe* I wouldn't have cut Rick's hand off. I don't know, it was such a cool moment that I decided to throw caution to the wind and just do it. Other than that . . . nothing. The book is more successful than I ever could have imagined and I'm still having as much fun (if not more) as I did when I started it, so I don't think I'd want to change anything.

Frisch: Since we last talked five years back, the cast of *The Walking Dead* has changed dramatically—only a handful of the characters from back then remain. Are there any "right" or "wrong" reasons to let a given character die? How do you know losing a cast member is better for the book than keeping them around?

Kirkman: I don't. I have a rule on killing characters . . . I do it without thinking. I kind of like that . . . it seems more real to me. If I ever kept a character around because I thought it would be good for the story, I'd feel like I was cheating. That's not how death works. It's supposed to be quick and

In a bout of instability, Carol talks and embraces a zombie in a moment that shocks her fellow survivors. From *The Walking Dead*, Book 4, by Robert Kirkman and Charlie Adlard; Image Comics, 2009.

sudden and disruptive. So I try to keep that in mind. Nine times out of ten, I know when a character is going to die many issues before it happens, but I try to never consider, "What if I kept these people alive?" Once I think of a good reason to kill them, I put it out of my mind . . . that's it, it's decided, they're dying. The only character I've ever given a stay of execution is Abraham, and that's because he was planned to die pretty soon after his introduction, but his character changed drastically shortly before he was introduced in the book . . . so I changed things around to suit that.

Frisch: As the series progresses and the characters—especially Rick—go through radical ordeals, make tough choices and sometimes do gruesome things, are you worried that the audience might get lost trying to find someone in the book to empathize with and root for?

Kirkman: That is a concern. I do try to make sure that I show their humanity as often as possible. I don't think any characters in the book have gotten to the point where they're irredeemable. If I feel I've gone over that edge of making the characters too unlikeable . . . I do my best to do something to pull them back over as soon as possible. I try to be very mindful of the fact that readers need someone to root for, but at the same time, this is a dark story, and I try to never pull any punches. We'll see.

Frisch: Do you think the book could work without a recurring protagonist like Rick? Is he expendable?

Kirkman: He could be . . . eventually. Maybe I've already said too much. Rick could die at any moment. That's a fact. Nobody in this book is safe. Whether the book could survive without him, or not . . . I hope to one day find out.

Frisch: At this point in the story, it seems the real danger for the cast often doesn't originate with the zombies anymore, but with other people—or with themselves. Were you always aware that this was going to be the direction of the series?

Kirkman: Yes. The zombies are something with a fixed set of behaviors. They're something you can learn to avoid. I always knew I wanted to get to a point in this book where people knew how to deal with them. They're still a threat, but it's something our characters are prepared for.

Frisch: As far as the Governor is concerned, who was the major villain for a couple of years, I think everyone probably expected a Western-style showdown with Rick or Michonne—and then, when the time came, things didn't go down quite like that. Do you consciously play with these kinds of genre expectations?

Kirkman: All the time. I try to steer expectations one way and then do something different. That's the writer's job, right? At the same time, I do try to sometimes give readers exactly what they want. I try to change things up as much as possible to keep people guessing.

Frisch: With serial fiction that's driven, to an extent, by a "big mystery," there always seems to be the danger of disappointing the audience when it's finally resolved, like, say, *The X-Files* did with the alien conspiracy angle. Is it a concern of yours, regarding the zombie plague, that readers might at one point demand a resolution, or might be disappointed with the one presented to them?

Kirkman: I've always maintained that the cause of the zombie plague is completely useless in the context of this story. I plan to never reveal it. So hopefully people won't be disappointed by that—because I've been saying that since the beginning. This book is about the characters.

Frisch: It seems you'd found a great balance between creator-owned work and work-for-hire assignments, with some very successful results on both ends. Why go through the hassle of joining Image Comics as a partner?

Kirkman: The hassle was doing work-for-hire. It just didn't suit me. I wasn't interested in it. All I wanted to do was creator-owned work. Also, there's that commonly held belief that you have to do work-for-hire to finance creator-owned work . . . which most people think never makes any money. But I was doing work-for-hire for Marvel, and it accounted for less than a quarter of my income and three quarters of my workload. I'd always wanted to work at Marvel . . . and I did it. So it was time to focus on what I enjoyed, which is doing whatever I want with no restrictions. I'm happier than I've ever been, and sales on all my books have gone up since I left Marvel . . . so things are great.

Frisch: From listening to creators, it seems that work-for-hire is what pays the bills from month to month, whereas creator-owned work is more something that pays off in the long term. Would you say that's a fair way of putting things?

Kirkman: For some, sure . . . but maybe they're just not putting the same effort into their creator-owned work that they are in their work-for-hire. I mean, sure . . . it's hard to start a career in creator-owned work and stay there forever. That's because creator-owned work sells almost entirely based on the popularity of the creator and very few creator-owned books take off like *Bone* or *Strangers in Paradise* and allow the creator to stick with it. I started out in creator-owned, gained some notoriety with it, moved on to Marvel, got my name out there a little more, and now I am able to make a living only at creator-owned books. I don't agree that you have to continue doing both . . . especially if it's not something you want to do.

The Geek's Guide to the Galaxy Podcast Episode 25: Interview with Robert Kirkman

JOHN JOSEPH ADAMS AND DAVID BARR KIRTLEY / 2010

From *Geek's Guide to the Galaxy Podcast*, November 11, 2010. Reprinted by permission of John Joseph Adams and David Barr Kirtley

David Barr Kirtley: Hello, and welcome to Episode 25 of Geek's Guide to the Galaxy!

John Joseph Adams: Hi, this is John Joseph Adams. I'm the editor of *Lightspeed* and *Fantasy* magazines, and I've also edited several anthologies such as The Living Dead and The Living Dead 2, and Wastelands, and some others.

Kirtley: And I'm David Barr Kirtley. My short fiction appears in books such as New Voices in Science Fiction and Fantasy: The Best of the Year, and my most recent stories are "Cats in Victory" in Lightspeed, "The Skull-Faced City" in The Living Dead 2, and "Family Tree" in The Way of the Wizard. And today on the show we'll be interviewing Robert Kirkman, who wrote the graphic novel series The Walking Dead, which is now a new hit series on AMC. And AMC just announced that they've picked up the show for a second season of thirteen episodes. According to their press release, "Since debuting on Halloween, The Walking Dead has broken ratings records, with the series reaching more adults age eighteen to forty-nine than any other show in the history of cable television." So we'll be talking to Robert Kirkman about his various graphic novel projects and about the new show, and stick around after the interview, when John and I'll be talking about some zombie stuff that we've watched recently, including The Walking Dead TV series.

Adams: Okay, so let's get Robert Kirkman on the phone.

Kirtley: Hi, this is Dave and John from Geek's Guide to the Galaxy.

Robert Kirkman: Hey, this is Robert Kirkman. How you doing?

Kirtley: Good. Thanks for joining us on the show.

Adams: Okay, so The Walking Dead puts just as much emphasis on survival as it does on battling zombies. Why did you decide to focus so much on the survival aspect?

Kirkman: I guess at my core I'm just a big girl that likes soap operas. The thing that I enjoy, the parts of the comic that I really like writing, are the emotional bits, the relationship stuff, the interaction between Rick and Carl. All that stuff. The zombies are really just there to trick dudes into reading it, is basically what it boils down to.

Kirtley: Could you talk about how much thought you put into the survival aspect. Did you study survivalism or anything like that?

Kirkman: No, I have no studies in survivalism. I Google enough to make it somehow seem realistic when I have to have someone dress a wound. One of the things I most like to do in the book is make things up in a way that seems realistic. In particular there's one scene where a guy dresses a wound, and I had friends that were like, "Wow, look at you, doing your research, that's amazing," but I really made up half of what the guy does because I thought it seemed cool. Because most of the time when I do research, I end up with things that aren't really exciting, like, "Oh, that's a really simple way to do that. Oh, you clean a wound by washing it out with water." That's dull. So I did something with tea leaves and wax, and I got a letter in from a guy that said that would actually cause it to get infected and he would have to have it amputated, but it seems like a nice realistic thing when you're reading the comic. And then to counteract how fake it is, I just don't print that guy's letter. [*Laughter.*] So that's how I do that.

Kirtley: So it's important that people shouldn't use The Walking Dead as a reference for medical school or whatever?

Kirkman: Oh, please, lord, don't anyone do anything from this comic book thinking that it actually works. I don't want to be responsible for someone getting their leg cut off . . . again. [*Laughter.*]

Kirtley: The Walking Dead is very convincing in the way that it portrays the strained emotions of the characters. Do you have any tricks for putting yourself inside their heads, and did you do any research into that, into disaster psychology or anything like that?

Kirkman: Well, I know a lot of troubled people, so that helps. But a lot of times it's just thinking about, "What I would do in that situation?" and doing the opposite, or thinking about what I would do in that situation if I were a crazy person. But, you know, if I were to always just put myself in that situation and do what I would do, everyone would behave the same way, so it's really just a matter of changing things up as best you can and trying to keep things believable. The other thing I do is I try to map out how characters react to certain things, and how their reactions are going to change over time based on other things they've experienced, so you'll see a character like Glenn react a certain way in the early issues, but as he goes through those experiences and learns, over time his reactions will vary later on in the series.

Kirtley: So a prison seems like a natural setting for a zombie story, but The Walking Dead was, I think, the first time I'd ever seen that done. How did you get the idea to have your characters take refuge in a prison, and what sort of benefits or drawbacks were there to using that as a setting?

Kirkman: You know, it kind of came out of the blood. It wasn't like a hard study I did to determine whether it was going to be a prison or—it was originally going to be a high school, because the high school I attended had a courtyard, and in the center of it there was a building basically shaped like an O, and I was going to base the high school in the comic book on that, you know, because the courtyard would be a place where they can actually grow food and have a little outside area that was fully protected. And then it occurred to me that high schools don't really have beds, and as I was writing it I was like, "Oh, and they'll take the principal's couch, and what, are they going to fight over that? They'll be sleeping on the floor, this is awful! There's like one room with showers in the gym but that's about it, and that's not good, and then it occurred to me that prisons and high schools are pretty much exactly the same, except you go to sleep in a prison, so that seemed like a more ideal thing for the story. They would have more things to actually live off of inside a prison, and it would be already be well fortified. It seemed like a natural fit. It is kind of odd to think that no one's really set a story like this in a prison before.

Kirtley: Have you spent a lot of time in prison yourself?

Kirkman: I don't really like to talk about that period in my life, but . . . yes. No, I've never even set foot inside a prison. That's why the prison is completely 100 percent inaccurate and made up in the comic book series.

Adams: How did The Walking Dead TV series come about, and what was the development process like?

Kirkman: It's funny, because the development process was very long and drawn out and very quick at the same time, because there was kind of a false start where Frank Darabont contacted me because he had a deal with NBC and wanted to do a pilot, and he was going to make the pilot of The Walking Dead, and it almost happened at NBC in 2005, but that fell through because NBC decided they didn't want zombies to be in the show, after they read the script, which is a funny story that he likes to tell, so I feel okay in telling it, but it kind of went into limbo after that, and there was some interest here and there but nothing ever really came together, and then about eighteen months ago Frank contacted me again and said, "What you think about AMC?" and I said, "Well, you know, I love me some *Breaking Bad* and some *Mad Men*, so I'm quite keen on AMC." And he was telling me that they were interested, and Gale Anne Hurd had been brought in somewhere along the way, and she kind of got everything back on track and brought AMC to the table and made it happen. So eighteen months ago we started out on this, and now there's a show that's going to be on the air in a week, so it was really kind of an unusually fast process from that point on.

Adams: How involved have you been in the production?

Kirkman: You know, fairly involved. I've gone out to the writers' room a few times, and spent a week here and a week there working with them, and then I actually wrote the fourth episode. So, you know, fairly involved. I'm an executive producer. I could fire Frank Darabont if I wanted to . . . I couldn't really. [*Laughter.*] I don't know. I should call someone and say I want to know. You know, I've been on set a bunch. I mean, my job to me is to make sure that the show is awesome, just because I feel that the people who read the comic book and like the comic book deserve the television show to not suck, and so I always wanted to have a hand in it just to make sure that everything was good for them, just because I feel like I owe them, and thankfully I haven't really had to do much because Frank and everybody involved were also out to do an awesome show, and their version of awesome is the same version as mine, and the show turned out to be pretty great.

Adams: What kind of changes should fans of the comic be expecting to see in the show?

Kirkman: Well, Rick is a duck. [*Laughter.*] And they all live in a spaceship . . . No, there's some cool characters that I kind of wish were in the comic book. Merle and Daryl Dixon are pretty awesome, and they're wholly original to the television series, and there's other characters like T-Dog and Morales and Jackie that you're not going to recognize from the comic because they're not in it, but they're welcome additions and they bring a lot to the show and there's cool stuff going on, and there's little storylines here and there that kind of crop up, and aren't from the comic book but they fit seamlessly into what the comic book has always been about, and if you have a poor memory you may not remember that they're not in a comic book, and so they don't really stick out in that respect. But there are a lot of things that Frank did that I'm just jealous of, where he would take a scene and add to it, where he would read the comic book and go, "You know what, Kirkman? That was a cool couple of pages, but I'm going to do this with it," and it's so obvious and awesome that I look back, I'm like, "Why didn't I do that begin with? Like, what the hell's wrong with me? So, you know, there's a lot of things like that that just kind of piss me off, so I'm a little bitter about the show.

Kirtley: So one recent issue of The Walking Dead featured a color story by Ryan Ottley. How did that come about?

Kirkman: Well, one of the most frustrating things about The Walking Dead series is that since day one, when I wrote a text piece in the back of the first issue about how I plan for this series to go on for years, and this is a zombie movie that never ends, yadda yadda yadda, I started getting letters from people that would say, "Well, you know, the third issue is pretty good, and I like these three issues, but I just don't see how you're going to get this to be interesting for a year." Or like when issue ten would come out it would be like, "It's been pretty good for ten issues, but I don't see how you're going to keep this story interesting, because it just seems like it can become repetitive and mundane, and not be able to keep this thing going; it seems like you're going to run out of ideas," and so I would start jokingly replying that I'm fully aware that I'm going to run out of ideas, I'm clocking that I will probably run out of ideas by around issue 75, and at that point I'm not going to stop the book, because I'm a sellout, I'm just going to add aliens into the book to make it more interesting, and that'll be my "jumping the shark" moment, and the book will swiftly be canceled after that, but for a time there will be aliens in the book. And it was all a big joke, and at the time, you know—issue 3, issue 10, issue 12—issue 75 seemed really far away, and it seemed like, "I may never make it to that, I mean, we'll see, who knows?" And so it was something that came up in the letters column—a lot of people would respond and be like, "You know, I'm going to read this book until issue 75 when the aliens come, and then quit." So I feel like the hard-core fans, the people who actually read the letters column, were very acutely aware that issue 75 was coming, and I didn't want to just not do anything, but I wasn't actually going to put aliens in the book, so I thought it would be fun to do an out-of-continuity backup story that was a fun gag that played off of the "aliens in issue 75" joke that had been running through the letters column for like seventy-five issues, and much to my dismay, some fans thought that it was in-continuity, and so I got some letters from some people who had never read the letters column, who hadn't even read the letters column in that issue, where it talks about how the story is just a gag, who thought that I had somehow decided that the book was in color now, and drawn by Ryan Oteley now, and featured aliens and science-fiction weaponry and stuff. I don't know, there weren't that many people who thought that. So I think most people just thought it was a funny gag, but I sure had a lot of fun doing it. It was kind of fun to write the characters in a different way, and seeing Michonne with a light saber was pretty awesome.

Adams: So it was recently announced that you'll be doing some Walking Dead novels cowritten with novelist Jay Bonansinga. What can you tell us about those?

Kirkman: The novels will basically be some expanded backstory for the comic book series, so they'll take place in the comic book continuity, and I don't really want to say who the first one is about just yet, but it's basically really awesome characters from the comic book series that aren't in the comic book series anymore, so it's people that . . . well, they've died. It's fan favorites that people want to know more about, and so we're going to be telling a really cool history of this character and how they came to the point where they were at when we met them in the comic book series.

Kirtley: So in recent years all sorts of new variations on zombies have appeared—fast zombies, zombie romance, zombie superheroes. What's been your take on all of this?

Kirkman: You know, the more the better. I actually like it. Zombie superheroes . . . I guess I was kind of a part of that. But yeah, I'm all for it. Zombie romance sounds a little gross. But I like zombies, and as long as it's good, I don't care if there's a zombie cooking show, as long as it's entertaining. I'm certainly not a zombie purist that can't stand running zombies. They're not right for The Walking Dead, I mean, that's not what the show or the comic book is about, but I really like the Dawn of the Dead remake. It's a really cool movie, and the fast zombies don't really bug me. It's ridiculous that they're busting through walls and stuff, don't get me wrong, but it works for that movie, and so I don't really have a problem with it. It's better than vampires, right?

Kirtley: So do you think that the zombies as we've seen them in The Walking Dead—the sort of Romero-style zombies—is that what Walking Dead is always going to be, or will there ever be any sort of other supernatural element introduced further down the road do you think?

Kirkman: No supernatural elements. I swear. You know, while I do think zombies of different variations are very cool, I don't think that they're cool for The Walking Dead, so the classic Romero zombies that we have now are not going to change very much. Now, we see in the comic books that there are different things that happen to a zombie over time, you know, in the comic book series there's even some that have grown a little bit lethargic and aren't quite as threatening as fresher zombies. But they're not going to be sprouting wings anytime soon, basically. Although that is a pretty good idea.

Adams: Your short story "Alone, Together" appears in my anthology *The Living Dead 2*.

Kirkman: Oh, we've got to plug your anthology, blah blah blah . . . [*Laughter.*]

Adams: Yes, we do. So . . . what was the process of writing that story like, and how is writing a short story different from writing a comic book?

Kirtley: And don't worry, we only have ten questions on this subject. [*Laughter.*]

Kirkman: No, it's a very good anthology, everyone should run out and buy it. It's the one with the blue cover. It's funny, I was actually in a bookstore waiting in line, and someone in another line across from the register was there buying the book, and I thought that was very cool, and I didn't say anything to them because I'm actually quite shy. But anyway, it's very different because when I'm writing a comic book, I can go, "Hey, Charlie, do something cool, they're saying this," and he turns it into an awesome panel, and people read it and they think, "Oh, that Robert Kirkman guy is a great writer, because he told Charlie to draw something cool," and I didn't really do crap, so comic writing is much easier, and then when you sit down to write prose . . . it's funny, that's actually the first prose I've written since high school, just because I've been busy, dammit, but you know, it's work, it's hard, because you have to like . . . take words and actually make them . . . read well, I guess, so there's a reason why Jay Bonansinga is working on The Walking Dead novels with me. I think it's a pain in the ass. But I had a lot of fun with it, and it's a good story, people should buy those books, right? It's a good story, right?

Adams: I agree.

Kirtley: Yeah, it's great.

Adams: Well, I put it first in the book, so obviously I thought it was pretty good.

Kirkman: Yeah, what's up with that?

Adams: So how did you first break into writing comic books?

Kirkman: I did a comic book and I published it myself. I was lucky enough to meet Tony Moore in seventh grade, and so I knew that guy, and was able to trick him into drawing comic books for me at a very young age. So shortly after high school the two of us started working on a book called Battle Pope, and then from that I started a publishing company called Funk-O-Tron, and I published that starting in June of 2000, and then did that book for about two years before I started getting work at Image Comics, and the rest is history.

Adams: How difficult was it doing that, publishing your own comic book starting from the ground up?

Kirkman: You know, in a lot of ways it was easy, just because there's not a lot of moving parts in comics. There's one distributor that distributes to all the comic book stores in the country, and there was a printer that was in Canada that most people used, and so I would work with Tony Moore to make the comic book, we would send that to Canada, and then that would be sent from the printer in Canada to the one distributor, and then it would go to comic book stores, so once you get that system down it's really a fairly easy process, but there's a lot of troublesome financing stuff that came into it, and then the actual production of a comic book is not something that people just know off the top of their heads—you know, what kind of paper to draw your pages on, how you make the word balloons, and different things that have to be done in order to turn a bunch of pieces of paper into a comic book, or things that I kind of had to teach myself, but it was a lot of fun, and it seemed to lead to something, but it was a very hard time in my life. By the time I started actually making money in comics I was about $50,000 in debt, and by "making money in comics" I mean I started making about $500 a year, so there were some tough times along the way, but in the end it all worked out swimmingly. I couldn't be happier.

Adams: What advice would you have for aspiring comic book artists and writers today?

Kirkman: Give up! [*Laughter.*] No, I mean, one thing that is much more prominent now than it was when I was starting out is the internet, so people these days could do exactly what I did, and instead of losing money by getting it all printed up and distributed and stuff, they could actually just put it on-line, and that's mostly free if you teach yourself how to do it, and spread the word through message boards that your website is there, and that's really the way I would recommend it. It's also easier if you're better. The better you are, the easier it is to break in, which I know sounds simple, but it's really hard to recognize if you're not good. If you can recognize that you're not good, that's really important, because if you're not good you can either give up or get better, and if you think you're great, you're probably not going to get better, and then it's never going to happen. Unless you are great, and then it's going to be easy. You'll probably have to play that back a few times to get it, but it all makes sense, I promise.

Kirtley: So what do you think about the current state of the comic book industry, and are there any changes you'd like to see made?

Kirkman: Well, sure, there's tons of changes. You know, on one hand I like it, I think it's cool, there's good comics being made, and everybody's having a good time. On the other hand it frustrates me that most people—it's harder to do creator-owned material, I understand that, but I wish that people were taking more risks with comics and doing more creator-owned stuff, and not simply just working for Marvel and DC, I mean, that's the main frustration that I have. Also I wish that the books of Marvel and DC were better. But whatever, there are a lot of good books coming out from them, so I probably shouldn't really complain about that, but I don't know, there are a lot of things that you could complain about, but I'm actually really optimistic, just because as we move into the digital era I think that the problems that we've had with distribution, getting books out to a larger audience, are going to go away, and as we start to reach a larger audience we're not going to be selling comic books to the same people we've been selling comic books to for the last twenty years, and so we're not going to try to sell original material to an audience that's predisposed to keeping their runs of Daredevil intact, and so hopefully we'll be finding people that are more open to create their own stuff and new ideas, and that'll make for a better comic book industry because people will be doing more original stuff, and I think more original stuff is really what we need.

Kirtley: And you've talked particularly about the comic book industry not doing enough to appeal to younger readers?

Kirkman: Yeah, I mean, that's another thing with mainstream comics catering to a fan base that is aging, they have kind of lost the younger audience, and so I wish that more people were doing books for a younger audience, and I'm happy to say that I'm working on a number of books that are for all ages, that I'll be rolling out soon, so I'm going to try to fix that problem instead of just complaining about it. But yeah, it's kind of sad that someone—you know, my son, for instance, if he were to see a Wolverine cartoon and want to read a Wolverine comic, that's a very hard thing for him to do. You know, the trade paperbacks in bookstores are a convoluted mess. It's not like in manga where you can go, "Okay, here's volume one and here's volume thirty-seven." If you go to buy Wolverine, there's thirty-five different trades with different names, and it's hard to figure out where to begin. I just wish that things were set up more for a wider audience and appealed to a wider audience more.

Kirtley: Yeah, and could you talk about some of the books that you've worked on besides The Walking Dead, and which of them would you most recommend to readers who are new to your work?

Mark's father tells his son two different stories and the second story (the truth) is preceded by a similar but less frightening image of Omni-Man. Left: From *Invincible*, Compendium 1, by Robert Kirkman and Corey Walker; Image Comics, 2015.

Right: From *Invincible*, Compendium 1, by Robert Kirkman, Corey Walker, and Ryan Ottley; Image Comics, 2015.

Kirkman: Well, I do another book called Invincible, which is a superhero title. It's kind of everything I've ever liked about superhero comics boiled down and put into one comic book. It's a universe-spanning superhero tale that you can get in pretty much all in one series. It's also been running as long as Walking Dead, so it's rapidly approaching issue 80, so that's kind of cool, and there's trade paperbacks available and stuff. The premise is that Omni Man is the premiere superhero of the world, and Invincible is his son, who has just reached puberty and gained superpowers, and Omni Man—he thought that his father was this alien from another world who came to help earth, but actually it turns out that he's there to conquer, and Invincible and he are at odds, and so he ends up having to fight his father, and that happens very early on in the series, so there's a lot more story that happens after that. And then I do another book called The Astounding Wolfman, about a werewolf superhero, that has recently come to an end. I decided to end that with issue 25 so that I could focus on some newer projects, and I think there will be four trade paperbacks available for that—that's one I do with Jason Howard. It's pretty cool. And I cocreated another book with Todd McFarlane called Haunt, that is kind of an espionage book with supernatural ghost elements added in. It's about a secret agent who dies, and then his brother who's a priest is able to see him and interact with him as a ghost, and together they're able to form a super secret agent that's got ghost powers called Haunt, so it's a lot of fun that book. People should try it.

Kirtley: So are there any other recent or upcoming projects that you'd like to mention?

Kirkman: I have a new imprint at Image Comics called Skybound, which is basically my corner of Image Comics to do whatever I want and bring new books into the fold and shepherd them out to the audience, and one of the first books we're doing there at that imprint is called Witch Doctor, which I'm very excited about. It's about a scientist who basically uses scientific and medical know-how to combat supernatural things—werewolves, vampires, monsters from other dimensions—with science, and so it's a very realistic take on a supernatural story, and that's written by a new writer by the name of Brandon Seaford, and an artist named Lucas Kentnor, who are doing this thing, and it's probably one of the smartest comic books I've ever read, and that'll be coming out probably—I want to say March or April of 2011. We're still trying to nail down those dates, but yeah, I think's going to turn a lot of heads, and it's definitely a unique story—it's got horror elements, but it's a realistic take on that stuff, which I think is really cool.

Kirtley: Okay, great. So, John, was anything else you wanted to ask?

Adams: No, nothing really comes to mind.

Kirkman: It's called The Living Dead 2.

Adams: Yeah, right, I was going to say, can we talk some more about how awesome The Living Dead 2 is?

Kirkman: It's really amazing. It's a great book.

Adams: Well, thank you. I mean, I don't know if you're just jokingly saying that to appease my ego or if you really mean it, but thanks anyway.

Kirkman: No, I wouldn't have agreed to be in it if I didn't like the first one, and I almost think the second one is better, and not just because my story's in there, I swear.

Adams: Well, that's nice of you to say, I mean, I'm glad you think so. Actually, a lot of people have also mentioned that, and I'm hugely flattered to hear that, just because The Living Dead collected so much of the classic stuff that bringing in all this newer stuff, it was really a challenge to follow that up, but . . .

Kirkman: Well, anytime I can read a new zombie story written by Bob Fingerman, I'm totally on board.

Adams: Oh really? Oh, wow. Well, I'm sure he'll be thrilled to hear that.

Kirtley: Actually, one thing that really struck me is that The Walking Dead is so grim, and in interviews you're so funny. I mean, do you have any . . . ?

Kirkman: I put it all on the page! No, it's weird for me too. I don't know, I get a lot of people that meet me and they're like, "Wow, I always pictured you as being more depressed." But, you know, I have a good life. I have healthy children and a friendly wife, and things seem to be going well, and I don't know where the shit in Walking Dead comes from, to be honest.

Kirtley: Are any of your other books that you do, are they humor? Do you do any humor writing?

Kirkman: Well, books I've done in the past have had kind of the humorous slant. My first book Battle Pope was obviously comedy. But those books didn't do well, and so I stopped. Actually, my most successful book is The Walking Dead, which is depressing as hell, so I think after having a few comedy books that fail and then having a depressing book that is kind of a hit, it kind of tells me that the audience is sad.

Adams: So how do you think you would fare in a zombie-apocalypse situation? Would you be one of the first to die, or do you think you'd do all right?

Kirkman: Oh, I would be one of the first to die. Yeah, people are like, "Oh, but you wrote that big comic, and you must think about how things would go, and you've probably got plans, right?" No, I mean, I know a zombie apocalypse isn't really going to happen, but even if there was any kind of end-of-the-world kind of thing that happened, I would be the first one jumping off a building. I mean, I love my kids, I'd try to protect my wife and kids and stuff, but especially if they were already gone, I'd be out the door. I mean, it's just not something I want to live through. You know, I'm a big giant sissy, and so I'm not going to be able to get through any of that stuff. I would be the first to kill myself. See, that's depressing, right?

Adams: I was going to say, that's a good happy note to end the interview on.

Kirtley: And that was our interview, so thanks so much to Robert Kirkman for joining us on the show.

Generation Z: Zombie Superstars Kirkman and Brooks Living It Up Among the Undead

AARON SAGERS / 2011

From *Paranormal Pop Culture*, January 2011. Reprinted by permission of Aaron Sagers

If George A. Romero, iconic director of 1968's *Night of the Living Dead* and the five follow-ups, is the king of the modern zombie movement, then Robert Kirkman and Max Brooks are the deans of the dead.

In October 2003, comic book scribe Robert Kirkman's Image Comics series *The Walking Dead* debuted as a monthly title. The celebrated title follows a growing, then declining, group of survivors from Kentucky to Georgia to Washington, DC, as they attempt to survive and rebuild lives after the dead refuse to die.

Kirkman was already an accomplished comic book creator before *Dead*, but only seventy-eight issues in—with no end in sight, he says—*The Walking Dead* is Kirkman's legacy. Alternating between occasional uplifting moments and many depressing, disturbing scenes, the ongoing story presents world where no main character is safe.

Kirkman's success with *The Walking Dead* led to *Marvel Zombies* in 2005, where he was given the freedom to turn super heroes Spider-Man, Iron Man, the Incredible Hulk and others into flesh-eating versions of themselves. On October 31, the televised adaptation of *The Walking Dead* premieres on AMC with a pilot directed by *Dead* fan/executive producer Frank Darabont (*The Shawshank Redemption*), and is perhaps the most eagerly anticipated show to premiere in the fall.

Not a month before *The Walking Dead* was introduced, Max Brooks' *The Zombie Survival Guide* was published in September 2003. Although previously an Emmy-winning comedy writer for *Saturday Night Live*, after Max Brooks wrote the critically-acclaimed bestsellers *Guide* and *World War Z: An Oral*

History of the Zombie War in 2006, he became known as an academic of the slow-moving undead. Far from being in the shadow of his father, comedy director Max Brooks, the thirty-eight-year-old is a zombie historian and lecturer who gives presentations on recorded living dead attacks throughout history, and offers suggestions on how best to survive an impending zomb-pocalypse.

With the *World War Z* being turned into a summer 2012 film, starring and executive-produced by Brad Pitt, and the *Guide* having been spun off into the *Recorded Attacks* graphic novel and zombie scanner iPhone app, Brooks has become a zombie superstar—all because the shuffling, rotting corpses from horror movies haunted his dreams.

Along with director Edgar Wright and actor Simon Pegg (*Shaun of the Dead*), Brooks and Kirkman are the Gen-X caretakers of the house that Romero built. Like Romero, both artists treat zombies as terrifying, slow-moving disasters—but it's the humans who play key roles as heroes, villains and troublemakers. The current fascination with the traditional living dead genre (fast zombies need not apply) which has bitten pop culture is directly related to the work of these two. It is perhaps, no small coincidence that my interviews with both were independently set up and scheduled back-to-back with them.

As a result, the responses from Kirkman and Brooks to the same questions ParanormalPopCulture.com asked them are presented here, together, as one interview.

ParanormalPopCulture: What celebrity/historical figure as a zombie would you like to encounter?

Robert Kirkman: As a general rule, I would not like to encounter any zombies in real life. But, if I were to pick a celebrity, it would probably be someone like Shirley Temple or somebody who's manageable. I'm not gonna be picking the Abraham Lincoln zombie or anything. That guy is far too tall and formidable. But, yeah, just somebody you know. Some kid that—what celebrity kids died of an early age, because I could probably pick them as zombies. I could probably handle that. I don't want to get bit. That's basically my problem . . . I would probably just run away. You know, picking a child zombie was probably not the best idea.

PPC: You know this is going to be the headline for the story: "Robert Kirkman Wants to Kill Child Zombies."

RK: It's really just because of self-preservation. And that's not out of any kind of desire to do that.

Max Brooks: [French painter Henri de] Toulouse-Lautrec because he's short and couldn't move very fast. [I would take him out] like I take out every zombie: with a shot in the head. And with Toulouse-Lautrec you just have to angle down instead of up.

PPC: What's the weirdest, off-the-wall question you get from people about zombies?

RK: As far as zombie related and stuff like that, I get the question a lot, "How do I think I would fare if there were an actual zombie apocalypse?" And I think people expect me to be like, "Well, I think I'd do really well because I write this comic book and there's this TV show coming out." I obviously know a lot about this. But I would jump off a bridge pretty quick just because I don't think I would last very long. And I wouldn't want to get eaten. It doesn't seem like the kind of world that I would want to live in for very long. So I would check out pretty quickly . . . take the coward's way out.

MB: Probably "What celebrity or historical person would you most want to meet as a zombie?"

PPC: So I have earned a place in the odd interview question hall of fame.

MB: I think you nailed it.

PPC: Are zombies actually your favorite horror genre? Or is there something you like more but you sort of fell into zombies?

RK: I just want to say that I'm glad this question isn't getting me to talk about my desire to commit suicide or kill children. So I appreciate that. As far as like a horror sub-genre, I guess, yeah, I really do like zombie movies quite a bit. If I were going to pick my favorite I would definitely rather watch a zombie movie than a vampire movie any day of the week.

MB: I'm just a zombie nerd who happens to think about this stuff . . . I'm a zombie fan before I'm a zombie creator.

Aaron Sagers: Why write these stories that are so focused on the people that survive horrific events?

RK: I put a lot into *The Walking Dead*, but it's not really just a horror thing. There are a lot of different characters; it's a very human story. I try to do just basically a straight drama that has zombies walking around in the background.

MB: The reason [George A. Romero] is the godfather of zombies—it's basically his world, we're just living in it—I think the reason that he is The Man, is because his movies are about people. And they are all about social commentary.

PPC: Why did you write the stories, then?

MB: I wrote them for me. I didn't expect anybody to really be into this stuff. My books are just answering my own questions. I went looking for a zombie survival guide, believe me. I wanted to read this thing and nobody had written it. And so, I wrote it for me. When it came time for "World War Z," all the zombie books and all the zombie movies and stories in general, comics and video games, they are all micro. They're all one story of one person—which is good, I'm not dissing that—but zombies in nature are big, they are global. I wanted to read a big, global zombie story with survivors from all around the world. And I couldn't find it. And I'm like, "You know what? I'm going to do it." I'm going to answer my own question. I am going to feed my own need. I think that's the thing with me: If I'm going to do it, anything with zombies, it's gotta be because I can't stop thinking about it.

PPC: There are people who actually believe the zombie threat is real, and are preparing for it with guns and bunkers. Is the appeal of zombies—and for some, and actual belief—that it's easier to discuss how to defeat the undead than it is to figure out how to solve the healthcare debate or financial crisis?

RK: Exactly. You can't just shoot the healthcare crisis in the head. It's a much more manageable threat.

MB: I think you have just nailed it right on the head. Hundred percent. I think why zombies are successful in general is because we live in very uncertain times, and I think we are constantly being assailed by crisis after crisis. I think most of these crises are really hard to get your brain around. How the hell did our economy suddenly melt down over night? And why is the planet melting? And what do these terrorists really want? I think there are so many complex issues with so many complex solutions. Something like zombies is a very manageable way of dealing with our apocalyptic anxieties. Because in a zombie story, the world still goes to hell, like it would in any other scenario. But, a walking corpse I can shoot in the head. I get it. I think it calculates our fears and gives us literally and figuratively a magic bullet.

PPC: At what point do you want to take people aside and say, "Yeah, I believe it's real but P.S., it's not real."

MB: I think that the reason the book is successful, honestly, when you take away all the compliments, I think the reason it works, is that when you take away the zombies, it's still a disaster preparedness manual. Which is exactly how I went about it. I went about it very realistically. I thought, OK, if zombies were actually real, forget movies, forget plot devices and gimmicks and drama. How would you really survive? So all the knowledge in there is knowledge that you would need in an earthquake or a riot or any kind of disaster. So the nice thing is there's nothing in there that is zombie specific.

RK: I don't want to believe that zombies are real.

PPC: [To Kirkman] Have you read Max Brooks' work?

RK: I was given the *Zombie Survival Guide* as a gift, and I just flipped to one page looking through it to see how it was formatted and stuff because I didn't really know how the book was done. It was a page about how you can fortify an apartment building by destroying the stairs on the first level and living on the levels above the first level—zombies wouldn't be able to get up there—but you've got a rope ladder so if you needed to get down or up, you could. I was like, "Oh my God, I could totally do that in *Walking Dead*; that's totally a practical thing that the characters could do and it's totally cool. And I can't do it now because it's in this book. Damn it!" So I closed the book and I decided I was never going to look at it . . . I didn't want to feel influenced by it, so I just avoid his work.

MB: [Responding to Kirkman] The poor guy is so paranoid about that. I met him once. The first thing out of his mouth is, "I didn't read it." And I'm like, dude. First of all, I don't care if you did. And I don't care if you do rip me off. George Romero would be the first guy to tell you he ripped off Richard Matheson . . . I don't care if you do rip somebody off. As long as you do something cool with it. Isn't that how it's supposed to work? I'll be the first person to tell you I ripped off Studs Terkel—shamelessly. He wrote a book called, "The Good War." It's an oral history of World War II where he interviewed survivors of World War II and he was a big influence on me and I shamelessly ripped him off.

PPC: When does the zombie work end?

RK: I don't really have an end in mind for *Walking Dead*. I could say, "Oh, it'll take ten years or fifteen years." But I could see it going twenty more years. Really, I set out as a young man to get into doing comics and writing comics for a living, and to get to tell stories for a long period of time over a number of years with the same characters and have complete control over those characters in that book. And I have exactly that. So with *Walking Dead*, I'm doing exactly what I set out to do. And I'm having the time of my life. I think I'll be able to keep the book going for a good long while.

MB: There's definitely zombie projects that I think of—not necessarily novels or stories, but there's definitely elements of zombie survival culture that I've been thinking of. And there's one I've been kicking around. Not a novel, not another big World War Zombie project. Nothing like that; just a little side thing. We'll see.

Talking "Dead": An Interview with *Walking Dead* Creator Robert Kirkman

EVAN O. ALBERT / 2012

From *Ace*, October 23, 2012. Reprinted by permission of Ace.

Two episodes into season three of AMC's zombie rating juggernaut *The Walking Dead*, and a week before creator Robert Kirkman will take the stage for his Behind the Lens lecture at UK's Memorial Hall, it's time someone asked him the question "What was it about growing up in Kentucky that inspired you to create this apocalyptic survival fiction?"

Kirkman says, "I grew up in a pretty rural area in Kentucky, so I was often left to my own devices, watching horror movies, reading comic books, and crafting my own stories and things like that. Just because, well you know, I like to say I didn't have a lot of friends. Being left on my own out in the wilderness allowed me to be able to think about survival and things like that. Maybe that led to it. Kentucky is a beautiful, wonderful place and in no way inspired the zombie apocalypse, but I think there must be certain aspects about the way I grew up that made me think about those things."

Kentucky might not have inspired the zombie apocalypse, but he agrees it does inform the distinct southern culture of both the comic and the series. "You see a lot of stories set out in Los Angeles and New York," he says. "I thought it would be a lot more interesting to tell a story about middle Americans. People that lives their lives. I'm fighting to try not to say 'normal people' but just average everyday people like I am. Firefighters, lawyers, or whatever—it's a lot more interesting. The cast of *The Walking Dead* is from places like Kentucky and Georgia and places like that. They are very much more trying to survive than solve the problem. I think that made the story that much more interesting."

With the comic nearly a decade old, and the series three episodes into the third season, fans of both know that *The Walking Dead* is all about the long game. Kirkman acknowledges, "It is a tremendous amount of work to keep it all straight. To know the backstories you've already told and bits of information about the characters that have already been revealed. Keeping track of that over the course of a story that in the comic book form has been told for nearly a decade now is somewhat of an arduous project. I will say that all the benefits to me greatly outweigh that. Being able to tell a long, involved story that unfolds over the course of many years and to be able to lay the groundwork for stories that will pay off years down the line is the most fun way of telling a story for me. I really enjoy being able to plan things out and to be able to set characters out and be able to build to huge impactful moments over the course of many years many issues and many episodes. It is so fulfilling to me that all of the work ends up being worth it."

Fans of both the show and the page also know that the paths of the two sometimes diverge, in a process not always solely controlled by the author. He says, "I am in the writer's room with a writing staff. We are all creative individuals and the fact that I worked on the comic doesn't give me any special treatment. We are adapting the comic book like any television show would adapt the source material. And when you are sitting there with a bunch of talented individuals and they are coming up with good ideas, I am wholeheartedly encouraging that kind of stuff. I am in the writer's room essentially telling my story for the second time. Anytime there is something new that can get me excited about it, I feel like those changes are going to make the diehard fans of the comic book just as excited as it does me."

Kirkman is a tireless advocate for independent writers and creators' rights. He says, "This day and age is a time where creators in comics have fought for decades and decades to create a system that allows them to own their creations and profit from their creations in a way that in the '30s through the '70s just was not really possible. I think there is a tremendous amount of opportunity for creators to steer their own destiny. I think that's what it's really all about: being able to write your own stories freely and being able to control your own stories and have them benefit you, as opposed to have them benefit a larger corporation is something that I think is somewhat unique to comics. There is certainly not a television network owned by people who create TV shows; that kind of thing is unprecedented in the entertainment industry. I really like that more and more creators of things are taking advantage of that in comics."

Keeping pace with the demands of a hit series, and a new issue every month is admittedly a juggling act for Kirkman, one he says is made easier by the fact that his career and his passions converge. (His new novel, *The Walking Dead: The Road to Woodbury* is also out this month.) "I like to say that I have a job and that I have hobbies, and my hobbies are the exact same thing that I do as my job. The time normal people would spend doing work and then doing things that they enjoy and having fun, I just cram all those hours together and that's my work. While I do work more than forty hours a week and that does sometimes get a little taxing, I absolutely love everything that I am doing. When I have free time, the thing that I most of the time want to do is work on stuff."

The Walking Dead Season 3 premiere—the goriest so far, in a show not known to overdo violence—debuted to bigger adult-demo ratings than any other fall series, a fact that is likely causing rival network execs to blush with schoolgirl envy, but they had their shot. Kirkman recalls how it all began. "The famous film director Frank Darabont, who did *The Shawshank Redemption*, discovered *The Walking Dead* at some point in 2005 and thought that it would be good for a television show. He got NBC interested and ended up writing a pilot script for them, which they eventually passed on. Frank and I from that point on started talking to different networks here and there from time to time over the course over a number of years trying to get the project green-lit. We were turned away by pretty much every network in existence until at some point in 2009 Gale Ann Hurd became aware of the project and wanted to turn it into a TV show. She teamed up with Frank and I and brought AMC on board . . . and from there it was a hop skip and a jump to being on the air."

So, how long would Kirkman last in a zombie apocalypse, and what would his weapon of choice be? His answer might surprise fans. He's no katana-toting Michonne. "My weapon of choice would be a high building I would jump off of, just because the thought of hanging around and fighting zombies the rest of my life is completely unappealing to me. It would be terrifying and nerve-wracking and I probably wouldn't survive long, and it would end up with me being eaten. I would probably check out pretty quickly. Before I did that I would probably use a baseball bat; it's pretty simple. A sword sounds nice but I don't really know how to use a sword . . . I've used a baseball bat before and I think that would be pretty deadly."

The Kirkman Effect: How An Undead Army May Recreate Entertainment

BRIAN CRECENTE / 2015

From Polygon, March 30, 2015. Reprinted by permission of Vox Entertainment.

Robert Kirkman, if not yet a household name, probably should be.

He is the writer behind the long-running, award-winning comic book *The Walking Dead*, and one of the people who helped shepherd that comic into what has become the most-watched basic cable television show in history. And like some sort of pop-culture hydra, for every one success he sees, two more seem to spring up alongside it.

Now a spinoff of *The Walking Dead*'s show, *Fear the Walking Dead*, is in the works. Cinemax purchased the rights to Kirkman's *Outcast* comic before it went into print, and AMC is working on turning a third comic, *Thief of Thieves*, into a show.

And that doesn't touch on all of the comics that continue to flourish on their own, or the video games, or the movie, or the tabletop game.

Kirkman is an industry.

But despite his many successes, his thriving catalog of works, his growing company and spreading reach, Kirkman seems haunted by the shadows of possible failure. And it doesn't seem to be just a fear of failing, but of letting down comic book fans, creators, comics.

In 2008, Kirkman did what at the time seemed like the unthinkable: He gave up a job at Marvel Comics to work full time at indie comic book publisher Image Comics.

Years later he explained why.

"The main reason, the reason I want to talk about now," he said in a 2013 YouTube video, "is I did it to save the entire comic book industry."

The nine-minute video, which has become known as the "Robert Kirkman Manifesto," delves into all of the things that Kirkman saw were wrong with the comic book industry.

No one, he said, reads books or watches movies and only ever aspires to create sequels to those books or movies. People don't get into those creative jobs to make *Pulp Fiction 2* or write *Moby Dick 2*. But that's how the business of comic books works, he said.

"We come into the comic book industry to create our own work and we eventually graduate up to Marvel, and that's the end of the story," he said.

What comics need to thrive are more independent comics, more people who create new ideas and own and control those ideas, the theory goes.

The video was the launching point for something that has always shaped Kirkman's career: creator activism.

Earlier this year, South by Southwest organizers contacted me to ask if I'd like to interview Kirkman on stage during the March show. Creator activism is the topic he wants to discuss, they said.

I ask him about it when we first meet over breakfast in a little hotel restaurant in Austin. It's the day before we're set to go on stage and talk in front of an audience about his ideas and creations.

The way Kirkman describes it, creator activism sounds like a strong belief that the best creative works come from the people who can maintain control of what they make. That, tinged with an underlying fear that despite his tremendous, almost unbelievable successes in comics, games, television, and soon, perhaps, movies, everything may at any moment come crashing down around him.

"All I'm saying is, creators should always try to keep their own best interests at heart," Kirkman says. "This is a tough gig. I'm two days away from not being popular. When your career's on a downturn, it's very hard to turn that around, and so writing and writing well and doing new jobs well—if you're working in video games or comics or TV or whatever—that's an essential part of having a career. But recognizing the opportunities that come along, because they're always happening, and knowing when to jump and when to pivot and when to change gears—it's an essential part of making it. No matter how popular or successful you are—I always try to keep in mind that there have been many people way more popular than I'll ever be that couldn't get arrested now.

"You have to be aware that that unrelenting, zombie-like force is chasing your career at all times. Do whatever you can to combat that."

FROM HARD-DRINKING PAPAL AUTHORITY TO THE SHAMBLING UNDEAD

In the beginning there was Walmart.

Kirkman grew up in a small town in Kentucky, and a single comic book rack lost in the back of the chain megastore's toy section was the only place he could buy comics. And Marvel was his only choice.

So, naturally, he was a Marvel fan.

By the time he entered high school, his tastes and the availability of comics in town had broadened.

"In high school I was going to comic shops, and so I would read some DC stuff," he says. "But it wasn't until later that I started getting into more independent comics and stuff like that."

By the time Image Comics sprung to life in 1992, Kirkman had built up a complex palate for comics. He followed the artists and writers and noticed that a lot of Image Comics' new books were being created by folks he read in Marvel.

"So I stopped reading all the Marvel books and followed those guys over," he says. "Being a big fan of comics at the time made me a little bit more aware of the creators' rights issues that were going on in comics, the fact that all these popular creators that I looked up to were being entrepreneurs and doing their own thing instead of continuing to work at the big companies. And so I think that because I was keenly aware of that situation at a young age, it put me on the path of always wanting to do my own thing."

That understanding of the shift in comic book creation mixed with a deep love of the medium inspired Kirkman to try his hand at comic creation.

"I read comics as a kid," he says. "To me, I don't know, watching movies is fun, watching TV is fun. But at the end of the day, I'd rather be reading a comic, I think. It's just a magical storytelling medium that I really enjoy.

"I like to think that I'm kind of an idiot, and so I didn't really have any real skills. I didn't go to college or anything. I had some menial day jobs and one of those was working at a comic shop. I realized from working at a comic shop that it would be really easy to actually publish a little comic and get it distributed, because there's only one major distributor that goes to all the stores in the US and worldwide."

So at nineteen, Kirkman teamed up with Tony Moore, a friend he'd known from seventh grade, to create their first comic. Kirkman wrote and did the layouts and lettering for *Battle Pope* and Moore did the art. Kirkman ran the publishing company out of his house in Kentucky, printing the comics in

Canada and shipping them through a distributor he knew through his days at the comic book store.

"From Kentucky I was publishing this little book that was all over the place, and because it was somewhat controversial it actually did fairly well," he says. "I guess I started doing comics . . . that's how I got into comics."

While plugging away on his self-published books, Kirkman caught a break, managing to get his hands on the phone number for Erik Larsen, creator of *Savage Dragon* and one of the founders of Image Comics.

"I knew a guy who was running a website that was doing interviews for people," he says. "The website never got off the ground, but I found out that he had scored an interview with Erik Larsen, so I went to him and said, 'I'm gonna do that interview!' I had never interviewed anyone before, but I'd read the comic. I could talk about it. So I got a little tape recorder and I called the guy on the phone, and did a two-and-a-half-hour interview with Erik Larsen."

After the interview, Kirkman says, he would mark on his calendar dates to call Larsen back, just to chat with him.

"I would just call him and be like, 'Hey, it's that guy that interviewed you, what's going on? How you doing?'" he says. "So we kinda hit it off. It was through being buddies with that guy that then I ended up being able to leg up and pitch new books to Image Comics."

While Kirkman says the pitches didn't always work on Image publisher Jim Valentino, it didn't matter because he would just go to Larsen with his failed attempts.

"I would call Erik Larsen and be like, 'I think this comic's pretty good!' He'd be like, 'Ah, yeah, we'll publish that,'" Kirkman says. "That only happened a couple of times. But if people tell you that nepotism doesn't help you get a foot in the door of any industry, they're wrong. Do whatever you can to make friends with people. Hard work is not the only thing that'll help you out. Definitely try to score as many favors as you can from people, and good luck trying to get my phone number."

Thanks to that contact and his work on *Battle Pope*, Kirkman began doing freelance work for Marvel and Image. Eventually, his work at Image became so popular, with comics like *Invincible* and *The Walking Dead*, that he stopped working with Marvel and became a partner at Image.

"I kind of became a cornerstone of their publishing plan or whatever," he says. "That eventually led to them making me a partner, and then once they made me a partner, that gave me the opportunity to build out my own company around the books I was doing . . . one of those was *Walking Dead*."

"BECAUSE I'M AN IDIOT?"

A successful line of comics, an incredibly popular television show, two more in the works and a movie about to be released.

Kirkman is on a roll. But his success has more to do with the freedom he enjoys in controlling his own creations than in his own abilities, he insists over our breakfast in Austin.

Later, on stage during our South by Southwest talk, I question that concept again.

"You have *Walking Dead*, obviously, which is super popular," I say. "*Outcast* is soon to be, it sounds like, a TV show. Both of those are properties that you've created. How do people look at this who are creators? How do they know that this isn't just because you're awesome and the stuff you make gets turned into great stuff? How can they maybe have the same chances you've had?"

Kirkman only pauses for a moment before responding.

"Because I'm an idiot?" he says. "If I can do it anybody, can do it. But I don't know. I'm having trouble answering that question. I think that valuing yourself and valuing what you're doing more than a lot of people do . . ."

Then he interrupts himself.

A lot of his success, he says, has to do with knowing when to wait and when to jump when a deal comes along. That's what happened with *The Walking Dead*. He passed on offers for a TV show, waiting for the right one to come along.

"Not doing that can lead to getting a bad deal," he says. "Marvel Comics is a good example. If they had waited two years before they did that X-Men deal, they would be in a much better position right now. But because they were struggling and in bankruptcy, they did that X-Men deal where they don't control a lot of it. They don't get to do a lot of stuff with the X-Men. The Spider-Man deal is much better, and then they did their own movies. Now they're Marvel and they're doing all this crazy movie stuff, but they don't have access to the X-Men because they gave that to Fox."

And that's it, Kirkman says, the key to success. It boils down to something pretty obvious on some level: When people make great things, they should maintain control of those great things.

SLIPPING THROUGH UNDEAD FINGERS

It's hard to peel Kirkman's thoughts on creator activism away from the nearly overwhelming successes of *The Walking Dead* and the creation of Skybound Entertainment, a new studio he created inside Image Comics.

It's like figuring out which came first: the undead chicken or the invincible egg.

Skybound was initially born out of a very specific need.

"It was really when *The Walking Dead* show was about to happen," Kirkman says. "I sat down with my manager at that time and was talking to him about being on the eve of *The Walking Dead* becoming this television show. I have all these opportunities. I'm at the center of the show, one of the executive producers. I'm writing all these comics. I'm gonna have all these opportunities to slip through the cracks. I was working with him and I said, I need somebody to help me do T-shirts when T-shirts are an opportunity, do merchandising and licensing and all these other things that are becoming opportunities for us.

"Through that we formed Skybound."

It was later, Kirkman says, that he realized he had perhaps accidentally created something that fit in neatly with his beliefs on creator ownership. Skybound allowed Kirkman to stay at the center of things as the creator of *The Walking Dead* while also helping him expand the brand into television, merchandising and video games.

"It became clear that we could take other creators and bring them into this system, and allow them to be more involved in their creations than any other company would allow them to be," he says. "Too often something gets optioned in Hollywood and they say, 'Great, you did a good job. Now we can do it better because we're the experts.' I think that by keeping me involved in [AMC's] *The Walking Dead* from day one, it led to that show having a bit more credibility.

"The creator's voice is still involved in the TV show, even though I don't make TV for a living. It was all new to me. I think that's something that Skybound is keeping at the core of everything it does. It's a big part of our success."

What started in the comics space, as a publishing imprint of Image Comics, has become something far greater. Not only is the company able to give creators a leg up, but it has the ability to both expand a concept across mediums and, in some cases, decide where a creation should first plant its flag.

"I try to think of Skybound as a company that I would have liked to have in my early days," Kirkman says. "When I was doing *Battle Pope*. If future me could have called and said, 'How about trying this and this? Let's do that,' I would have been thrilled. That's kind of my goal there."

That Skybound is so inexorably connected to *The Walking Dead* has also helped the company grow and get people to respond.

"If you call somebody and you say, 'Hey, we're Skybound, we want to do Walking Dead this or Walking Dead that,' it helps you get in the door," Kirkman says. "That's something that we've had a tremendous opportunity with. If I do something with *Thief of Thieves* or *Invincible* or *Manifest Destiny* or all the other things we're doing, people already want to talk to us because of *The Walking Dead*. We're able to use that opportunity to get those other things through the door when we otherwise wouldn't be able to."

As Skybound's aspirations continue to grow, the company is building out its portfolio of internal talent as well, hiring people who can help usher through original creations not just in the comic, television, and movie worlds, but also in video games. Last year, Skybound brought on Dan Murray, a former vice president at gaming-centric transmedia company Foundation 9 Entertainment, to head up the company's interactive division.

FROM TRAIN WRECK TO GAME OF THE YEAR

That the only two currently existing big *Walking Dead* video games can serve as a perfect case study for the importance of creator ownership is, perhaps, just a lucky bit of coincidence.

In 2012, Telltale Games reinvigorated adventure games with its release of the highly praised *The Walking Dead* video game. The game, which was followed by a successful second season in 2013, garnered game-of-the-year awards from the likes of *Wired* and *USA Today*—and *Polygon*—and was praised for its strong writing, acting and use of the source material.

In 2013, Activision published the Terminal Reality–developed first-person shooter *The Walking Dead: Survival Instinct*. It was, to put it mildly, a train wreck. Racking up an average score of just 32 on Metacritic, the game was eviscerated by critics for its bland settings, broken mechanics, and terrible writing.

How did two games born out of the same source material have such wildly different results?

One was created with the help of Kirkman; the other wasn't.

"We had nothing to do with that," Kirkman says, when I bring up *Survival Instinct*. "That was the Activision/AMC game."

Survival Instinct, it turns out, came about because of what Kirkman calls a "very unique licensing situation."

"Skybound has licensing control of *Walking Dead* outside of the television show," he says. "We can do our own games, T-shirts, whatever, based on the comic book series. Then AMC has their own licensing division that licenses the television show. Much the same way that *Lord of the Rings* was in a similar situation. The difference being, the game that AMC did was not very good, and the game that we did [with Telltale] was awesome."

Kirkman jokes that the Telltale game is a title that he shouldn't take credit for, but does anyway.

"It's a fantastic game," he says, adding that he plays the game and keeps up with development. "It's weird for me, because I'm in calls and story meetings and stuff—'Hey, we're gonna do this. We're gonna kill this person.' But then when I play the game I'm like, 'Hey, they did that well.'"

He says he's also been playing Telltale's *Game of Thrones*.

"I haven't gotten the second chapter of the *Game of Thrones* game yet," he says. "But I did play the first *Game of Thrones* chapter, and at the end of it I was like, 'Whoa, what happened? What's going on?' And then I realized, 'Oh, this is what it's like for people.'"

Kirkman says he doesn't think Activision's flop harmed the property or the potential of future *Walking Dead* video games, because people nowadays understand some of the complexities surrounding licensing. Murray, president of Skybound Interactive, added that while some people bring up how bad *Survival Instinct* was, it just creates an "opportunity for a conversation."

"The strategy that we're trying to go out there and do is, we're not just a licensing shop," Murray says. "We're more in the spirit of a production shop. We're trying to augment development in a lot of different ways. I've gone and out and talked to developers and it's been a very easy message to sell, because we already have a relationship directly with Telltale. It proves that by having the creator involved with the developer, the product became much better. We were able to stretch it into something that a lot of people felt was something new. It felt like a new story, new characters, almost like a new IP within this existing universe. A lot of times with licensed products, you don't have that. The developer doesn't have the flexibility to do that."

And this comes at a time when licensed games seem to be on the way out, or at least not nearly as popular and successful as they once were. Murray says the key is making sure you pick properties that deserve a video game.

"Whether you're building an adventure story or a platformer or an RPG, it doesn't matter," he says. "If you're looking to come up with the game first, what is it that creatively dictates what you should go out there and try to do? Versus the other way, which is typically where you get a license and then you look at ways to milk money out of it. It becomes a business proposition first. If you focus on the creator first and dig in with the creators and the developers, instead of treating them as contractors, and allow them to own the property and own the business around the game, then you have a different conversation as far as how you treat them as partners."

That bucks the traditional approach to licensed games, which often are tied to the release of something, typically in hopes of helping to promote it.

"We look at things in a much different way," Kirkman says. "We're trying to make sure that all these games exist because they're good games, as opposed to because it's a popular license. A good example of that is this *Air* game we're doing."

Air is an upcoming movie created through Skybound that will star Norman Reedus (who plays Daryl Dixon on *The Walking Dead*). But the game itself won't have Reedus in it. In fact, the game won't even be a retelling of the movie's story.

Kirkman says they avoided that because it would have created a derivative experience, not an additive one.

"What we're doing instead is taking the story of what *Air* did, taking the writer and director of that movie, or the cowriter of that movie, Christian Cantamessa, who's big in video games, and he is actively participating in producing this next game that's going to be set in the same world with different characters who have their own story," Kirkman says. "The video game is not going to be a derivative experience where you have to watch the movie or understand the movie. It's going to be something where you can experience both things separately. The game itself will have its own complete story experience that will fulfill any kind of enjoyment without being dependent on the movie."

The game, which is due out sometime this year on Steam, tablets, and potentially consoles, is in development by Gaming Corps. The company's previous works include *Kill the Dot* and *Riddick: The Merc Files*. The game is meant to be an episodic adventure-mystery title that is taking a page from Telltale's approach to game development.

A DOZEN GAMES IN THE WORKS.

Skybound is awash in comic creations, but it also has an entire division dedicated to gaming headed up by Murray.

"My hope is that all of them will be realized. Because of the type of deals we're putting together, we're not doing game development—we're not doing deals in the traditional sense where there's a timeline with all these restrictions and forcing people into that. We're doing games of many different scopes. Not everything is a big Starbreeze game or a Telltale game. We're trying to find ways to integrate into existing games with DLC packs."

An example of the latter would be the recent deal with Argentinian developer Pixowl, which introduced *Invincible* to mobile game *The Sandbox*. The add-on for the game is an example of the smaller things Skybound wants to do. How the deal came about also shows how easy the company can be to work with.

"I was speaking at this conference called the Gaming Insider Summit," Murray says. "During the panel, [cofounder Arthur Madrid] from Pixowl raised his hand and asked me some question. From there we had a conversation. It didn't take very long for us to do that deal, because I saw the game and saw right away how fun and unique it was. We had an existing audience. We were interested in what we could do with *Invincible* as far as introducing it to the game space. It felt like that was an excellent way to do that."

Of the dozen things Skybound is currently working on in games, only a few have been announced.

There's the work with Pixowl, which continues. There's continuing work with Telltale on its series. (Murray calls Telltale the company's "premier partner.") There are a lot of Skybound characters in indie multiplayer game *IDARB*. (Murray sees this as a way to introduce a cross-section of the company's characters to a game in a "more playful way.") There's the *Air* project and a couple of other announcements coming this summer. The biggest traditional game the company is currently working on with a developer is the *Walking Dead* title being developed by Swedish game maker Starbreeze Studios, Murray says.

Kirkman says the Starbreeze game is Payday-esque but with a much grander scope. Starbreeze's *Payday* and *Payday 2* are cooperative online games that have players working together in first-person shooters to pull off heists. Murray says Skybound and Starbreeze will have a lot more to share about their game at E3.

"What can I say? Not much," Murray says. "I think it's safe to assume that we're going to be telling a wide variety of non-linear sorts of entry points to *Walking Dead*. I'd look to what they've done in the past and see where that is heading. We're not just going to leverage *Payday 2*. They're going for a much more ambitious approach to it. The team has come up with some big ideas.

I can tell you that it's not going to be a small game. It's not going to lack for innovation.

"These games start and then they build; that's the point."

I ask Murray what Skybound's appetite is for games like that—big AAA games.

"It's interesting," he says. "There's this divergence going on right now where there are AAA games, but that space is seemingly shrinking into an almost atrophied thing that's not changing very much. Then you have this massive indie scene that's always changing, but it doesn't produce a Call of Duty. The AAA independent game studios, like Starbreeze, they're still out there. A lot of them are still making big traditional games. We're having conversations with all those folks. They're all looking at what Starbreeze has done. They've been extremely successful. A lot of them have been making headway going into this transition, where they can take a bit more of a front seat in how they run their games business over time."

So the ambition and desire is there, Murray says, but it takes more time to figure out how to fund those titles.

All of Skybound's approach to gaming seems centered around that important relationship between original creator and creation. It's what drives the decision and what prevents Skybound—at least so far—from helping to create a crappy licensed game.

"The key that I think is important," Kirkman says, "is that we're not doing, 'Hey, it's Daryl Dixon running around shooting zombies because you like Daryl Dixon,' or 'It's Rick Grimes doing this because you like Rick Grimes.' We're telling our own stories and doing our own things, almost as if they're original games. *Air* is a movie. It's cowritten and directed by Christian Cantamessa. It's about Norman Reedus' character and Djimon Hounsou's character in the world that they're in and all the different things that happen to them. The game takes place in the same world, but it doesn't feature the same characters. It has its own story. It has its own entry point. Christian, who came from the video game world, is working directly on the game as well. And so instead of it being a derivative experience where you kind of enjoyed a movie so you play the game, and it's not as good as the movie, we're doing a thing that's its own experience and stands on its own as a cool game, as opposed to just being a licensing barnacle to this popular movie.

"That's what we try to do in all our things. We try to come up with some way to make it exist in its own right, as opposed to cashing in on the success of *Walking Dead* or whatever we're doing."

The same is true for Telltale's game. Telltale's staff can, Kirkman says, come to him at any time and run ideas by him. They don't run their concepts by someone who's thinking about how the game can be made valuable; they're running it by the person who cares deeply about his own creation and knows on some very deep level what does and doesn't work.

"Because I understand every facet of the *Walking Dead* world, I know when you're breaking those parameters and when you're playing in them correctly," Kirkman says. "I'm able to give Telltale the leeway and the freedom to do what they do well, as opposed to trying to dictate to them what I think *Walking Dead* should be, to a certain extent, if that makes sense."

Traditionally, licensed games have been terrible because they are often pinned to a set release date and with a set motive in mind; everything else is secondary.

"That's the simple answer right there," Kirkman says. "Most licensed games have some lackluster element to them because the licensee says, 'You have to hit this date. Game's not good? Nobody cares.'

"We'll just push things back to make sure it's good."

FROM COMICS TO BEDSHEETS, TELEVISION AND FABRIC

"There's this soulless corporate idea of transmedia, but then there's also an organic, almost accidental transmedia, which I think is a little bit truer," Kirkman says when I ask him how Skybound isn't simply a transmedia company.

The difference seems to be both in the intentions and how the many medium-crossing deals come about.

Where typical transmedia deals involve carefully plotted rollouts of a brand to comics, movies, TV, bedsheets, you name it, what Skybound does is more based on what the team thinks makes the most sense, not necessarily what makes the most money.

In a way, a big part of Skybound is about protecting creators from companies looking to snag a property and transmedia it.

That lesson all comes back to *The Walking Dead* for Kirkman. He says he had a lot of opportunities popping up as the comic made the leap to the television show. They all promised small chunks of money in return for small amounts of rights for that property.

Holding out, making sure you retain your rights to a property, doesn't just mean you'll make more money in the long run; it also means your creation will continue to flourish as you continue to shape it, Kirkman says.

"Holding those rights was more valuable than taking those deals," he says about his early days discussing *The Walking Dead*'s future. "And so it kind of got to a point where I was defending this thing with *Walking Dead* that was very important to me. But by defending that it gave me the opportunity to do the stuff I'm doing now."

That also means that Skybound, which started out as an imprint of Image Comics, doesn't always think a new creation has to start out as a comic book. That's in part because Kirkman, who still values comics most, doesn't want to use the medium as a means to an end. For instance, he doesn't want comics to become a proof of concept for a movie.

"That's something that we'll never do," he says. "If we come up with an idea that's perfect for TV, but doesn't really fit in the comic space, we just won't do the comic. While we are working in video games and TV and movies and comics, not everything we do has to plug into every one of those sections of the entertainment world. We're just trying to make the best stuff possible."

In terms of his take on what makes a good video game, Kirkman says he thinks there are a lot more opportunities than people realize.

"There are certain out-of-the-box ways of thinking that people don't necessarily do," he says. "I think there are games where people are like, 'That could never be turned into a movie.' But they just haven't thought of the right way yet. I'd say there are definitely some things that can't translate. I'm not going to box myself in by saying something I've done could never fit as that, because we just haven't thought of it yet. But I feel like there are certain things that should never be.

"Like, what's the *Destiny* movie? The beauty of *Destiny* is building this character and inhabiting this world. If we were just watching those random guys you create talk to each other, I don't want to see that movie. 'Cool helmet, bro! I couldn't get those boots! I worked really hard.'"

Essentially, Murray says, it comes down to that initial creative idea.

"Everything begins with what Robert was saying—does this make sense as a comic, a game?" Murray says. "You start with the one idea. What we try to do is find creators in those fields, and if it makes sense to go in that direction, find that creative property."

And it's important for Skybound to find those creators and those properties before someone else snatches them up, like the Marvels and DCs of the entertainment world.

Murray says they use a sort of network of creators to help scout out future projects. In the video gaming world, that means finding studios that have made a transition from simply creating games for publishers to running a game both as a business and entertainment product.

They're also scouting indies. Earlier this month, Skybound Entertainment announced it was teaming up with IndieCade, which some call the video game industry's Sundance, to create programs to bring more awareness to indie gaming projects, and that it's also exploring the idea of creating a video channel for IndieCade nominees and winners.

"We're talking to a lot of young developers or, I should say, new development teams of certain kinds, some of them veterans in the game space, about new ideas," Murray says. "We're having conversations. A big part of our transition from where we've been, as far as leveraging our portfolio and having these conversations with multiple potentials, is new IP. It doesn't matter as far as the scope and the size. What matters is the idea, whether or not it fits with what our fans want. When we look at things, it's not about what we see as an opportunity for us as much as, it's an opportunity for our fans to engage with us. That's where you build a path to success."

In some ways, this seems all about Kirkman trying to pave that path to success he used. To make it easier for ambitious, talented creators to find their success. And he sees that happening on its own already to some degree with video games.

"The technology has gotten to a point where I feel like teenagers are making games and putting them online," he says. "The pipeline for getting them to consumers and the technology with which you create them is very much coming to the space where I was when I was making comics.

"I knew, from working at a comic shop, how to make a comic and how to get it into comic stores. Now video games have gotten to a point where kids who are about nineteen can say, 'I know how to make a game and get it in front of people.'"

And services like YouTube, Twitch, Hulu and Netflix are in some ways doing that for television.

"It's getting to a point where a network is basically just a website," he says. "It's very easy to build a website. YouTube and things like that are making it very easy for people to make shows and movies and things like that. We're moving into a place where people will be able to create their own content and own it all and control it all in the same way you do in comics. That is a huge transition. It's leading to all these amazing indie games that are doing crazy business and are fun and innovative."

Comics, too, continue their march to more creative freedom.

"I think that *Walking Dead*, to a certain extent, has made people more aware" of indie comics, he says. "They were always aware of the possibilities of doing creator-owned comics, but having *Walking Dead* out there and my dumb face on Conan O'Brien and all these weird things that have happened to me makes people a bit more aware of how easy it is. Honestly, I am a moron. If I can do it anybody can do it. Someone like Brian K. Vaughan is infinitely more intelligent than me. The future of something like *Saga* can dwarf what I've done with *Walking Dead*."

THE FIX

Kirkman has his creative touch involved in myriad things, but he remains faithfully, loyally, a comic book creator first.

"Comics are a medium that is dependent on an individual; ten people can read the same comic and all get a different experience out of it," he says. "I think that's awesome. Because the pacing and so many other things, the inflection on dialogue and all this other stuff, is based on you. That freedom for an audience member to kind of control their experience is really awesome and unique. You might read them at a different speed and get a different thing out of them. I think that's the coolest thing about comics."

But as he's grown as a creator, it's obvious that his early ambition, that drive to fix the comic book industry, has grown to encompass all of these other fields.

When I ask him about that, if his goal has broadened to include the other things he works on—TV, movies, and video games—he falls back into the blunt honesty powered by that fear.

"I don't know," he says. "My goal is to not be homeless, so I think in that respect I've succeeded. Anything after that is gravy. So I don't know."

Kirkman knows he's not an expert in television, movies, and games, so the notion of expanding what he says about comics to them might be absurd. But . . .

"But I do think it's somewhat ridiculous that you can create a TV show and not really have an ownership stake in it," he says. "I would say that a long-term goal for me would be to try and get to a point where I can self-finance shows in the way that I self-finance comics, own shows in the way I own comics. That's, in a sense, an unobtainable goal. But even though that's something that will probably never happen, I like to give myself something to work toward. That's probably the end goal.

"In comics, I think things are changing. Image Comics in particular, nobody would have expected eight years ago that there would be this number of amazing, ground-breaking comics coming from the absolute top creators in the field coming out of that company. There's probably, like, thirty really important comics coming out right now that people will be talking about for decades. That's all coming out of one company. I think it's because of the creator rights deal that Image gives. Skybound is some part of that. But I think in a sense that's transforming the way comics are done, which is going to change the industry for the better for years to come."

Robert Kirkman Talks Hope and Betrayal in *The Walking Dead* #150

JESSE SCHEDEEN / 2016

From *IGN*, January 15, 2016. Courtesey of Jesse Schedeen and IGN. © 2016 IGN Entertainment, Inc. All rights reserved.

Recent issues of *The Walking Dead* have explored the aftermath of the Whisperers' brutal attack and Rick's uphill battle to prevent his people from launching into a destructive war against an unknown enemy. The solicitation for issue #150 promised a big betrayal, and that moment came when two citizens of Alexandria attacked Rick in the middle of the night. But despite having only one hand and a bad leg, Rick proved capable of defending himself.

After waking up the next morning, Rick's first order of business was to deliver an impassioned speech to his community about the need to stick together and avoid slipping back into the darkness and cruelty that characterized the early years of the zombie apocalypse. He also revealed that he would be spearheading the formation of a military force to protect the city and finally punish the Whisperers for their crimes.

It was a key moment for Rick, and it offered renewed hope that civilization really can rebuild. However, the final shot of Rick's former enemy-turned-adviser Negan hinted that maybe our hero is headed down a dark path.

IGN: I'm sure you never pictured this series reaching 150 issues when you were first starting out. Is it surreal now to think you've been writing *The Walking Dead* for that long?

Kirkman: Yeah, there's a weird duality to it. On one hand, I'm like, "Oh my god, I can't believe we made it to #150! That's so many issues! I can't believe we've been at this for over a decade!" And on the other hand, it really does still feel like we're just getting started. Which is almost scary at this point, but I've got a lot more stories to tell. It's interesting. At the same time I'm feeling like "Oh my god! I've been doing this forever!" and "Oh my god! I have more stories!"

IGN: There's always this assumption that milestone issues like this are going to have something big going on inside, whether it's a major death or a status-quo change or whatever. But I feel like with this issue you guys weren't specifically setting out to do something shocking. You were treating it more like another chapter of your ongoing story. Was that kind of the philosophy you went into it with?

Kirkman: It's one of those things where I don't want everybody to always be expecting a big thing to happen. We had a monumental thing happen in issue #144, and shoehorning a big event into the series just because this is issue #150 seemed like a mistake to me. That said, there is a titanic, monumental shift in Rick Grimes at this point. We see Rick using this horrible thing that happened to him—this attack—to basically manipulate the people that are under him. The shift in his thinking and the way he's going to be leading these people moving forward has serious repercussions. I think people will look back on #150 as a huge turning point in the series that changed the book quite a bit, even if it doesn't necessarily seem like it right now.

IGN: Rick's speech was great about laying out what I think is the main conflict of the book now, talking about him trying to lead his people forward rather than sliding back into the chaos they dealt with for years.

Kirkman: Yeah, there's definitely an honesty to that speech. Those are definitely things that he believes. But doing it in that moment, making sure he was still covered in blood, using that attack to solidify his power and make everyone rally behind him. These are all things that he's, to a certain extent, picking up from Negan. He's picking it up from seeing how that guy manipulated others. This is definitely a big change.

IGN: With that last page there's definitely an unsettling quality to what's happening, and the reader has to wonder if Negan is becoming a bad influence on Rick and might cause him to eventually go down that same path.

Kirkman: Definitely not a great thing to be getting Negan's approval.

IGN: I want to talk about Alpha and the Whisperers for a minute. Alpha seems like a very different villain from someone like Negan because she's conflicted and seems to have some regrets about the things she's done. Did you feel like the book needed a change of pace after so many years focused on Negan?

Kirkman: Yeah, and I also want to make sure that all of our big villains are as different from each other as possible. I would argue that Alpha—she's

As Rick rouses his people to prepare for battle, Neegan, his former enemy, articulates his approval. From *The Walking Dead*, Book 13, by Robert Kirkman and Charlie Adlard; Image Comics, 2016.

definitely evil. She's definitely done a lot of bad things. But I would say she's more conflicted than any other villain we've encountered. Negan 100 percent prepared to do all the things he was doing. There was no conflict within him. He's very confident and sure of himself. Alpha, not so much. She's assembled this group and things have gotten away from her, and she's made a lot of compromises to hold her group together. There's a tremendous amount of regret she feels over all the things she's had to do to keep her group operating. That's something we're going to be exploring a lot moving forward. We're going to see a lot more of the Whisperers after #150 and beyond.

IGN: I know the series isn't really big on flashbacks or anything like that, but are we eventually going to learn more about her past and her relationship with her daughter and things like that?

Kirkman: Yeah, there's a lot to be revealed there. We're not against flashbacks, and we have done them from time to time. It's not something that happens very frequently, but I wouldn't completely rule it out in her case. Regardless of whether it's a flashback or not, we will be finding out more about what it is that makes her tick and that unique relationship she has with her daughter and how she came to be who she is.

IGN: Alpha might be the main villain of the series right now, but you have kept Negan around, and he's started to play a more prominent role in the book again. Did you feel like he was too fun and unpredictable a character to not keep around?

Kirkman: I guess I'm having a lot of fun writing Negan, but I'm always very careful not to grow too attached to these characters. Just because I don't want to artificially keep them around just so I can keep writing them when, by all other indications, their story has already been told. I strongly feel that Negan's story hasn't completely been told. There's a lot more to be done with him. Most recent issues were sowing the seeds of other storylines. Without revealing too much, there's a whole lot more of Negan ahead of us.

IGN: This issue culminated with Rick's speech and the official formation of their military. Going forward, is that what the major focus is? Does the book become sort of a boot-camp story?

Kirkman: That's one aspect of the story, but there's going to be a lot more going on than that. We're gearing up for another big conflict. We've had big conflicts in the past in this series. There was the attack on the prison or the big "All Out War" storyline. Now that we're ramping up for another big confrontation between two big groups, we're going to see everything in a much different light. The formation of the military and Rick's new plan to combat the Whisperers and put that situation to rest is all part of a larger story of them continuing to figure out how to live long-term.

The Whisperers have proven to Rick that the infrastructure of the military and a peacekeeping force that has an offensive side to it and can keep them safe on a larger scale—this is something that's necessary to their continued survival. While that military is being developed to handle this very present threat that's there right now, I think Rick is always thinking long-term and seeing that this is a piece of civilization and infrastructure that needs to be brought back from the dark ages, so to speak. It's all part of that larger story.

IGN: I think my favorite element of the book right now is Carl's character arc and this idea that he's growing up and growing apart from his dad. Will that also be a big focus as you move forward?

Kirkman: Carl has now hit that age where he wants to be his own man and he wants to live on his own. And while he is still very young—he's not an adult by a long shot—this is a different time. In much less civilized times, people did grow up faster because they, frankly, didn't live very long. I think the world of The Walking Dead does mirror that in a lot of interesting ways. Carl has always had a level of maturity that's not present in everyday kids, based on the situation that he's living in. This is a further continuation of that. That will be a big part of the story moving forward. A lot of people talk about him, "Oh, he's replacing Rick as the main character of the book!" I don't know if we're necessarily there yet, but I would say that he's possibly a much more central character to the story than he ever has been in the past.

IGN: I do sometimes wonder if we'll look back on the series 10 or 20 years from now and realize it was more about the story of Carl than it was of Rick.

Kirkman: That's entirely possible. [*Laughs.*]

IGN: One of the announcements you guys made last year is that Brian K. Vaughan and Marcos Martin are teaming up for a digital spinoff comic. Is there anything more you can say about that right now or when we might see it?

Kirkman: I know it's being worked on right now. I've read the script, and gosh darn it, it's absolutely amazing. It's a fun prospect for me to have Brian K. Vaughan come in and write one single issue that people will say is the best issue of The Walking Dead ever, blah blah blah, even though I've written 150 issues. But I'm very confident. I can handle that kind of criticism. So that's fine. It's really great. I think people are gonna love it. Marcos is drawing it right away. I think he's working on it at the same time he's doing Barrier. I don't know when it's going to be released, but when it's done it'll come out.

One of the cool things about Panel Syndicate is that their release schedule can be very flexible because of the online nature of it. There's not any kind of big production that factors into it. We'll be able to market and release that in a pretty shocking and startling and very cool way. It won't be promoting something and then ordering something and then shipping something. That aspect of it is possibly the most fun for me. So when it comes out it'll be a surprise, and people will be able to enjoy it. On the record, when it comes out it'll be amazing.

Robert Kirkman on the "Really, Really Ugly" History of the Comic Book Industry

ABRAHAM RIESMAN / 2017

From *Vulture*, November 13, 2017. Reprinted by permission of New York Media. Abraham Riesman/Vulture.com.

Nearly ten years ago, Robert Kirkman recorded a manifesto. In a video entitled "Mission Statement by Robert Kirkman," the writer and creator of Image Comics' The Walking Dead—at the time just a comic book—spoke about why he would no longer work for the so-called "Big Two" publishers, Marvel and DC. His plan was to only make comics that would allow him to own the underlying intellectual property, rather than let his destiny be controlled by corporate behemoths. It proved to be a turning point in the recent history of sequential art, inspiring other creators to also take control in an industry that has long sucked up ideas generated through cheap labor.

The historical injustice done to comics writers and artists is one of the main focuses of Robert Kirkman's Secret History of Comics, a documentary series that debuts Monday night on AMC. It's a collection of stand-alone docs, overseen by Kirkman, about salient tales from the industry's past. The first round of episodes tackles stories ranging from writer-artist Jack Kirby's battle for cocreating much of the Marvel universe, to the rise and fall of diversity-oriented Milestone Media, and the saga of Kirkman's own beloved Image Comics. We caught up with him to talk about how 9/11 affected superhero fiction, what potential topics didn't make the cut, and finding out that actor Michelle Rodriguez is a huge geek. (Note: This interview was conducted before the comics industry was rocked by news that DC editor Eddie Berganza had been accused of sexual misconduct, which led to his suspension by the company.)

Abraham Riesman: What were the origins of this show?

Robert Kirkman: Well, AMC recognized how successful Preacher and The Walking Dead and various comic book–related things have done on their network. Also, outside of their network, comics are very popular on TV. So, they came to us and they said, "Would you guys be interested in doing some kind of comic book–focused docuseries? We don't really know what the subject matter would be, but we really wanna explore this material in a little bit more depth." So I started thinking about all the stories that comic book creators tell after hours about the history of comics, or things that they've hear from a friend, or that happened to them, or different creator stories, and it's all quite fascinating. Some of it not quite appropriate to put on TV, to be completely honest. There's a wealth of stories out there that are completely untold, and they all intertwine with these characters and stories and events that have kind of taken over pop culture. It was a really great opportunity to peel the curtain back, and show how much hard work and dedication have been put into these stories and the medium for many, many decades, and how that has resulted in this pop-culture goldmine that is driving the entire entertainment industry today.

Riesman: What was your exact role with the show? Each episode has a different director, so I'm curious about what your influence was.

Kirkman: I worked with the directors and some of our research teams to try and figure out exactly which subjects would be the best to tackle and what angles that we would explore within those stories. I really just kinda oversaw the project. I kinda consider myself, maybe, the comic book ambassador. I knew that, because my name was gonna be on this, and because I'm a very entrenched member of the comic community, it's on me to make sure that this is accurate as possible. I can't tell you how many times I've been watching a History Channel show on comics, and I'm like, "That's not how that happened." Or, "That's not what happened there." Or, "That's totally wrong there." So it would be embarrassing if that were to happen here. With that said, I'm sure that there's gonna be some aspect of one of these episodes that I slipped up on.

Riesman: Yeah, I mean, I had my share of nitpicks.

Kirkman: You're gonna have to send me a list of the things we got wrong.

Riesman: I mean, for example, the Jack Kirby and Stan Lee episode had them making up at the end of Jack's life. I wrote a profile of Stan last year and it seemed pretty clear to me that they still weren't on great terms back then. But we'll leave that aside for the moment. Was it hard to get DC and Marvel to play ball, given that a lot of the episodes are pretty critical of them?

Kirkman: A little bit. DC seemed to cooperate a little more than Marvel did. We got access to [DC copublisher] Jim Lee for the Image episode, which we're very grateful for. They were very involved in the Milestone episode because they're doing a Milestone relaunch. But, y'know, I think that a lot of the worst things that Marvel and DC have done in their history, hopefully, are behind them. I think that it's different people at the helm at this point, and I think they recognize that. So, it wasn't too terribly difficult. And it's not like the people that work at DC don't think that [Superman cocreators Jerry] Siegel and [Joe] Shuster were given the short end of the stick.

Riesman: Along those lines, why do you think the comics industry has broken the hearts of so many creators?

Kirkman: I don't know. If you go all the way back to vaudeville, the entertainment industry, as a whole, is absolutely brutal. I'm sure you could find some horrible stories in the world of book publishing. It's just such a profit-driven endeavor that people tend to get steamrolled until there's an awareness in the creative community that builds up that can prevent that. I think that things are on a much better footing in modern times; in the history of comic books, you can see that it was a really, really ugly business.

Riesman: Yeah, I was gonna ask: What do you think the comics industry needs to do better these days?

Kirkman: I think the main problem is that when Marvel and DC Comics first started and everybody was creating all of these characters, there were not set work-for-hire rules, there were a lot of verbal contracts, and there was not a clear understanding as to what these creators were actually doing. So, some creators understood that they were collecting a paycheck, other creators did not quite have that understanding, and that led to some very ugly business. I think that, nowadays, there aren't creators that work for Marvel and DC and create new characters for them without being fully aware that that's completely work-for-hire, and those characters are going to be owned by those companies. That's why you see so few new characters coming out of Marvel and DC, because people are aware of how it works and it just doesn't happen. But I think there are companies like Image Comics that offer great alternatives to the larger publishers that retain rights. And so, at the very least, there are options in the industry now that weren't present before. So I feel like we're at a pretty good place.

Riesman: One of the true delights of the series is the fact that Michelle Rodriguez keeps popping up. How'd that happen?

Kirkman: You never know, when you bring people in, how they're going to play, but she had such an enthusiasm, and was very knowledgeable, and was definitely into all of this stuff. We started realizing, "Oh, she's got a lot to say about a lot of different subject matter." And so, that's why she got more and more prevalent in the episodes.

Riesman: For the Wonder Woman episode, did you guys reach out to Jill Lepore, who wrote the big book about the character? I was surprised to not see her in the piece.

Kirkman: You know, I honestly don't recall. I'd have to check with the director.

Riesman: Why did you decide to do an episode about 9/11 and the war on terror? That one came out of left field for me.

Kirkman: We were just trying to think of moments in history where the comic industry had a pivot point. I think that's something that anyone watching the episode can relate to because we all know where we were during 9/11. It's a big part of all of our lives, but we also are all pretty familiar with how the world changed as a result of that, and how our perception of the world changed. It's interesting to explore how that affected the comics world, and how the comics world changed the kind of stories that were being told, and all the different aspects of that. So just to see how something that we're all so familiar with affected this medium that a lot of people aren't quite familiar with. It seemed like an interesting episode.

Riesman: How did the episode on Milestone come together? That was the highlight for me. It's a story that hasn't been told nearly as much as the others. Why did you choose to do it?

Kirkman: One, race is such a huge issue and has been for a long time, which I think is one of the themes of the episode. And it's such an important story. We didn't want everything to be about the '30s, '40s, '50s, or '60s. We didn't want it to be all the early days of Marvel and the early days of DC. We already had a Wonder Woman episode, a Superman episode, and the Marvel episode, and so we wanted to try and make sure we were covering a lot of different eras in time. The Milestone story is just an absolutely great story. I mean, the story of those guys getting together and doing this—Denys Cowan and his childhood friend [Derek T. Dingle]—it's pretty remarkable. So as we sat down to figure out what stories we would tackle, there was a point where we had fifteen different episode ideas, and as we were narrowing things down and cutting things out, the Milestone episode just kept rising to the top. It became pretty clear early on that it was an episode we were gonna have to do.

Riesman: What were some ideas that landed on the cutting room floor?

Kirkman: Well, I would have loved to do an episode about [writer-artist] Frank Miller. I think that his life story, especially his story with comics, is something that is really very important. I'd love to do an episode focusing on [writer] Alan Moore. One of my big ones was [writer-artist and Spider-Man cocreator] Steve Ditko, and we really struggled with Steve Ditko 'cause I wanted to put that in the first batch of episodes, but he's so press shy, and there's been so little done with him over the last few decades that it's hard to do something that isn't a direct copy of the thing that Jonathan Ross did for the BBC. So that was a difficult one, but I'm hoping that we can figure out a good angle and do it, because I think that Steve Ditko, sadly, is becoming kind of a forgotten architect of the comic book industry at this point.

Riesman: I wrote a profile of Ditko last year and managed to get him to open his office door for me. Before I could even finish saying "Mr. Ditko," he closed it.

Kirkman: At least he opened it.

Riesman: What did the show teach you about the comics industry? What did you learn that you didn't know?

Kirkman: Jeez, man, gosh, that's a tough question. I'm hoping that I knew a lot of things going into this, because if I didn't, I never should've done it, but I don't know. It is a tough business, and if anything, I think the best lesson for me to take from this is that, no matter how popular The Walking Dead gets, it's just gonna be a . . . I could definitely be a forgotten creator at some point, or just be an interesting story some person tells. It's interesting seeing the cycle of popularity, seeing just how long the time span of these characters actually is. I'm aware that Superman's been around since the '30s, but when you really get into it and you start studying the story of Siegel and Shuster, it really kinda shows you . . . The Walking Dead, as cool as it is being at the center of it as I am, it's really just a drop in the bucket in the history of comics. And so I'll be lucky if it ends up being more than a blip. I think it's a little bit more than a blip. I mean, one of the things that you really come away with is what we were talking about earlier, which is that creator rights are in a different place now than they were, and The Walking Dead was a real turning point for that. You being able to control your own destiny with that.

Riesman: Would you ever do an episode that's just about making The Walking Dead?

Kirkman: I mean, I don't know. I would prefer someone else do that one.

Off Panel 47:
The Comic Life with Robert Kirkman

DAVID HARPER / 2018

From Off Panel #147, *SKTCHD*, March 19. 2018. Transcribed by Terrence R. Wandtke.
Printed by permission of David Harper

David Harper: Yo, everybody. Welcome to *Off Panel*, a weekly interview podcast about all things comics. Joining me today is the writer of comics like *Outcast, The Walking Dead*, and *Oblivion Song*, which just debuted in comics shops everywhere. It's Robert Kirkman. Thanks for coming on, Robert.

Robert Kirkman: Hey, thanks for having me. I'm very excited to be here.

DH: Well, before we dive into *Oblivion Song* and everything else you have going (which is a lot), I want to start with where you are as a creator. One of my favorite questions in comics is: I'm always curious about why people do comics. I mean why is comics the medium that they want to tell stories in? You're at an interesting point. You're at a point where you don't really need comics anymore. So my question for you is why do you keep coming back? What is it about comics that really speaks to you as a storyteller?

RK: It's hard to put it into words but, I don't know, you grow up loving a thing and it's got a special place in your heart; it's something that's real meaningful to you and all that kind of terrible nonsense. I don't know. To be completely honest, it's a laziness thing too because I'm comfortable writing comics; I'm comfortable with the way I tell stories *in* comics. And so creatively, I'm very fulfilled because I can sit down and it's very relaxing to go, "Okay, I know how panels break down, I know how to tell stories in still images." So when I get ideas in my head, I very much think of them as comic book ideas.

Just because of that level of comfort, when it comes to writing TV pilots or working on movie scripts or any of that kind of stuff, it's like pulling teeth because I have to train my brain into reminding myself that people can nod.

That's one of the biggest notes I would get when I started working on *The Walking Dead* was like, "Well you know you can do this without dialogue, right?" I'd be like, "Oh yeah, I forget things move. I'm very sorry. Oops!" And so I find those formats to be somewhat nerve-wracking.

But comics, it's just something that I really enjoy, and I'm also really addicted to getting art back from artists. I love looking at dailies. It's really cool watching a TV show and it's all fun and everything, but nothing really compares to seeing your scripts interpreted by an artist, seeing the things that they add. Being able to come up with just absolutely crazy, ridiculous things and see them pull it off and make you look good. I mean that's always fun. I don't want to be too negative on myself, but I'm also very lazy, and it's just so thrilling to type eight words and turn it into a massive double-page spread that an artist turns in, and you're like, "Oh my God! This is so much fun; I really enjoy this."

I get this a lot with the whole "You're in television now. Why would you slum it in comic books?" It's one of the most offensive things that happens to me in interviews. I'm not saying you did that, don't get me wrong. I know that you love the comics but these people that don't know comics think of it that way. It's a medium that's driving all of entertainment now. We should have a little more respect for it. I feel honored to be able to continue to do comics.

DH: That was one of the things I was going to ask you: whether or not it grates at you to be perceived . . . sometime it's like there's the comics creators who have success in other media. Mark Millar is a good example. He has a Netflix deal, he has all these other things, these big deals. I actually have to admit—I've said this on the podcast many times—I love Millar's stuff. His comics are super fun. There's an extreme value to that when not every comic needs to have an end-of-the-world intensity. You just want a romp. But sometimes people are like, "His comics are just storyboards for his movies." And just personally, I don't think there needs to be this ghettoization of the idea of the cross-platform thing. Nor do I think that the idea that comics are like slumming is this weird thing. I think Mark is like you, just doing comics because he loves comics.

RK: I hope so. I think so. It's also funny because one of the things . . . it's like a chicken and the egg thing. Are Mark's comics just meant to be pitches for television shows and movies, or are they so well put together and so streamlined and so structurally sound that they adapt so easily to those things? I think that you can say, something like *Chrononauts*, there's pretty good structure there, there's pretty good character beats and a pretty good arc. You can see how that could seem how that would work really well as a movie, but it's really just a hit-the-ground-running, very streamlined, impressive way to tell a story in a comic. I don't know if that's just his writing style or if that's something he's specifically doing. It's unfortunate for someone to look at something like that that is just universally appealing and then figure out some way to crap on it: which is kind of what a lot of people do these days.

DH: I like that you mentioned that fact that you love getting art in because in the first issue of *Oblivion Song*, I really like your write-up in the back of it. How you were waiting for Lorenzo De Felici. It seems like for me as an outsider, you're always in pursuit of finding a next amazing artist. Like the idea of you and Cory Walker having conversations about that. Would you say that you're an art nerd? Is that a big part of your fandom of comics for yourself?

RK: Oh, for sure. I enjoy reading the stories, and there is nothing better than a comic that's extremely well-drawn and extremely well-written, but I've definitely bought more comics just for the art than just for the writing. I've almost bought more comics just for the lettering than just for the writing. [*Laughs.*] It's an art form, and I think that that's the stuff that entertains me. I don't know. I love working with new artists. I love that grace period where you're figuring out how artists interpret your scripts, what they're capable of, and all that kind of stuff. It's just a really exciting process. Being able to draw a line in the sand and go, "Okay, this is as big as we can get," and then continually try to cross it and see artists rise to the challenge is a lot of fun. I mean fifteen years of trying to break Ryan Ottley! There's no better thing. And then having him continually go, "Oh my God, I had no idea I could do this: four thousand characters on a double-page spread, good to go." "These three guys are going to fly through a planet and smash it, and that's going to take eight consecutive two-page spreads; have a good time." It's the best.

DH: I was just going to ask what are the eight words you actually wrote for destroying Viltrum? I mean was it more than eight words? I don't really know how you work.

RK: Yeah, I'd have to look back at the script, but every now and then it's a little more than that. And unfortunately, sometimes it's a two-page spread that's like two pages typed. It's extremely rare. Let's be completely honest. At the end of the day, it's really just a paragraph.

DH: One thing I'm curious about your work at this point is the impact success has had on your approach on comics. Look at *Oblivion Song*. You're doing things a bit differently. You already have twelve issues in the can. You're starting the thirteenth according to the write-up in the back of the first issue. You're doing the collector's edition of the first issue and doing a massive overprint instead of a series of other printings, not to mention I was just at

Comic Pro [the Comics Professional Retailers Organization Meeting]; retail-ers were just over the moon about the fact that you gave them not just a PDF but a trade to read and know where this book is going. That is a cool thing. There are not many creators that get to do these things. Do you think that as a creator in a unique position you're looking to take risks and try new things when it comes to your comics work?

RK: Yeah, definitely. I think that it's great to be able to do those things. Being in this position and having the ability to do that is . . . it kind of makes it my responsibility. It's all cyclical. Anything that I can do to help retailers to help sell my product, it all just comes back to me in the end. So I'm helping them, and I'm helping me by helping them. Anything I can do to get a project on a solid footing as early as possible is to me a worthwhile endeavor.

One of my favorite aspects of Image Comics as a whole as an ecosystem is that we're all always as creators trying new things. Rick Remender will try something that I will sometimes in my head be like, "Well, that's kind of dumb, I don't know why he'd do that." And then it works, and then I'll do it six months later. Same with Brian K. Vaughan, same with Ed Brubaker, Jona-than Hickman. We're all working on our own books but we all communicate. I think the best example of this—and I've talked about it before—*Saga* was forty-four pages for the first issue. I was out to dinner with Brain K. Vaughan, and he was telling me, "I just want to get people hooked right away: give them as much story as possible so that they know what to expect and impress them by, 'Oh my God, I got two issues for $2.99 and so I'm going to support this book.'" And I just looked at him and said, "This is pointless, man. Your book is going to sell anyway; you've got all this heat from doing *Y: The Last Man*. You're coming in and doing this great thing and Fiona Staples' art is so awe-some. Why wouldn't you split that in two issues? It's ridiculous." And he's like, "Nah, nah, I'm gonna do it." I told him he was stupid. So then he does it, it works, it really did hook an audience and paid off in dividends over the years.

So when I was doing *Outcast*, I was having trouble cramming what I wanted to do in the first issue in the first issue. And I was like, "I'm just gonna do the *Saga* thing and that issue is forty-four pages." If I can do a ridiculous statue with the first issue and that works, if that helps a book sell, I've tried some-thing dumb that maybe I shouldn't have done that other creators can try to do. If this galley, which is difficult . . . you know it's hard to work on a book for many years behind the scenes, and it is a risk. But if this galley edition that we sent out to retailers makes *Oblivion Song* more successful than we perceive it would've been otherwise, then we can do that with other books. It's all about finding these tricks and trying to make these comics sell better so that we can continue to do them for years and years.

DH: I like the idea that you're all learning from each other. It's like you're all individual test kitchens and once you see something that works, you're like, "Oh man, I gotta implement that in there." I think there's this interesting dichotomy in the way that people view Image. They either view it as Image is a traditional comic publisher where they own what everybody's doing—not own what everybody's doing but have an awareness of what's going on every single day—or that they're completely . . . like nobody pays attention: like you're an island of Kirkman, there's an island of Remender, there's an island of BKV. It's kind of funny. I never really thought of it that way, that you guys were talking about it and maybe studying what each other is doing so that you can learn how to do your books better in the future.

RK: Yeah, we do our best to make sure that we're all doing cool things and pay attention to each other. And if we see somebody across the street doing something, then that becomes . . . we're always looking for things that work. That's the thing in comics. You send a poster to retailers. Does that work? You overship a book. Does that work? You want to find things that help the retailers sell the books. Image is . . . honestly, I came from self-publishing, and I spent a little bit of time working at Marvel—the less said about that, the better. Anyway, there are these people that are just like, "Image is basically self-publishing, and it's an umbrella," and it's not true.

It's the best of both worlds. You have all of the structure and all of the marketing and marketing assistance and production assistance that you would get from any other publisher, but you also own everything completely and you have complete freedom. I mean freedom to do whatever you want and try whatever you want. Eric Stephenson and I are constantly talking on the phone on how we wish that this creator wouldn't do that, we feel that it might hurt their book, but they are really adamant about trying it. And once a creator says, "I want to try this, I want to try that, I want to do this," then you get 100 percent support from the company. And it's such a unique environment. It's a really remarkable thing. I feel like a shill now, but Image Comics is absolutely the best thing ever.

DH: I do think it's interesting though because it definitely enables—especially if you're in a certain position—to take risks that you wouldn't otherwise because you can do different things. One thing I'm always interested in is that comics are so adaptable. They can be different things. They can be different formats. There can be different release schedules, different genres, different styles of story. It's like having that kind of freedom allows you to do different kinds of things. One thing I had one of my patrons ask about was *The Passenger*, the graphic novella that you and Charlie Adlard were doing (and I'm not going to get into that because I'm sure that that's somewhere). But do you feel like when you're contemplating new projects that you try to explore not just what the best story would be but the best format and the best way to release these books? Is that an important consideration as you're looking to roll this out?

RK: Yeah, that's a huge part of it. I mean figuring how many pages you want it to be, figuring out how long you want the series to be. Even down to, from project to project, I do slight variations on storytelling. If you look at Outcast, the panel structure with those little micro-panels that we throw in, is a little bit different. Sometimes, I'll talk it over with an artist and be like, "I want this to be a really dense book, let's try to do seven or eight panels a page, really try to do something really kind of weird." And they'll say, "I don't really want to draw seven or eight panels a page." And I'll say, "Okay, we'll do four panels a page." But figuring out how a story lives, the format, is a huge part of the fun.

DH: So let's talk about *Oblivion Song*. Like I said in the intro, it just came out. One thing I'm curious about is something we already mentioned, and that's the fact that you guys are already basically thirteen issues in, which is insane. That's wild lead time. I have to ask, was it a little strange this week releasing the first issue? I mean when did you even write the first issue?

RK: When did I write the first issue? What year? I think—it's 2018 now—so I think it was June of 2016.

DH: Oh wow. I'm always really amazed by the people who release comics in the book market like First Second for example. Their books are basically finished six months to a year before they're released. And you're to a certain degree in the same place as that. Is it a little disorienting seeing this book come out? I mean do you have to revisit it yourself and be like, "Yeah, that's what the first issue was"? Is that disorienting at all?

RK: A little bit. Not really. The thing that's disorienting is that it's not a secret anymore. You get used to having this secret project that you've been working on for a very long time, and it's out and people are talking about it. That's what's weird. It's like, "Oh, oh, people are talking about this." It's great but *Oblivion Song* is a fairly complex story, and it's fairly fast paced, but part of the reason that I'm terrible to have a conversation with, and every once in a while I stammer a lot in an interview, is because I keep all this crap in my head. It's not a matter of "Oh, I have to go back and figure out what this first issue is that I wrote a year ago." I know the first issue better than I know the twelfth issue because I'm constantly looking back and paying attention to what's going on and monitoring things. And I do that on all my books. I don't know where I'm going with that. But I remember it, I remember all this crap because that's the priority in my life. I don't remember my wife's favorite cereal [*laughs*], but I do remember what happened on page seven of *Oblivion Song* #2.

DH: That's awesome. I always . . . there's this amazing Kate Beaton comic from *Hark! A Vagrant*—I forget what it's called, it's like *Man-Child 2063*—and the first panel is an old couple sitting. And the woman says, "Do you remember when our child was born? It was beautiful." And the guy says, "No," and he says, "Do you remember *ThunderCats*? That was awesome." And that is always what I think of when I think of comic fans because I can tell you when Gambit's first appearance in the *X-Men* was but I can't tell you who that person's name was that was in my class ten years ago. That's the magic of comics. It's incredible.

RK: Yeah.

DH: So for listeners that don't know, what is *Oblivion Song* all about?

RK: Dear God. I still haven't distilled this down to a sound bite. It's frustrating, but it's a complicated idea, so whatever. Basically, ten years ago there was this event called the Transference where a large chunk of the Philadelphia land mass basically traded place with the land mass of another dimension. So, three hundred thousand people on that land mass suddenly saw the city in the distance around them disappear and be replaced with an alien world. All the people on earth saw the land mass in the middle of the city disappear and be replaced with this small chunk of an alien world that was covered in monsters. It's this big cataclysmic event.

Eventually, scientist Nathan Cole comes up with this technology to bounce back and forth between dimensions, and the government funds his team to start going over there and rescue people. And they rescue people for nearly a decade, but as the years go on, as they rescue fewer and fewer people, they eventually shut that program down. And as the story starts in the first issue, Nathan Cole has this technology that he's keeping together with spit and duct tape. His funding has been pulled, and he's working with these scientists who help him out so that they can get samples from the other dimension. And it's just the three of them that are helping Nathan go in there every day. He goes in the dimension that eventually becomes known as Oblivion to rescue people, and it's something that is kind of ruining his life. He's absolutely obsessed, and he's living in a world that just wants to forget this event that happened. They just want to move on. They just want to live their lives. But he keeps trying to find people because his brother is lost over there and he won't stop until he gets him back.

DH: I have to ask, have you ever watched *The Leftovers*?

RK: Yes.

DH: The part about the first issue that I like the most—or the concept even—is the exploration of how people react after these sorts of—it's a rare thing but when a huge part of your world is taken away—how do you re-act, how do you move on? It is always interesting to see people respond to these massive tragedies. It's kind of like in *The Leftovers* when 2 percent of the population disappears, it doesn't seem like a huge amount, but it's just this random cross-section of people. For *Oblivion Song*, a portion of this entire city was taken away. It's really fascinating in the first issue; you're seeing the difference between Nathan who can't move on versus the rest. I think it's a really interesting and fertile territory to dive into.

RK: Thank you. It's a lot of fun; it's a fun world to explore. You kind of think about things like 9/11 or income inequality or global terrorism; people just get used to things in a really odd way. It's the greatest strength and the greatest weakness of us as a civilization. We are very adept at normalizing things and going, "Okay, this is the foundation of our lives now, and let's forget about that other stuff and move on." And it's sometimes not the best thing to do.

DH: Absolutely. And Nathan is not good at that. I did want to ask about your approach to writing because something I've always noted about your work is how, for me, you feel character first. It feels like everything kind of comes out of that. With *Oblivion Song* which is a big sci-fi kind of idea, it really feels like it's built around its lead, Nathan Cole. Would you agree with me? Would you say that your writing style is character first, or am I just wildly off base there?

RK: No, I 100 percent agree with that. I mean I hate plot. I think that plot is terrible and boring. Plot is really just so that it's not people talking in rooms the whole time. But the character stuff, that's the part that interests me. I think if you really pay attention, I think that most of my plots are really half-assed. Well, you've gotta go over here and you've gotta do a thing. Great. And now we can just sit around and talk about our feelings.

DH: Yeah, for *Invincible* which is big superheroics—I was actually reread-ing it recently because I was writing a piece for Skybound about *Invincible* at its end and everything. One of the things that really stands out is there are a lot of times when it feels kind of sit-com-y, just kind of like Mark hanging out with people. And I think that is why people love it because it's like the old

Marvel comics ideas of relatability. Superheroes work better when you can see yourselves in it. I think all stories really do. You want to have . . . for stories to succeed, you have to have a way in, and the only real way in is through people. It's not like I can associate with half of my city being taken by an alien landscape taking it over; that's not relatable.

RK: Yeah, exactly, that's a really universal thing. It's all about . . . it makes the story more interesting too if you care about the characters, if you worry about their well-being. That's really the secret sauce of *The Walking Dead*. It could just be characters just going through a meat grinder all day long. Oh, look at the gore, that's cool. But if you're really worried about a character, if you really care about a character, if you've grown very close to reading a character's story, then you're really invested in them—well then that's when you can really torture an audience. And that's the most fun.

DH: Yeah, I was actually gonna bring that up. It does seem like you're unafraid to break your own toys. With your stuff—I feel like this is a semi-silly question, but it's also one that I think some writers fear—how important is it for you to be unafraid to literally kill your own darlings, to break everything so that we can move forward and see what pieces are left?

RK: That's the most important thing I think. You can destroy a story. I think if I had killed 90 percent of the characters in *The Walking Dead* in the first year, people would be, I don't know where this book goes, I don't know what to do here. Don't overdo it, but, yeah, I think it's all about surprising people, and I think putting characters through their paces and pushing them to limits that people don't expect; that's the thing that surprises people the most. So yeah, take out an eye every now and then.

DH: It's funny that you mention that because I actually have a question that's specifically about Carl's eye later that associates with something. But I was curious, I had a listener question about your personal affinity for Eric Larsen and *Savage Dragon*. And I think that's one thing that people sleep on about *Savage Dragon*, is Eric was never afraid to break things, to change things up. And with *Savage Dragon*, he's been doing it for twenty-five, twenty-six years. Is that something you always wanted to do, or was that something that was partially like, "Oh man, this Larsen guy, he kind of showed me that that is really impactful and something I like to see in stories"?

RK: The epic tale of *Savage Dragon* he's been telling since '92; it was one of my favorite comics in my youth. That's been a huge influence on me, even with *The Walking Dead* where you wouldn't necessarily notice it: the same cliff-hanger structure, the same two-page spreads. It's all . . . the way that Eric moves a story, the way that Eric is constantly surprising people is definitely an influence on everything I do. That's the kind of entertainment that I've always gravitated towards: things that are shocking, startling, disorienting. I mean that's really the stuff I enjoy. But anyone out there that actually wants to do comics and hasn't read the first hundred issues of *Savage Dragon*, you're missing a bed stone of comic book greatness.

DH: It's funny that you mention *The Walking Dead* has that influence in there because naturally I would think *Invincible*, but you're right, it still does have the similar structure.

RK: *Invincible* is the obvious example, but I think that people would be startled to realize just how much of the structure of *The Walking Dead* comes from the way that Eric has told a story.

DH: That's one of the things that people do forget, is that you're not straight aping it or anything. Everybody who is a creator is ultimately a mix of a lot of the influences that have informed them. That was one of the things that was injected into your work. That's one of the things that I think people sleep on is that fact that you—we talked about it from an Image piece—you grew up, Image was your jam, that was your thing.

RK: For sure; absolutely.

DH: That was for me too—although I have to admit I was obsessed with Jim Lee at the time; that was the way I went. But I am curious (going back to *Oblivion Song*), what made that a story you wanted to tell? I read somewhere that—I thought this was really interesting—you did an interview where you said it exploring what Jack Kirby doing Batman would be like. That was some level of inspiration. What made that a concept that was interesting to you?

RK: That was the initial nugget. The other thing that's somewhat unique about *Oblivion Song* is that it's an idea that I've been tinkering with for—Jesus—fifteen years. It was an idea I had before I ever worked at Marvel, and it was an idea that I was going to do a book about, but during my four or whatever years at Marvel, I was limited to however many creator-owned books I could do because of my contract there. I had a bunch of stuff that I would just tinker with behind the scenes and never actually do, and *Oblivion Song* was one of them. It started because I read this article about how Kirby had never done Batman and what a crazy run on Batman it would have been. So I was starting to think about *The New Gods* and what Kirby would have done, what new devices and tech that he would have given Batman, thinking about Batman flying around on one of those Orion sleds. I was like, "Oh yeah, that would be a fun book to do: a sci-fi Batman." *Oblivion Song* couldn't be further from a sci-fi Batman than you could get, but he does kind of have a cape, I guess. Yeah, I guess that just goes to show how an idea can start in a certain place and then over time, evolve into something completely different.

DH: It is really interesting to see that because when I saw that I had already seen the first issue, and I thought, "Man, that doesn't seem like totally reflective of it." So how did . . . I am curious . . . in the back of the first issue, you talk about how you met Lorenzo De Felici, or you found out about him through Cory Walker. I do want to give a shout out because Lorenzo is staggeringly good. I'm kind of astonished that I've never seen his stuff before. He's very reminiscent of James Harren for me, and James Harren is basically my favorite artist. I'm curious: how did the book evolve from that original idea, but also once Lorenzo . . . did he have an impact on how you approach the story once he came in?

RK: Yeah, for sure. The world itself doesn't really exist until the artist is brought in. You know, I had vague ideas of "this guy does this," and I had that opening scene and I knew where I wanted the story to go. But as far as what the creatures looked like and what their physicality was and how you interact with them, that's all stuff that comes from seeing his designs and all that. And also, the characters, Duncan and Bridget: it's almost like hiring a good actor. You're working on a television show and you hire an actor that rises about the plan that you had for that character; then, you change the plan for that character. Melissa McBride as Carol on *The Walking Dead* is a good example of that.

So when I see how Lorenzo draws Duncan and Bridget, you know, I can do a lot more with these characters. They're really interesting-looking characters. Lorenzo, I was telling him about Duncan and I said, "He lives in Oblivion for like five years, he actually spent a lot of time there, so he's suffering from PTSD; he's got some real issues that he's dealing with." Lorenzo was like, "What if he still wears his shoes." [*Laughs.*] I was like, "What do you mean?" "What if he still has these ratty old shoes that he wore all the while he was in Oblivion." I was like, "That's great. He's got this little personality tick, where he only feels comfortable if he's still wearing those ratty olds shoes." It's stuff like that where there's visual things like that a comic book writer might not initially think of. And so Lorenzo has been adding little stuff like that too.

Every now and then, he'll send me some story ideas. There's some very cool stuff that will be coming up in the series, significantly later, where he was like, "What if this happened with the belt?" or "What if this happened with the creature in the other dimension?" Just little ideas for scenes, ideas for action sequences, things like that. It's all very useful. And look man, at the end of the day, I get credit for that stuff anyway, so who cares?

DH: It does seem like you have a long legacy—this is gonna sound like I'm talking about you stealing stuff—but with Cory Walker . . . It's funny because I was writing that piece about *Invincible*. It just seemed like Cory Walker was gone and it was just Ryan Ottley, but it sounds like he was always a sounding board for you about this stuff, right?

RK: Cory has a really great story sense. I mean he would tell me that he doesn't but he's really good at keeping things unique and good at keeping things unexpected—which is great. We did this miniseries, *Destroyer*—I'm gonna get blue for a minute but it was a mature book. Page four of *Destroyer* was a splash page of Destroyer stabbing a guy with a gun, and the gun's coming out of his back, and while he is stabbing the guy, he is saying, "Guns are for pussies." It's a pretty iconic moment in that series, and we started working on that, and Corey said, "I think it would be pretty funny if he stabbed a guy with a gun and was like, 'Guns are for pussies.'" And was like, "Oh, yeah, that's great, that's great." It's one of the marquee moments of that book. I'm feeling like I'm not getting any credit for the things I come up with. It's fine, it's fine.

But anyway . . . and one of the things with *Invincible* that was really key on his part was he was just like, "You know, all these books are about teen romance, and he's got a girlfriend and blah, blah, blah. Let's hold that off. We don't need to see that." It's such a trope that's done in . . . He's very good at keying in on tropes and avoiding them. So that's why—I don't think it's until issue 14 or 15 of *Invincible* when Amber comes in. And I was very clearly steering toward a relationship with Atom Eve early on in the book, but his notion of holding off on that allowed me to do a lot of interesting stuff with Amber and continue to see that relationship with Atom Eve. And by the time you get to—gosh, when do they actually get together?—issue 40, there's such a real friendship that's been built between them. Their relationship is a lot more nuanced and a lot more real. The audience is really invested in them getting together because it's taken so long. It's really a much better thing than if I had them start dating in issue 8.

DH: Rereading it, you can actually kind of see how you're setting up the threads early on. Actually, one thing—this is a super random aside—there is this line in one of the first ten issues of Invincible, and basically you allude to Robot going bad right in the beginning. There is a conversation between Atom Eve and Mark—I'm trying to remember what the line was—it was basically like you were just calling your shot where eventually later on your good guys could turn. That might be going too far back but was that you alluding to Robot?

RK: No, definitely not. Larsen and I talk about this from time to time. You just throw stuff out there every now and then and if you're constantly rereading your work, you pick up on things like that and play off them. And it's very easy to build a tapestry that looks like you've planed everything and isn't exactly there. That said, there are things—like issue 34—there's this version of Guardians of the Globe that comes from the future to save Mark when he's been stranded in another dimension. And that, very much, set up some things with different characters with joining Guardians of the Globe forty issues later, and I knew exactly where I was going with some of that stuff. There are things in the last issue, 144, that were set up in issue 54: Mark goes into the future and encounters Immortal when he's king of the world. We did a lot of stuff where we had very far-reaching plans, things that happen years in advance, and then there's other stuff that we just came up with on the fly (and it just looked like we had it planned).

DH: It is funny. You easily could have just claimed that as just being a genius of storytelling, that you were planning Robot the whole time, and I wouldn't have known any better because it just kind of worked out that way. It's great.

RK: You know, I'm trying to be honest here.

DH: So back to Lorenzo. Lorenzo's amazing, but how did he become the guy for the book, and what made him the right fit? You described him as the person you've been waiting on. What made him that person?

RK: Because there are mundane, human parts of the story of *Oblivion Song* and that's a skill that is . . . that a lot of artists have. And then there's epic, crazy, explosive parts of *Oblivion Song*, and that is a skill that a lot of artists have. There's a very difficult aspect of *Oblivion Song* that's world building, it's monster creation, it's creating an entire other dimension, and that's something that specific artists have. Finding those three somewhat unique traits in one artist is pretty difficult, and going through Lorenzo's *Deviant* art, his normal people look interesting; that's a talent. Sometimes people draw great-looking superheroes and great-looking monsters—you put a guy in a business suit and it's like, "I don't want to look at that. That's no fun." And so his people are interesting. He's got really cool, really unique creatures that he's drawn that I've found on his site, and he's got cool splash pages and cool action shots and stuff like that. He was someone that was extremely well-rounded and could do a book that has all of these different elements thrown into it.

DH: He's a staggeringly good character artist, and given the fact that I'd never experienced his work before, I was just kind of astonished. You have this guy that comes out of nowhere for me and he's fully formed. He can tell a story so well, and that's a rare characteristic in an artist. A lot of times, that's the kind of thing they really have to build at because that may not be as natural to people. Was he a working pro before you met him, or was he just kind of a guy on *Deviant Art* that Corey Walker just happened to find?

RK: He was a working pro, but he had done much less work than I thought that he had done. He had a ton of different pages from different projects on his site, but because I'm not Italian, I don't know what they're publishing over there. I thought I was looking at Italian Arthur Adams or someone that has been around for decades. For all I knew, Lorenzo De Fellici was sixty-five years old. I really had no clue. I actually hesitated to talk to him a few times because this guy is doing his French albums and Italian comics. Who knows if he wants to work in America? Who knows if he wants to work with me or anything? And you know what, I'm just gonna do it.

And I knew that he was doing a *Dylan Dog* comic at the time because he had been putting pages of that on his site. But what I didn't realize was that he had mostly been a colorist. He's actually colored some random issues of *Spider-Man* for Marvel in the mid to late aughts—is that what we're calling those now? And then he's colored a bunch of stuff in Italy, and he was actually trying to break in as an illustrator. So he had done *Dylan Dog*, and he had just taken a gig doing this French album called *Infinity 8*, I think. But I caught him very much at the beginning of his career just as he was starting to explode overseas. So I nabbed him and brought him to America. So all those amazing Italian and French comics that you were going to get from him, those won't exist now. I feel very proud about that.

DH: That's great. So I did want to ask about your collaborators in general. You worked with Ryan Ottley, Cory Walker, Paul Azaceta, Bettie Breitweiser is a golden god in my mind (the best colors in comics), Charlie Adlard. Those creators are astonishingly great, but you look at Paul on *Outcast* versus somebody like Ryan on *Invincible*, and they're very stylistically different. And obviously, you don't want the same thing for *Outcast* that you want for *Invincible*. But is there something you look for in specific? Is it just filling all those roles that you were talking about before, where you can do the storytelling, and you can do the small scenes, and you can do the big scenes, or is there something else that you look for in particular?

RK: It's a few things. With Paul on *Outcast*, you look for those things like *Oblivion Song*: can he draw monsters, can he do action, can he do normal people. But with *Outcast*, are his pages moody, can he do emotion? And *Outcast* is really . . . it's remarkable that it's as successful as it is because it's people in cars. There's exorcisms from time to time; it has cool intrigue, it's very moody,

Even though the demon threat is, at best, implicit, the depth of composition creates an ominous cliffhanger. From *Outcast*, Book 1, by Robert Kirkman and Paul Azaceta; Image Comics, 2016.

and I'm very proud of the book. But it's Paul's art being interesting to look at that keeps you moving through that story because it is a very grounded, human story. It's people in shirts for God's sake. There's not even a sword in the entire book.

DH: Even the demons are just people in shirts.

RK: Yeah, so you need to have someone who can carry that. And it was difficult to find someone who could do it on *Outcast*. But there's also this other aspect, which I think is about fifty percent of it: does the idea of getting art from them excite me? There are artists that I enjoy that I love looking at their comics, but then I'm like do I really want to write stories? I'm fine looking at art from other books for that person. It's a really intangible thing where I look at Paul's art, I look at Ryan's art, I look at Charlie Adlard's art, I look at Lorenzo's art, anybody I'm working with, and I just love seeing this stuff. I must see more of this stuff. There's an excitement to it that makes them stand out to me.

DH: I was actually really appreciative when *Outcast* was first announced. I was a huge fan of Paul. I love the Mignolaverse, the *B.P.R.D. 1946* stuff was totally my jam. I actually thought that *Graveyard of Empires* was a really great book, and I felt like he was the type of artist who was just waiting for the right project for him to become a big name in comics. I feel like he was an artist's artist, but he had not quite hit it big, and that guy is just an absolute killer, and him and Bettie are just perfect together.

RK: Paul's a weird case because I always loved his work. I didn't even realize when I started talking to him that he had never done more than five or six issues of anything. He just traveled from book to book to book, and it was something that didn't even occur to me as a fan of his. So when we were talking and I was like, "Yeah, a regular monthly series." And he was, "Oh, I've never done one of those." And I was, "What? Hold the phone! Are you kidding?" So yeah, convincing the artist, giving them the platform, the ability to sit in a place and relax in a place and keep doing work in that one place, I think is really cool. The fact that he is working on thirty-five or thirty-six of *Outcast* . . . it's great that he has this big, long run and it'll keep going for a while.

DH: It's been cool seeing how he's evolved. You look on all of your books and you can see that Ryan Ottley, my God, that guy goes from never-heard-of-him to he's the best superhero artist ever. It's cool because with Paul, he didn't have a chance to really dig into a big project, and you see him evolve and get more comfortable with the way you guys are telling stories, and you guys working together. And it's just fantastic seeing that. I want to talk briefly about the ending of *Invincible*. And I don't want to go into spoilers or anything because of trade readers, but I do have a question about endings. Sometimes stories can outstay their welcome. I always think of that Harvey Dent line from *The Dark Knight* where you either die the hero or live long enough to see yourself become the villain. Was it important for you to end *Invincible* before it became tired and wasn't something that you really enjoy doing . . . just kind going through the motions almost?

RK: Yeah, that's why I want to end it before I got to a point where I was just going through the motions. That really wasn't that much of a concern. I still love those characters. It's actually hard not writing issues of that book right now. I think it was just . . . when you do these books, *The Walking Dead*, *Invincible* (fifteen years old), it's a constant struggle to build the story and continue to top yourself. I feel like if you look back at the run of *Invincible*, every twelve issues we were telling different types of stories with different scope. And things would get a little bit crazier and a little bit elevated, and there was a progression there. It's a little easier to do in *The Walking Dead* because—I'm trying to think of an example—there's a tractor trailer with flame-throwers. I can do that! It's very small stuff that continues to elevate the world of *The Walking Dead*.

Once we're cracking planets apart and fighting on the surface of the sun, you kind of run out of places to go. So that was a concern. And then I had started writing toward an end as an exercise because after we got through the Viltrumite war and all that stuff, I didn't really have this far-off event to build toward. So I was trying to come up with what the far-off event I would build toward would be to keep the story moving: to make sure I was moving toward a goal so that I could build to it. I was just artificially like, "You know what? I'm gonna pretend that I'm gonna end it at this point and I'll work towards that."

And as I kept working toward that and—I'm trying not to go too into the weeds with the writing process—but once you have the endpoint in mind or once you have a goal in mind, as you're getting there, the story just keeps getting deeper and deeper. Because when you're writing the first part of that, you're writing all the other parts along the way, and so by the time you get to step fifteen, you've been working on step fifteen since step one. Things just get crazier and crazier and more dense and more dense as you go. At least, that's the way I work. As I'm getting close to that ending, I'm like, "Oh, this is really working out, this is really cool. Oh, now I've come up with this part and now I've come up with this part and now I've come up with this part." And it got to a point where I was like, "What a minute. If this isn't the ending, I don't know how to top this."

Then I started to realize, you know, *Invincible*, it goes against type. It's always been poking fun at what Marvel and DC does. It's always been about tricking the audience that is very well versed in Marvel and DC books, to think I'm going in a certain direction and then changing it and going in another direction. That's what the book has always been designed to do: to subvert what you expect of a superhero comic. And what better way of doing that then ending an epic superhero series that theoretically could have gone to a different creative team and could have gone on thirty years, but instead just ends. I got really excited about that—and also Ryan Ottley wanted to draw Spider-Man.

DH: That's a good reason. I do have to say, you were talking about the subversive part of it, and I have to give you a lot of credit. I was a little dubious about "Reboot" when I first heard about it, but man, that one really threw me for a loop. You took the idea and you made it so much more emotionally harmful—in a good storytelling way because of the way it payed off and everything. I imagine that that was one that people were a little of dubious of. "Oh my God, is *Invincible* running out of ideas? Is that what's happening here?" Secretly, you were just subverting another idea.

RK: That was a lot of fun too because a reboot is essentially running out of ideas. "Well, we can't take this story forward anymore, so we're going to start over and do it again." I feel like we're poking fun at a thing like reboots because I think there is a large portion of the comic book audience that hates reboots—as much as DC Rebirth and the New Fifty-Two is working now and has reenergized characters that have been around for eighty years. You also run the risk of alienating people. It was a lot of fun with the ramp up to "Reboot" and the marketing of "Oh yeah, we're alienating you. We're totally redoing everything. Everything that you loved about *Invincible* is gone now." And then now doing that. It's kind of like when we did the "Death of Everyone" storyline, it was all about making fun of the death of Wolverine and the death of Superman. When you do a story like that, you know the ending. But everyone still gets excited, and everybody still goes and buys those stories. It's like, "I'm pretty sure Wolverine's gonna die at the end of this." And so, I wanted to do that and then not kill anyone.

DH: That's the perfect misdirection. You did those things all the time with *Invincible*. I loved the words above the title that you would always have. It started out with the "Girls, Acne, Homework, etc., etc.," and then it slowly became "The Best Superhero Comic in the Universe!" It was just really funny. It seemed like it was always a throwback to the old school "World's Greatest Comics Magazine," the *Fantastic Four* thing, so kind of making fun of it to a degree.

RK: It started out just "Girls, Acne Homework, Superhero . . . Supervillains; When You're a Teen It Pays to Be Invincible," I think was what the first one was. That was literally just, "Please, dear God, buy this comic. This is what the comic is about." It was just, "Can we do anything else on the cover to give someone a sense of what this comic is so that they will buy it?" And then, he ended up not being in school and not . . . I guess he was a teenager still, so we ended up having to change it and then it just became, "Let's show people what the tone of this book is." The tone was very serious at times, but for the most part, we were trying to have a fun atmosphere to the story, and so it seemed like a good way to give the people what they were getting into when they picked up a copy.

DH: I just have a few more questions. I'll go quick on these ones but I did want to ask one more question about the *Invincible* ending. Let's be fair. You gave Mark one hell of a hard time through the series. With the ending, did you want to give Mark a semi-happy ending after giving him such a hard time for so long?

RK: Yeah, yeah. I don't know; it was a couple of things. Wanting to subvert expectations because I think that having read many, many years of *Invincible*, people were like, "Well, this is going to be bloody. He's gonna have the goriest moments ever in the last issue; it's gonna be ultraviolent, and it's gonna be really depressing. Everybody's gonna die." And I knew people were expecting that, so that's why there's next to no violence in the last issue. It's all happy. But I love these characters. It was as much me saying goodbye to these characters as it was me sending them off into the sunset for the audience. To me, Mark and Atom Eve and Terra and Marky, they still live in my head and they're still doing things—which makes me sound like a psychotic lunatic. But I didn't want to destroy their world on the way out. I like the idea that they're living happily ever after and going on adventures that no one ever reads. For my peace of mind, it just felt like a good way to end things.

DH: I don't know if you were a *Parks and Recreation* fan, but it reminded me of the finale of that show which is about as big of a compliment to an ending as I can get. A lot of times, they end with some level of finality, but it was just like your story *Invincible* ending with "to be continued," that life would go on. It's fantastic.

RK: I think there is some resolution to it. I really tried to make some resolution to it because literally every other thing that I've ended has ended with, "Yeah, this isn't an ending." *Astounding Wolf Man* ends with we set up Dracula and pretend that Wolf Man is gonna fight Dracula soon, and then they go off on another adventure and then it's like last page: goodbye! I love endings that

With rhetorical and artistic elements drawn from Marvel's Silver Age, this splash page demonstrates the playful self-consciousness of the series. From *Invincible*, Compendium 1, by Robert Kirkman and Ryan Ottley; Image Comics, 2015.

aren't really endings but with *Invincible*, God damn, I just tried to make there be some kind of closure. But you're right. [*Laughs.*]

DH: No, no, no. There is but they're not all dead which is . . . I was in the bloody camp. I thought everyone was gonna be dead by the end. One thing I wanted to ask about: I told you I was gonna bring up Carl's missing eye. I had this experience one time where I was in my local comic shop and there was a couple who were looking through a box of *Walking Dead* comics. They'd had laid them because *Walking Dead*, the TV show, was so popular. They looked at this cover that had Carl missing an eye on it and they said—I remember this very specifically—they said, "This comic is wrong. Carl had an eye." And I remember just thinking it was really hilarious but at the same time, you have a fair amount of other people working in your sandboxes, in iterations of each existing in other mediums. What is that like for you to see all these other takes and head-canons for fans that you've created but you don't necessarily have complete control on?

RK: It's super weird and super nerve-wracking. I'm constantly meeting with the Telltale people on the game, and I'm like, "No, that's better than anything I've thought of." "That part's not fun." Especially if I'm in the writer's room on the show and they've taken a story of mine and added something to it and I'm like, "Well, of course, if I had my story to build off of, I would come up with something that good. But damn it, I didn't think of that the first time around. God damn it." That stuff's frustrating, but it's really fun and it's really gratifying. The audience part of it is fascinating. I don't remember exactly what it is. Somebody put it on Twitter. I'm sure it's attributed to somebody, but I feel like it's so true but it was like, "the fan arc" and how fandom interacts with something. It was like, "I love this. I own this. I hate this. I want to destroy this." And I do feel like people are going through that with *The Walking Dead*.

For the most part, we're in the "I own this" phase, but we are very much getting into the "I hate this" phase with some people. But the "I own this" stuff is interesting, where somebody could be in a comic shop and be like, "Well, that's not right. That's not Carl." Whatever. I fucking made Carl; I can do whatever I want with him. What are you talking about? I get Twitter response sometimes like, "The story shouldn't have gone in this direction." I'm like, "Who are you to tell me that?" If I want the story to be something that you don't like, that's my right. It's a fascinating journey to be on with *The Walking Dead* 'cause there are so many people that have their opinions, watching it, and there are so many people behind the scenes that are working on it. It's a very, very weird experience.

DH: It's funny that you mention the Telltale series because I'm a massive fan of the Telltale *Walking Dead* series. I think it's genuinely amazing. I was gonna ask you, were you a little upset about how good of a character Clementine is? I actually think she is one of the best characters in modern fiction. She's so good.

RK: No, it's great. I didn't really have much of a hand at all in her creation but she's still part of the overall *Walking Dead* tapestry, and that's cool. I didn't have all that much to do with the creation of Daryl Dixon, but he's part of *The Walking Dead* and that's cool. They're not as cool as Michonne! Whatever. It's amazing. The fact that people can come and play in the sandbox and add cool stuff like that, that is really awesome. I have people constantly that are tweeting me or talking to me at conventions like, "Don't take this the wrong way man but those video games, those are my favorite version of *The Walking Dead*." And I'm like, "I don't care. If that's what you like, it won't offend me." I don't want every single person to be comic book *Walking Dead* fans, first and foremost. I love that there are people who prefer the TV show or the novel series or the video game. To me, it reflects on the strength of the brand. That, at the end of the day, is what you want. You want people who support all forms of *The Walking Dead*. Otherwise, the entire house of cards is gonna collapse.

DH: The funny thing about the Telltale games for me is the fact that playing them—it's like being a parent simulator for me. I'm not a parent, but I sadly told my wife about this. I have this one overarching rule for those games, and it's I do whatever benefits Clementine. It's really weird how it works, but that's the nature of a good story.

RK: Yeah, they crafted this really interesting and at times vulnerable character, and you're really invested in her survival.

DH: So the last question I want to ask—this is a super random one but I have to end with it because it's my very specific interest. I love "Letter Hacks" in *The Walking Dead*. I'm a huge fan of letters columns in general. *Invincible*'s one was great; you and Sean have a great rapport. I do have to ask, of all of your letter writers, is Andrew J. Shaw number one in your heart?

RK: Oh, Andrew J. Shaw. At this point, he's really the only one whose name I remember. The guy . . . he is so fascinating. He's the absolute best. He's written a letter to almost every comic I've ever written. None of them are positive, and yet he remains a loyal reader, which is amazing. And every now and then, I will get a positive letter from Andrew. And I'm just like, "Man, what did we do? He actually like this issue." Letters are usually like, "Yeah, not my favorite book this week." The best part is that he doesn't know any of the characters' names and he doesn't really follow the story very well at all. It will be issue 85 and he'll be like, "I don't know who the black woman with the swords is, but I guess she's pretty cool." Really? You don't really know who Michonne is at this point? What are you doing? So that stuff just cracks me up.

But the dedication to comics and the dedication to letter-writing, because he also writes . . . you also see his letters pop up in Marvel books and all kinds of different Image comics and stuff. I just love him; he's a big part of my life. And Mackiewicz does not like him. Mackiewicz will actually not print letters from him, and I'll notice it, and I'll be like, "We haven't seen any Andrew Shaw letters in a while. What's going on?" And he'll go, "Fine, I'll put some in. Jesus." So that's always fun. I wanted to—I'll try not to talk too long; I know you're trying to wrap up. I wanted to fly him to Comic-Con one year and just do a panel where I talk to him about comics. Then I was like, "I don't know. He could be kinda stabby. I don't know how normal this guy is. Who knows?" And if he's listening to this podcast, hey, contact me. You've got the email addresses that get to me. Can I talk about this publically? I recently found out that Donny Kates worked with him at a comic book shop.

DH: No way!

RK: Yeah, Donny Kates worked at a comics shop in Texas, and Andrew J. Shaw worked at the store with him. So now, I'm finding out more details about this person, which is just great. So yeah, Andrew J. Shaw, a big part of my life—probably more than he realizes. [*Laughs.*]

DH: I don't know if you know this, but I wrote a feature about him. I actually talked to a lot of people.

RK: I think I heard about that, and I meant to read it, and I never got around to it. I'm glad you brought that up.

DH: I actually interviewed a bunch of people, creators in comics and editors in comics and stuff, asking, "Have you ever got an Andrew J. Shaw letter?" And everyone, yes of course. Sebastian Girner, I think it was, made an amazing point where—maybe it was Sina Grace—one of them said, "He's very strange, and he's got all of these negative things, but there's one thing to be said: he buys everyone's comics, and he keeps writing, and that takes some passion." He's such a fascinating character to me. I do have to admit though, Robert, at one point, and I think I asked Sean about this, there was a part of me that was like, "Is this Robert actually? Did he create this character?"

RK: First of all, that is so offensive. How much free time do you think I have? How in the world could I possibly be writing into all these other comics as Andrew Shaw? It's ridiculous. But at the same time, it flattering to think that I could concoct all the various, different letters that he's written without revealing . . . yeah, it's definitely not me. I will admit the only time I ever did anything like that—and this is a funny story—when I first started at Image. I had done this book called *Battle Pope*, that I had self-published, that is fairly offensive. It deals with the pope, it deals with religion, it's somewhat misogynistic. Looking back on it now, I regret some things. But it's still funny.

So anyway [*laughs*], I had started doing books at Image and there was a retailer that wrote in to Eric Stephenson and said, "Yeah, I'm not gonna support any of Robert's Image books because there's no editorial oversight on his books, and this guy's clearly a lunatic. I mean look at *Battle Pope*. So I'm not gonna be buying *Tech Jacket*, *Superpatriot*, or any of this stuff." And so I basically created a fake editor. If you look at the early issues of *Tech Jacket*, there's an editor credited and that's just a made-up person. Then, I came up with this gag where every issue I would fire the editor and hire someone new. And so the first letters column, it's like, "Hey, I'm . . ." and I took the name of a friend from high school. "I'm Chad Manyon, and I'm the new editor of *Tech Jacket*, yadda, yadda, yadda." He'd do the whole letters column and then the next issue, I would go, "Hey sorry, Chad, I had to fire him. He wasn't doing so great. So I just want to introduce the new editor, here's this guy." And then that editor would do the column. And then the third issue, fired him, new guy is taking over. And then we would get letters like, "Man, this Kirkman guy is an asshole, firing these editors." And I was like, "Well, that backfired." That taught me my lesson. I haven't done anything like that since.

DH: That's probably a good plan, especially as your star has risen because then people would probably figure it out. I love the idea that that guy probably just thought you were a megalomaniac who was repeatedly firing editors over and over, like you were just a huge diva effectively.

RK: And I was just trying to have fun. I don't want people to think I'm an asshole. Whatever. But I'm definitely not Andrew J. Shaw.

DH: That's probably good because all email you might feature is just so that you can give it a read. My favorite part of that feature is that I actually tried to find him, to see if I could interview him for the piece. I ended up finding a different Andrew J. Shaw who also reads comics but lives in Australia. And he was super pissed about the other Andrew J. Shaw because it ruins Andrew J. Shaws' names everywhere. The only letter he'd ever written was into *Daredevil* after Andrew J. Shaw wrote a letter crapping on the book, and he was like, "I just want to say that Andrew J. Shaws aren't always jerks. I love this comic and yadda yadda yadda." And this guy's whole vibe was just, "I'm the real Andrew J. Shaw, and this guy's a jerk." There was this amazing continuity. The premise of my whole article was basically that Image Comics's greatest villain was actually Andrew J. Shaw, and I feel like that Andrew J. Shaw from Australia would 100 percent agree with that.

RK: So think about this. I'm Andrew J. Shaw. I'm not, but just as an example. I'm Andrew J. Shaw, I think I live in Texas (I have no idea), I buy ninety comics a month, I write letters to all of them, David Harper writes an article about me. Has he not read it? I mean how has he not reached out to you? It makes no sense to me. Who is this guy? He's clearly plugged in. Is he gonna listen to this podcast? Is he gonna comment on it? Is he gonna write a letter where he mentions—I have no idea! It's just so bizarre. You think this guy would have contributed to your article, but who knows? He could be a hermit. I've got nothing. I can't stop thinking about him.

DH: I think he's a character honestly. I think it's a construct. I noticed that there were actually Andrew J. Shaw tropes to his stuff. Like you were talking about, "It's not the best issue written" but he's always done ones where he'd crap on another comic in the process of complimenting you and it would be like a backhanded compliment. There a lot of backhanded compliments. It's really fascinating.

RK: You think it's all an act.

DH: Maybe. He's like the Andy Kaufman of comics basically.

RK: To be honest, that's Mackiewicz's theory too. He doesn't like printing his letters because he's like, "It's just a shtick." I like to think it's his personality. I like to think it's all real. But who knows? Maybe it all just is an act.

DH: I could have just done an Andrew J. Shaw exploration podcast. I could do this for hours. The guy's so fascinating to me.

RK: Let's do it. *Off Panel* with Robert Kirkman, part two, all about Andrew J. Shaw. [*Laughs.*]

DH: Oh my God, I'm all about it. Robert, thank you so much for coming on. I appreciate it. Thanks for going on a wild journey of Andrew J. Shaw and *Oblivion Song* with me.

RK: Thanks man. That was a lot of fun.

ICv2 Interview: Robert Kirkman, Parts 1 & 2

MILTON GRIEPP / 2019

From *ICv2*, January 2, 2019. Reprinted by permission of Milton Griepp. © 2019 Milton Griepp, ICv2.

We caught up to *The Walking Dead* writer and creator Robert Kirkman last week in the run-up to the launch of the second arc of *Oblivion Song*, his latest comic series. In Part 1 of this two-part interview, we heard his thoughts on the state of the comics market, on continuing series vs. miniseries, and on the creation of and early response to *Oblivion Song*. In Part 2, we talked about the impact of first issues on the market, about *Oblivion Song*'s new arc, about the *Invincible* movie and TV series, and about Skybound's game business.

ICv2: You're an Image Comics partner and one of the bestselling writers in both the comics and book channels. What are your views on the current state of the business?

Robert Kirkman: I don't ever want to be adding to the chorus of doom and gloom. I think that the comic book industry has suffered from this overall air of, "Oh, things aren't going well. Everything's going to the toilet. What are we doing?" That seems to be something where there's think pieces on all the news sites, creators get together and bitch about things. That's all fun and everything, but overall, I take a pretty positive view of things. I think that there are still opportunities and there's obviously bright spots where sales spike up, and you see people doing something right, and getting rewarded for it. I like that, because I think it would be hard to deny that we're not currently in a down period.

I'm certainly seeing that our numbers internally are in just a slight slump. I think that maybe that's a market correction of the boom in creator-owned comics that we experienced five or six years ago.

Things will level out, and then things will come back. It's all cyclical. We're definitely in a down cycle right now, which is unfortunate, but I think we'll come out of it just fine.

ICv2: That's basically the question we ask when we're talking about the overall market: do you think this is a cyclical change or a secular one? It sounds like you're in the first camp.

Kirkman: Yeah, it's something that has happened many, many times before. Also, I could sit back and say (this might be a little controversial, you're recording this, aren't you) I feel like a lot of the complaints come from people not recognizing their age, and not recognizing the fact that over time, we're going to lose touch with what it is that is at the core of this industry.

I've been doing this for almost twenty years now. I don't know, I feel like I'm getting up there. It's very easy for me to go, "There are less books being published now that are exciting me, and therefore that is a problem." You have to recognize that as we get to this advanced age, that the industry is not necessarily going to be catering to my tastes, and that is absolutely fine, and the way things should be. So when you hear the complaints, sometimes it's like, "That's just old man-ism. That guy needs to calm down." If there's less comics for them, then that's good, because there's fewer of him. I try to be mindful of that as much as I can.

ICv2: Let's talk about *Oblivion Song*. We took a look at the numbers, and it looks like that's your second-best selling title of the books you're working on now, behind only *The Walking Dead*. Why do you think it's getting the response it is?

Kirkman: Like with everything that I do, I try to come up with something that's somewhat unique. I try to look for things that aren't really being serviced in the industry. There are a wealth of science-fiction books out there, but [this is] something that has a very visceral monster element to it, and has heightened action, but also has really quiet character moments. I think *Oblivion Song*, more than anything else that I do, actually does provide an audience with the things that *Walking Dead* provides without copying it (to a certain extent), because *Walking Dead* does have cool action moments and big spectacles, but it has a lot of quieter moments (some would say too many).

I don't often do things that appeal to the *Walking Dead* audience. I'm always trying to do things that are different. With *Outcast*, I try to make things as slow-burning as possible, and really get into the character development. That doesn't necessarily appeal to everybody that is into *The Walking Dead*, and likes watching people shoot zombies. With *Die! Die! Die!* I'm trying to do something that is a really edgy, weird, espionage story. That ended up being very niche. I think *Oblivion Song* just plays to the strengths of what I do well in *The Walking Dead*.

ICv2: What was the process of building the world? When does the artist come in? What are your respective roles in building the world?

Kirkman: The overall skeleton of things is something I come up when I'm coming up with what my next project is going to be, or crafting the overall structure of the story. I always try to bring in an artist, a co-creator, a partner, as early as possible.

Especially with something like *Oblivion Song* where everything is so visual, it's almost hard for me to continue writing the story before I know how the world is going to look. That dictates how the world is going to work; story comes out of that.

In the case of Lorenzo De Felici, he was very hands-on from the get-go, where I would just go, "I don't know, it's a different dimension that has different vegetation. I'm thinking they might be mold or fungus-based, just as a visual reference."

He hit the ground running with, "Here's how the animals work. Here's how their structures and body types are, and here's how the different animals relate to each other, so that they look like they're from the same world."

He really rolled the sleeves up, really came up with all of the visual elements, and fleshed out that world to a point where I could just sit back and say, "OK, I'll throw these creatures in here. Oh, it looks like these creatures do this kind of thing." And it's great, because once he did that initial work, I knew exactly how much I could lean on him. It got to a point where I would say, "OK, we need a little creature that does this for this scene." I would just write that into the script, knowing without too much lead time he could handle that, and work something into the story that would fill the need of what I need in that scene. He's been essential.

ICv2: In terms of a given story, what do you give him? Do you give him a full script, plot, page breakdowns?

Kirkman: I write in full script. On the surface, my scripts can be somewhat restrictive, just because the way I write, I picture the page; I'm basically describing the page as I view it in my head. I'll go as far as to say, "There's a wide panel here. There's three small panels below it. There's a wide panel at the bottom."

A lot of that is only there because I know how much dialogue I'm putting in a panel, and that's going to dictate the panel size. I know I'm writing the action in a way that sometimes, you'll need a bigger panel to service the action, sometimes, you'll need a smaller panel. I always make it clear with the artist. That's just so when I'm writing, I can picture the page, and I know that I'm not putting too much information in a panel, or not too much information on a page.

That layout is really just for me. Once the script is turned in, I have some artists that change the layouts completely. I have other artists that follow it somewhat. Some artists say that it helps. Some artists are like, "Yeah, I just completely ignore that, and do my own thing." And that's always fun. I feel like if I wasn't on top of what structurally fits on a page, I'd be going crazy, and writing scenes that wouldn't really work. It's important to me to go that extra mile, and throw that structure in.

ICv2: Then as you're building out a world, do you ever think about how the world you're creating will adapt into other media, or is it strictly a comic book?

Kirkman: I have to make it strictly a comic. It would be very easy for me, because I am well-versed in how productions go at this point, to go, "Oh, well, I'll make this monster smaller, so it can be a guy in a suit, instead of a CG thing."

Or, "Let's change the world this way, so that it'll work better on a set." There's different things that I could do to make a production easier, but that would be limiting to the comic space. The beauty of doing a comic is that you don't have those limitations.

I'm always very mindful of anytime anything like that creeps into my head of, "It would be better if you did this." I end up pushing myself in the opposite direction because I want to stay, quote, true to the streets, unquote, if that makes any sense.

I don't want to feel like I'm a Hollywood sellout by structuring my comics for other mediums. That's why later on in *Walking Dead*, you get things like pet tigers. That was because I was like, "Oh, it'd be cool if this guy had a weird pet." Then I'd be like, "Well, I don't know. That's not going to really adapt well in the show." Then I'd be like, "Don't be a sellout, Kirkman. Give them a tiger." You could even argue that I would have thought a tiger was too outlandish if the show didn't exist, but because I didn't want to feel like I was editing things for the show, I went that extra mile, and crossed that line, and actually put a tiger into the story. It might actually make things even crazier, because I try to do that.

I could have smaller monsters in *Oblivion Song*, if I wasn't worried about the idea of trying to cater things for another medium. That's when I end up with giant, four-story monsters, and all kinds of insanity that would possibly only ever work to its fullest in comic book form.

Survivors on the Oblivion planet are surrounded by massive monsters and yet happily declare, "Now, this is living!" From *Oblivion Song*, Volume 1, by Robert Kirkman and Lorenzo
De Felici; Image Comics, 2018.

ICv2: You're starting a new arc, which we want to ask about, but before that, we want to ask about how you handle new arcs. Unlike a lot of publishers and creators, you start a comic series, and just keep going. You don't do miniseries. When a new arc starts, it's just a new number in the series. Can you talk a little bit about why you do it that way?

Kirkman: I feel like that's the preferred method of comics. A lot of things I do just based on myself as a fan. That's what I would want. I don't want to have to track, "Oh, well, this number one came after this other number one." Then, "Oh, but that other number one came in between those two number ones." You break the system of following a series, or even collecting, because collecting is an aspect of our business that I don't think is bad. We are writing stories and crafting narratives that you want people to enjoy, but comic books have that added bonus of also being a collectible.

You want to have somebody that goes, "Oh, I got issue 36. I got issue 89. I got this whole run. This is totally something that I love having." I'm into that myself, as a comic book collector. I don't want to have those starts and stops in a series.

While I recognize that some publishers think that you get a little bit of extra juice every time you start something over with a new number one, I think if you actually look at the data, it more often than not provides a jumping-off point.

You can watch attrition really kick in as you keep restarting those books. Unless it's a massively different and popular creative team that's taking over with the new number one, it's something that I'm very much against.

I think that you want to make following the series as simple as possible. I very strongly believe that the reason the *Walking Dead* television show has led to a huge spike in comic book sales is because anyone can go into a bookstore and comic book shop and say, "I want to read *Walking Dead*. What do I do?"

They go, "The book with the number one on it. Find the book with the number one on it, whether that's the hardcover, the compendium, or the trade, and try that. If you like that, come back and get the one that matches it with the number two on it."

It's that simple. If you look at any of the DC shows, Marvel movies, Marvel shows, or a lot of the other stuff coming out . . . Somebody loves *Spider-Man: Into the Spider-Verse*. They walk into a bookstore, and they're like, "Hey, I want to buy a Spider-Man book. Where do I start?"

They're like, "Well, I like the Dan Slott run. Buy his number one," or, "Well, you really want to get this Visionaries book with Michelinie and McFarlane. That's got a number one." There's forty-five different number ones. It's very unclear where a novice fan would actually begin their journey into comics, which I think is a really bad thing. It's a disservice we've done to comics as a whole.

Keep things simple. Volume one, volume two, volume three. Stick with it. That's the way I prefer to do things.

ICv2: We were talking about how you keep your comic series running rather than starting with a new first issue every time you start a new arc. Circling back to the macro discussion for a second, do you think there's any correlation between the huge number of number ones we have out there, and the fact that sales are a little soft right now?

Kirkman: Yeah, I think it does get to a point where it's a little overwhelming. I've talked to younger creators starting off in the business. The reason I usually bring this up is because I feel like this is something I even did wrong.

When you start catching a little bit of heat and you've written a comic book, then you start another comic, and then you start another comic, you're bringing that audience with you from series to series. That's how a new writer or a new artist is going to build an audience.

For writers especially, because they can do multiple projects, when you start doing two series a month, three series a month, four series a month, five series a month, you're going to get to a point where you hit a critical mass, where your fan can't read everything that you do.

If you're a fan of seven different writers, and they're all doing five to six to seven different series every month, that's going to break the bank. I always tell creators, "Recognize your output, and try and find that sweet spot," because once your fan base stops buying, once they get to a point where they can't buy every book, then they're not going to buy as many as they would otherwise. If you're doing four books a month, and they can buy four books a month, then you do a fifth book, and they can't buy that, then they're just going to go back to buying two books a month. It'll actually make them buy less of your stuff, I feel.

The industry as a whole, because you have all of these new series and all these new books coming out, and you have Marvel and DC, Image, and other publishers publishing so many books, if you can't buy every Marvel comic (because you're a Marvel comics fan), you're going to buy infinitely fewer Marvel comics. You're only going to cherry-pick the ones that you want.

The glut in the market, with us publishing so many books, is driving people to buy less and less comics. If I'm an Avengers fan, and it's impossible for me to read every Avengers book, well, then I'm only going to read the one or two that I really love. If there's only three or four, I might buy all three or four, just because I loved knowing that I have explored every corner of that world, and I'm getting every inch of that story.

ICv2: You're starting a new arc on *Oblivion Song* in March. Tell us a little bit about where you're taking the story.

Kirkman: With all of my books, I try to make sure that the story progresses as much as possible, and that you are getting rewarded for your investment. The characters are changing. The status quo is changing. There's a new narrative coming into place, and you get a sense that this journey that you're on is progressing, and you're going to new places.

That's something that we're doing in a big way, starting with issue 13. There's a lot going on with the other dimension, Oblivion. It was a big mystery for the first twelve issues exactly what was going on there: how it is that the transference happened?

A lot of those mysteries have been answered in that first twelve-issue macro arc. As we dive into issue 13, there's a little bit of progression of time. We've got some new characters that are coming into the forefront that are venturing into Oblivion, and finding more and more things about it.

There's this element of the Faceless Men that are these seemingly intelligent creatures that live in Oblivion that people haven't really encountered very much, that are only seen on the fringes of things in the first twelve issues. Those characters are very much coming to the forefront, starting in issue 13. That's going to complicate matters exponentially for the people on Earth, as they find out that Oblivion is actually far more dangerous than they ever could have imagined.

[Note: Kirkman sent us this additional comment on the launch of the new *Oblivion Song* arc after the interview and asked us to include it: I just failed to mention that [*Oblivion Song*] issue 13 and the volume 2 TPB collecting issues 7–12 will be shipping on the same day. That's something we do to help retailers build readership in a new title. It's something that worked very well with *The Walking Dead* in the early days. The hope is that a reader who hasn't tried the series, sees that they can get all caught up very easily right away by buying the trades and the current issue.]

ICv2: You said earlier you write for yourself as a fan in some ways. For a store owner, which is a big part of our audience, who is the customer you think is the best fit for *Oblivion Song*?

Kirkman: It's hard to say. There are those lapsed readers, those people that have been reading comics for a very, very long time, and aren't necessarily happy with the current things that they're getting. Maybe that's from Marvel or DC, maybe that's from somewhere else.

I think that all of Image comics are trying to offer a very valid alternative to people that just read Marvel and DC comics. Just being realistic, there are a huge number of fans that are really just into superhero comics, love reading those two universes, and that's their main bread and butter. When they think of comics, that's what they think of.

Oblivion Song and other books, *Walking Dead*, many, many comics that Image publishes, they have the spectacle of big superhero comics, they have the nuance of big superhero comics, but they're offering things just a little bit different.

I like to think of Image Comics as a whole as a great alternative to people who maybe have read thirty years of *Captain America*, and are like, "This is starting to get a little repetitious. I think I need to move on." Image should be the thing that they move on to.

ICv2: At one point there was an *Invincible* movie in development. Now, more recently, there was a deal for an animated series. What's going on with adaptations of Invincible?

Kirkman: They're both very much still in process. There is not any news I can discuss right now, unfortunately, but the *Invincible* animated series is deep into production. I'm reviewing animatics; we're working with overseas studios; we're very far into casting. There should be some big announcements coming up very soon.

While we don't have a set release date, or I can't publically say the set release date just yet, I'm hoping that by the summertime we'll have a big marketing push that begins, and there will be a steady stream of advanced looks, cool reveals, and things leading up to the launch of that series.

The movie is happening alongside the animated series. I'm in constant contact with Seth Rogen and Evan Goldberg, who are writing, producing, and directing that movie with myself and my team at Skybound. That's something that is absolutely ongoing, and things are looking really good. I couldn't be happier with what Seth and Evan are doing with the world.

In some amount of time, there's going to be a lot of Invincible going on all over the place, which is really exciting for me.

ICv2: And then for our game-retailer readers, we should ask: Skybound's gone into the games business the last couple of years. How did that come about? Are you a gamer? How did you decide to go into games?

Kirkman: I like games quite a bit. Shawn Kirkham and David Alpert at Skybound are probably a little bit more into games than I am. We've had a lot of success with *Superfight*, so that opened up that world to us. It was something that we really wanted to dive into.

I think that with James Hudson coming in, we've done a really great job of bringing more and more games into the Skybound ecosystem. It's an area that I think Skybound handles really well. We've had a lot of success with it, and so I think we're going to keep doing more.

It's something that our team is very passionate about. I come by the office, and people are playing games nonstop. Testing out new games, and figuring out new things to do with games. It's something that we all enjoy.

ICv2: Anything else you want to get out there to our retailer audience?

Kirkman: I always want to make sure that I just voice how much I appreciate all the hard work that they do. I feel like it's a reciprocal relationship that we have between Skybound and the retailers. I recognize the sacrifices that they make in order to support the product that we do. The fact that I can launch *Oblivion Song* and *Die! Die! Die!* in the same year, in two very different ways, and they're both embraced.

I love the feedback that we get from retailers. I hope that they recognize that we do listen to the feedback. We make adjustments constantly based on what we're hearing, and we make plans based on things that we've heard from them at our retailer breakfast that we do at San Diego and New York Comic Con. I feel like we've got a really good relationship with them.

I hope that they understand just how much we appreciate what they do, and how we hope to continue the successful partnership that we've been building for many, many years.

APPENDIX: INTERVIEWS WITH ROBERT KIRKMAN COLLABORATORS

Artist August: Ryan Ottley (Interview)

DAVID HARPER / 2011

From *Multiversity*, August 3, 2011. Reprinted by permission of David Harper

Ryan Ottley, the artist of Image Comics' flagship superhero book (and arguably the best superhero book in comics), is our featured artist on today's Artist August interview. Ryan was *Multiversity*'s favorite artist of 2010, and he hasn't slowed down in 2011.

We're extremely pleased to have chatted with him, and check out after the jump as we talk about what it's like to work with Kirkman, how he fell in love with comics at first sight, and finding out who would win in a fight: a Sea Bear or a Grizzly Shark. Well, all of that and more.

David Harper: Can you look back on your life and recall the single moment that made you want to work in comics? Or was it more of a natural progression that led you here?

Ryan Ottley: It happened instantly the first time I saw a comic. Seriously, I was always into drawing. But at age fifteen when my cousin Bryan showed me my first comic, an issue of the *Amazing Spider-Man* drawn by Todd McFarlane, I felt the movement and energy and I thought instantly that I wanted to draw comics someday.

DH: Who or what has influenced the development of your art?

RO: A key factor for me in getting better was no social life. It really does work. I highly recommend it to anyone wanting to break in. No friends, okay maybe one good one, but just draw hours a day. Learn everything you can. I was highly influenced by all comics I read, then by anatomy books and just drawing from life.

DH: It's rare for creators to stick on one book for extended periods, yet since issue 13, you and Robert Kirkman have been rocking *Invincible*. What about the book has kept you so close to it? Have you ever been tempted to move in another direction?

RO: Issue 8 buddy, don't go skimming off issues of my run now. Here's a run down of how and why I'm still on *Invincible*. I started as a fill-in artist for one issue, issue 8. Robert dug my speed so he kept me on. I was just happy to be drawing any book. I was a hungry artist ready to work, after issue 8 was done and Robert wanted me on full time, he sent me the first seven issues to read. I loved it. Amazing stuff. Every script after was a joy to work on.

I still thought I wanted to work my way up some comic ladder and make it to Marvel or DC someday, that was my dream job since I started reading comics and it was just something ingrained into my thinking that every artist's end goal is to work for the Big Two, that's the top rung, that's as high as anyone could go! And many still feel that. I plugged away on *Invincible* every month, had many chances to leave and work at the Big Two, did one small thing at DC but my desire to work there started to dissolve. Robert and Cory made me part owner of *Invincible*, I was getting paid more than I would anywhere else, I don't have all these bosses telling me what to do. It was just friends making comics the way we wanted, no rules. And I realized I've had my dream job all along.

You basically decide what is top to you, if you grow up thinking working for a large corporation is as high and far as you want to go, then go for it. Or you can be the few who build their own corporation, work independently and take a bigger risk. It doesn't work out for everyone, but when it does it can be pretty great. I honestly don't think there is a better superhero book than Invincible. And I doubt anything could ever make me leave.

DH: How would you say your art has improved since you first started on *Invincible*?

RO: I think it has improved a lot, but there is still a long way to go. There is always more to learn.

DH: You were *Multiversity*'s Artist of the Year in 2010, and anyone who reads *Invincible* understands why. The Viltrumite War might have been one of the best arcs in terms of superhero visuals ever. How was it working on that arc in particular, and is it less exciting for you to draw a conversation than it is to draw a father and son exploding a planet?

RO: Anything is fun to draw if you are in the right mood. It's an artist's job to make what they are drawing enjoyable to draw. Even if it sounds boring you need to convince yourself that there is a fun way to draw it. If not, an easy page could take forever to draw and then you'll hate it. Of course action scenes are more enjoyable for me, the reason why I got into comics was because I felt the movement and action on the page, so working that out is always fun. The Viltrumite War was crazy, I definitely enjoyed it and it was a ton of work at the same time.

DH: Since issue 51, you have been working pretty consistently with Cliff Rathburn and FCO Plascenscia as your inker and colorist. How is it working with the two of them, and how important is it for you to have an inker and colorist that complement your styles well?

RO: Both Cliff and FCO are an amazing help with everything. It was tough inking myself for so long, I felt I couldn't get better at pencilling if I was always this rushed to finish both pencilling and inking every month. So getting Cliff on board was crucial for me to become a better penciller. And Cliff is just a better inker than me. FCO always added that energy I always wanted with my art. He's been great.

DH: How is it working with Kirkman, a guy many consider the greatest writer in comics today?

RO: He's a great dude, I'm still amazed at his will to work as much as possible and do as many books as he does, even now with his TV show he still thinks comics are the better place to work, and more enjoyable to make. He's been awesome to work with, I really wish there were a lot more writers like him. Someone that is talented and loves comics this much that they want to make new original content.

DH: *Invincible* features new characters being created constantly, sometimes on an issue-to-issue basis. Who have been some of your favorite creations so far, and is the act of developing new character looks all of the time fun or stressful?

RO: Battle Beast, Conquest, Gravitator are ones I like most. Aliens and monsters are always fun to create as well. It can be stressful at times because I feel I have this deadline looming over me for the comic so when I need to design someone and I'm not figuring out the design right away I get frustrated. So yeah, sometimes it's fun, sometimes it feels like I have no idea what I am doing.

DH: Gun to your head, you have to answer: who would win in a fight, a sea bear or a grizzly shark?

RO: Jason Howard and I have had this conversation a few times. And we both agree the bear would win. Sharks only have a mouth, a bear has teeth on his hands and feet as well so in the end a shark is nothing more than a giant delicious salmon to the bear.

DH: Does feedback (both positive and negative) with fans and critics via social media push you as an artist?

RO: I've heard many say we should never listen to reviews, good or bad. Just work and be happy, don't care what others say. Ignore them all! I can't do that. I read reviews, I like it when it's positive, if it's negative then yeah, I take some things to heart. But really, I am my worst critic. I try to get better because I'm not satisfied with my current ability. And the day I am is the day I stop progressing. So, I never want to be satisfied.

DH: Comics, even with increasing acceptance amongst the mainstream, are still a niche medium. With that in mind, have your friends and family always been supportive of your pursuit of a career in this field?

RO: Oh definitely. My mom and other family members read everything I do, it seems their least favorite thing was Grizzly Shark. My mom almost started crying at the sight of a family getting eaten by a Shark. But other than that she's way proud!

DH: What would be a dream project for you? Any particular writers you're dying to work with or titles you'd like to take a stab at? Perhaps a personal project you just want to see come to fruition?

RO: Dream projects these days for me are original content with a writer that creates something awesome and original or myself doing it all. I have ideas, the problem is finding time in between a monthly gig to do them. So every once in a while you'll see me do a one-shot here and there.

DH: Desert Island question: one book, one album, one film and one comic. What do you take with you?

RO: Book of Mormon, yes I'm Mormon. Vivaldi, I listen to a lot of rap and metal but I love classical as well and that just seems like the best choice for desert island all alone music. *Cast Away*, that way I can study over and over how he got off the island. Probably *Sandman*, been meaning to reread all that, now I'll have time on my island.

DH: Who are your favorite artists working in comics today?

RO: I love what Cory Walker does, anything he does I just gush over. He has more skill than any artist alive, I don't know how he does what he does. Another artist like that is Sean Murphy. I love Stuart Immonen, Moebius, Frank Blanchard, Diddier Cassegrain, Claire Wendling, any artist who is French seems to blow my mind.

DH: What projects do you have coming up?

RO: Every issue of *Invincible* is a new project to me, I love it and I know everyone else will as well. I have side projects on my mind that I have to get out sometime. There is a short eight-pager I'm doing right now for an anthology but not sure when that's going to be available, so I won't say anymore on that yet.

I do have an art book that I just had made called *Violence and Pinwheels*. I will make that available to order in August sometime. Just like my last art book *Violence and Piggybacks*, I only printed a certain amount, not to be reprinted. So if you want the book and missed out on the first one then order quick, see me at a con or buy from me off my website. Thanks!

NYCC 2015: Interview with *Outcast*'s Paul Azaceta

STEVEN BISCOTTI / 2015

From *What'cha Reading*, October 16, 2015. Reprinted by permission of Steven Biscotti.

Last Friday, during a busy afternoon at New York Comic Con, *What'cha Reading* had the opportunity to speak with Paul Azaceta, the popular artist behind the unsettling visuals of Robert Kirkman's latest title—*Outcast*. The already year-old comic by Skybound and Image is soon to be a television series on Cinemax; its only added to the intensity of fandom that the New Jersey-based and Cadence Comic Art-represented artist has encountered. So, on this crowded and more attended than SDCC event, we found Paul Azaceta at the Skybound booth and spoke to him about everything from his experience at this year's New York Comic Con, to the visual development and approach to his work, and just how you could obtain one of his original pieces of art.

What'cha Reading: Paul, it's been a little while since we last saw each other. New York Comic Con 2014, Royal Collectibles . . .

Paul Azaceta: Was it? I can't remember. They're all a blur to me. I remember you, but I can't remember if you asked me where and when.

What'cha Reading: Sure. Well how is New York Comic Con 2015 going for you?

Azaceta: It's going really well. It's only the second day and it's been so crazy already. Usually like Saturday is the real crazy day and it kind of builds up, but yesterday, the first day, I came in and it was packed and I was like "Man, I can't even walk." It just seems like it's getting bigger and crazier every year. My brain is mushed already and I still have two more days to go.

What'cha Reading: There's a massive turnout. Do you find that going from last year's comic con to this year's that there is a difference in fan reception, in particular to you and your work?

Azaceta: Last year was the debut of the book and I know there was a lot of attention. There was a lot of excitement and nice people saying nice things, but more just with anticipation. But this year there's been twelve issues now, so a lot of people are coming up now and saying, "I love the book. I loved it." There are more people who have read the book and fans of what the actual book is as opposed to those that say "This looks pretty cool." Now it's a real kind of fandom because they're reading along and they can't wait to see what's next. It's a really cool other level of readership, I guess.

What'cha Reading: I think to be involved with this book, one that had such a presence at this past San Diego Comic Con, especially with the show, that must be exciting.

Azaceta: It is exciting because we're going to do a show and we have all of that. It's been amazing. There are no complaints and I can't say anything but good things about this amazing kind of ride into Kirkman's world. I really appreciate what he's done and how he's given me the opportunity to do the book. We've known each other for years and he didn't have to think of me for this book, but he did and it's been great. I wish I had a more interesting answer.

What'cha Reading: I remember last time we spoke you were four or so issues in.

Azaceta: Probably yeah.

What'cha Reading: That was during the Royal Collectibles signing.

Azaceta: Yeah, I was probably up to four. At least a whole issue ahead. So I was probably on issue 4.

What'cha Reading: How far into it are you currently?

Azaceta: Right now I'm going to start issue 15. Twelve came out a little while ago, and then the trade for the second arc just came out. Taking a little break between arcs helps me to get ahead because deadlines start mounting, so by having those little breaks it helps me get ahead again. It's a vicious cycle of deadlines.

What'cha Reading: I could imagine. Now I believe you have a lot of freedom when it comes to character design and creature development within the series. Do you find that affects deadlines at all in the sense that there are certain aspects that you want to go full on with, but then maybe you have to reel yourself in on?

Azaceta: The fact that our world that we created, me and Kirkman together, created from scratch is something that takes time. You know, you work on Spider-Man for instance, and everyone knows that Spider-Man looks like Peter Parker and the Daily Bugle . . . Marvel, at this point, has design layouts and schematics of what they want it to look like. A lot of that thinking is already done and you go in there and make it cool.

What'cha Reading: Kind of like your work on Electro in the Spider-Man arc "The Gauntlet?"

Azaceta: Yeah, yeah exactly. And that one too, the arc I did there, with the Daily Bugle there was a computer file, a community file that I could look at and see exactly what the Daily Bugle was supposed to look like. And even outside of that, New York City too. I could just look around because I live here. I actually live in Jersey, but I'm right across the river so all of that stuff there's not a whole lot of thinking whereas with *Outcast* the book is based in West Virginia so that's a place I've never actually been. So a lot of that is Google Maps and looking at books that Kirkman sent me. Again, with *Outcast*, a lot of it is designing it from scratch. When he says there's a new character, a lot of that is then figuring out what does he look like? What is his posture like? I like to get into the acting and the character of it so I don't just think "Oh, this guy likes to wear a red shirt." That's not enough. I like to think "Is he a very confident person? When he walks into a room, is his head held high? Does he lean forward? Is he very aggressive?" With Kyle, he's very introverted so unless he's trying to take an active role, most of the time he's standing behind the character or characters. He's never really standing up straight and so things like that you really have to think about. I love that stuff though because I really get into it, but that definitely eats time. It's a little easier now because I've done twelve issues so a lot of that is established, so it goes faster now. But in the beginning, there was a lot of that where I think it took longer because of that. Coming up with and creating his house, I drew a floor plan because I was going to be drawing it how many times throughout the whole series, so I might as well draw a floor plan because it would make some kind of sense. I could go on and on. It's the whole concept of world building. I guess that's what they call it?

What'cha Reading: It's interesting because you're dealing with subject matter that's been explored in film and in literature and different mediums. And then you have Robert Kirkman who's essentially this master of horror, character drama, and suspense. You're dealing with demons and the devil and characters like that. How much of that was discussed in terms of the visual concept?

Azaceta: Kirkman had very specific ideas on what he wanted to do with the people who were possessed and the demon and stuff. He wanted to do it in a way that I think that the horror and stuff that we like is more atmospheric and creepy and suspenseful. It's not necessarily a giant monster jumping out at you or gore and stuff like that. With the possessed people, he didn't want it to be with horns, but just where they're a little off. We were talking about that and how he wanted that. It's creepier that way. A weirdo standing on a corner staring at you could be a hundred times creepier than some crazy monster. A crazy monster you kind of write off as "Oh man, that was crazy!" and then you tell your friends later on. But a creepy guy on the corner, later on you think about it, and when you're going to go to bed, it really sticks with you more. So we talked about that kind of stuff, and then with the demon stuff we discussed the idea of how it would be formless and how you kind of see stuff in it, but not really. It doesn't really have its own thing. But we thought about showing the actual demon where we keep picking at it so when we get to the climax . . .

What'cha Reading: Without spoiling anything, could we expect anything with a form?

Azaceta: I don't want to spoil anything, but I can say that . . .

What'cha Reading: That it evolves?

Azaceta: Yeah, there's an evolution of it. As we reveal more you see how they work and what's going on and stuff. Why Kyle seems to be targeted so much and all the stuff like that. It definitely escalates. I was just talking about the next arc and how I'm having a lot of fun with it. Issue 13 is bananas with all the stuff that goes on in that one and then with the following issue there are so many turns with the characters because a lot of the first few issues was establishing stuff, but now we get to pay off on some of the seeds we've planted. We get to put them through the ringer and that's a lot of fun. I don't know. I'm excited.

What'cha Reading: I've been reading since issue 1 and I love it. I know there are many that are very interested in it and there are many that love owning and collecting original art. I know Cadence Comic Art is . . .

Azaceta: Cadence Comic Art, that's my art dealer. Paolo.

What'cha Reading: And that's still the preferred way to obtain your work?

Azaceta: I don't get into selling my originals too much, but I do have some and he does have some of my stuff. Some of my *Outcast* stuff. I'm probably going to give him some more stuff. The other thing too is that I didn't know if anyone was going to want *Outcast* and then we had a lot of buzz so now I think maybe they'll want to buy the original art. I didn't know if anyone was going to care so I thought maybe I'll hold onto it in case something happens and if it does catch on. Everything appears to be going well so maybe now that people will actually want it I'll give him some more stuff. It's weird because it's not being protective, it's just more that since I create the art, the actual art is the printed comic book. I don't know. I don't have a definitive answer as to why not, but I do like to give out and try to sell some. I've got people asking so I guess I'll throw him some more art.

What'cha Reading: So CadenceComicArt.com?

Azaceta: CadenceComicArt.com and he reps a bunch of great artists and I'm one of them.

What'cha Reading: Yes, Paolo's great.

Azaceta: He is and he's a cool guy and that's why he reps me. If he was a jerk, he'd probably still rep me, but I wouldn't like him as much.

What'cha Reading: Thanks again Paul for speaking with us today.

Azaceta: No problem.

What'cha Reading: Thanks again and, we like to ask everyone this, so *what'cha reading?*

Azaceta: I'm so happy to be a part of Image. The lineup they have is incredible. I'm behind on *Deadly Class*, I know that. That's one of my favorites. The new *Southern Bastards* hardcover came out and I want to get that.

Interview with Charlie Adlard, Comic Book Laureate

TOM INNIS / 2019

From *Voice*, April 24, 2019. Reprinted by permission of Tom Innis.

Tom Innis: Could you first introduce yourself to the reader?

Charlie Adlard: My name is Charlie Adlard and I am a cartoonist.

Innis: Is that how you describe yourself, a cartoonist?

Adlard: Whether you do what I do, or whether it's something like Shultz, with Peanuts, we all caricature to different levels, I believe we're all cartoonists. A spade's a spade.

Innis: What does your job involve? Give us the typical outline of a day, if there is one?

Adlard: I'm very much a guy who's quite comfortable in routine, so actually I do have a regular day, it's just a nine-to-five day that people do with normal jobs. Basically the kids go to school, I come home, I get to work, kids get back from school. I might have to stop when they get straight back from school, but usually around the 5:30 p.m.—6:00 p.m. time I will stop.

Innis: So what are you doing in that time?

Adlard: If I'm working on a book, for example *The Walking Dead*, it's a monthly book, so I have twenty pages to draw plus a cover, so I basically have to divide my time into working out how many pages I can do a day, factoring in various things such as holidays or other appointments, and making sure I can do the work in the time allotted.

I like to get three pages done a day, that's generally my goal, and I get frustrated with myself if I don't achieve that goal—regardless of deadlines.

Innis: Will you keep working if you don't meet that goal?

Adlard: I do, otherwise I will just be frustrated for the rest of the evening, so I end up sneaking back into the studio, regardless. All of this has benefited my efficiency, it's just this attitude I have, other people don't and that's cool—I wish I didn't. I kind of admire people that can just drop tools and they know they can catch up.

Innis: What was your career path into this job? Have you also worked outside the industry?

Adlard: I've always drawn comic books since I was around six or seven. My dad bought me a copy of the *Mighty World of Marvel* in 1972, which was a British reprint of the Marvel comics from the early to mid-sixties, and that was the sort of thing that started me off. Then I just drew comic books all the way through school.

I always knew this is what I wanted to do—my only talent is doing what I do, to be honest. When I was at school I was brutally average in academia, and I was terrible at sports, so art was the only place I could excel at, and I think my teachers could see that. I remember my teacher at prep school saying, "I can't teach him anymore," probably because I could draw better than she could, but I never quite knew what she meant.

When I left school obviously there were no courses for comic art. I assumed the natural route was university, so I was looking at art colleges. I did my art foundation at the Tech and then ended up going to Maidstone Arts College to study film and video.

So I did that, and came out with a degree—with no idea what to do with it—so I moved to London. I was trying to find work in the film industry, but I could only get work as a runner, which disillusioned me a bit. I was the drummer in a band, and I tried to make it work for a while, but it eventually fell apart—not in a dramatic way, but the opportunity doors started closing, not opening—so I moved back home. While sitting there thinking, "Hmm, what am I going to do now?" I thought, "I could try this comic lark," and as soon as I put pen to paper, I realized that this is what I needed to be doing.

From there, it took me about three years to break into the industry. I spent that time beavering away at home building up my portfolio, as in this line of work you needed to show sequential art, not just individual images. I took my work to conventions and eventually landed a job.

Innis: What's great about your job?

Adlard: It's my hobby! I'm basically being paid to do what I love.

I've had the odd "normal job" when I was in London, but that's it. But I've had probably no more than three months of my whole life doing what you'd perceive as a normal job. The rest of my life has just been having fun and getting paid for it.

Innis: What do you find most challenging?

Adlard: Deadlines are always challenging in a lot of ways, but because of my own weird way of working, when I set my own personal deadlines, I find that more challenging than the actual deadlines themselves.

Sometimes working at home is not the best way of achieving goals. Sometimes there are general disturbances you get at home that you wouldn't get in an office. People who wouldn't ring you when you're in an office are more likely to ring if they know you're at home.

Innis: What are the highlights of your career to date?

Adlard: The laureate is a real highlight.

Innis: Ok, so let's move onto that. You were announced as the comic laureate in 2016. What does that mean?

Adlard: As the comic laureate you represent the industry and promote comic books generally as a genuine form of literacy to everyone, but with a main focus on education with teachers and librarians who are able to carry on the message.

What I want to make clear though is that comics aren't a specific form of reading for kids and people who find it hard to read, or don't want to read. They are for everyone, and they're just another form of reading. In France they call it the ninth art, that's how well it's regarded.

Innis: What is some of the work you have undertaken as your role of laureate?

Adlard: In addition to presentations and interview panels, the stranger ones were where I had to go and talk to the 'unconverted'. What I found though was that I had to be weary when I got an invite, and wonder whether they want you to attend on the basis of being the laureate, or if they want you there because of *The Walking Dead*. I think my predecessor, Dave Gibbons, had the same issue—do they want him there because he's laureate, or do they want him there because he drew *Watchmen*. Am I going to be there to talk about comics, or am I going to be signing books?

The only people you're talking to in that situation is the converted, so what's the point? I'm talking about how comics should be literal and everyone is just there agreeing with you anyway.

Innis: Do you have any words of advice for Hannah Berry, who has now taken your place?

Adlard: She doesn't need advice, she's an incredibly capable person. She'll bring a different aspect and personality to the role, and she's a great speaker—much better than I am! And I hate saying this as it sounds slightly belittling—it's not meant to be—but she doesn't have the baggage that Dave and I have from *Watchmen* and *The Walking Dead*, so when she's brought in it will be about her role as the comic laureate.

Hopefully that will make her role a lot more important in certain ways, and she will be able to get out there and talk to people.

Innis: Do you think the success of franchises like the Marvel Cinematic Universe, or the *Walking Dead* game by Telltale Games, has helped foster new interest in comics?

Adlard: Everyone thinks that, because of the success of things like the Marvel Cinematic Universe, the comic book industry is just about superheroes, and that's perpetuated by people buying those comics just because of nostalgia. There is this small base of—typically older—people buying these comics because they have disposable income, and that leads to the regurgitation of the same old things, and children are coming up through that. It's not helped that the movies are so bloody popular!

Innis: But the audiences aren't then going back to the comic books.

Adlard: *The Walking Dead* was a bit of a game changer, but I've yet to see something come up behind it be as successful at doing something else. I don't know whether that's the industry not capitalizing on that success, or if it's people still being of that mindset that they can handle one property that's not superheroes.

Innis: You've spoken before about your dislike of the phrase graphic novel. Do you not think it could have use as a means of distinguishing content more aimed at mature audiences, for example *Watchmen* or *Fables*?

Adlard: No, I don't think that at all. The phrase was coined in the '80s by people wanting to get into the book market. For some reason the book market didn't like the term comic, but they seemed to accept the term graphic novel, and now I think the term has become a byword for pretentiousness, with artists saying they don't draw comics, they draw graphic novels. It just feels like a pointless intellectualization of what we do.

It sort of goes in parallel with me calling myself a cartoonist as opposed to a comic book artist. Why separate myself from somebody that does the same sort of thing—it's just this big broad church, and why can't we call comics comics? We're all the same.

Innis: Have you noticed any changes in the industry? If so, what?

Adlard: Other than the rise of graphic novels?

As the wider medium of literature has found, people don't want to read physical things as much as they did twenty or thirty years ago. The comic industry from when I started was selling in the millions, but has since imploded. We suffer the exact same problems that anyone else in the book market does.

I'm talking specifically about the US and UK markets here, to be clear, but I think we're suffering from the malaise of people not wanting to read anymore. In the UK, at least, we've always had this attitude of comics just being for kids—which is fine, but I want them to be for adults as well; I want comics for everyone. That's why the comic laureate role was created, to convince people that there is a genuine argument that they're a genuine form of literacy.

Innis: Do you think that attitude is changing?

Adlard: It is changing something in a country that has been socially engineered to think another way, so it's one of those things that is so ingrained in society that it is going to take generations to change. You can't change these things overnight—I can't come along and suddenly everyone says "Oh yeah, let's start reading comics." It's still embarrassing to take out a comic on the tube—or even a graphic novel!—and start reading.

Innis: What is one comic franchise you would love to work on, or an author you'd love to work with?

Adlard: I'm already doing both! I'm working my good friend Robbie Morrison, a writer who also lives locally, and we're going to be doing a crime thriller—no fancy elements or a specific genre. Hopefully it's going to be published in France first, as we'd love to do a couple of ninety-plus-page books in a hardcover—something they do more over there.

We've actually worked together on a few things over the years, but I guess our most "famous" thing was a book called *White Death*, which is almost twenty years old! It was a book set in World War I, set in the border of Italy and Austria, and the title of the book refers to the canons they fired into the mountains to cause avalanches, which they termed the white death, and it was about turning nature into a weapon. I actually drew it with charcoal and chalk on grey paper, so it was incredibly different from what I would normally do. I mean it sold bugger all, but it's still out there!

Innis: You've been granted the ability to send a message to sixteen-year-old you. What do you say?

Adlard: Avoid all of the other stuff you wasted your time with! No, I'm joking, it's all experience, and you have to experience failure as well as success, but I would say forget about that, comics are what you wanted to do, stick to that, son.

Innis: Do you have any advice for young people interested in doing your kind of job?

Adlard: The opportunities out there nowadays are much more—when I was doing it there wasn't the internet—but I still think your best opportunities still come from physically getting out there, going to meet editors and people in the industry, because then they'll remember you.

Build a portfolio, and make sure there is sequential art. By all means stick in some nice pictures as well, to show you can do other things, but it's essential to have three or four pages of sequential images. You don't need much—editors don't want to spend days reading a proposal, and they don't want to spend ages going through artwork. Just choose three or four of your best pieces.

If it's taking you a week per page, you're not going to get paid! At the very least, you should be able to draw a page a day. Obviously when you work you'll get quicker and quicker as you get used to it.

And be persistent without being annoying. You've got to be determined, but you can't ring someone up every day.

INDEX

ABOUT THE EDITOR

Photo by Kevin Ramos

Terrence R. Wandtke is professor of literature and media studies at Judson University in Elgin, Illinois, where classes taught include *Comic Books and Graphic Novels* and *Media Theory*. He has directed the school's film and media program, served as the area chair of Comics and Comic Art for the Popular Culture Association Conference, and currently acts as the editor of the Comics Monograph Series for the Rochester Institute of Technology. He is author of *The Comics Scare Returns: The Resurgence in Contemporary Horror Comics* and *The Dark Night Returns: The Contemporary Resurgence in Crime Comics* and *The Meaning of Superhero Comic Books*; he is editor of the collections *Ed Brubaker: Conversations*, published by the University Press of Mississippi, and *The Amazing Transforming Superhero: Essays on the Revision of Characters in Comic Books, Film, and Television*.